Praise for
PR 2.0

"An 'easy read' filled with practical examples of how marketing professionals can leverage these new tools to enhance PR activities. The 'Interviews with the Experts' sections were especially useful in helping to highlight how companies have benefited from *PR2.0*."

Maura Mahoney, Senior Director,
RCN Metro Optical Networks

"*P.R. 2.0* is a must-read for any marketing or PR professional. It is filled with expert advice, real-world examples, and practical guidance to help us better understand the new media tools and social networking concepts available and how we can use them for our specific branding needs. This book is excellent for someone who is trying to understand the new web-based media and social networking concepts, as well those who are experienced in applying the new media tools and are curious about what everyone else is doing and what tools are producing the best ROI. This isn't a book filled with simple tips and tricks—it's an essential guidebook for the marketing/PR professional to better understand the new media options and how to apply them effectively to achieve results."

Jenny Fisher, Director Sales and Marketing
Operations, Catalent Pharma Solutions

"Wading through the thicket of expanding Internet tools—from MySpace to Facebook, from Twitter to Flickr—is no easy challenge. And once you finally understand these strange new art forms, how the heck do you harness them? Answer: You buy this book. Deirdre Breakenridge knows the Net—how to measure it, monitor it, and use it to maximize public relations performance. Best of all, she explains it in a style that even a Luddite can comprehend."

Fraser P. Seitel, author of *The Practice of
Public Relations* and coauthor of *IdeaWise*

PR 2.0

New Media, New Tools, New Audiences

DEIRDRE BREAKENRIDGE

Vice President, Publisher
Tim Moore

Associate Publisher and Director of Marketing
Amy Neidlinger

Acquisitions Editor
Martha Cooley

Editorial Assistant
Pamela Boland

Development Editor
Russ Hall

Digital Marketing Manager
Julie Phifer

Marketing Coordinator
Megan Colvin

Cover Designer
Chuti Prasertsith

Managing Editor
Gina Kanouse

Senior Project Editor
Lori Lyons

Copy Editor
Chelsey Marti

Proofreader
Lori Lyons

Indexer
Lisa Stumpf

Compositor
Nonie Ratcliff

Manufacturing Buyer
Dan Uhrig

Library of Congress Cataloging-in-Publication Data

Breakenridge, Deirdre.
  PR 2.0 : new media, new tools, new audiences / Deirdre Breakenridge.
    p. cm.
  ISBN 0-321-51007-0 (hardback : alk. paper) 1. Public relations. 2. Mass media and business. I. Title.
  HD59.B743 2008
  659.2—dc22

                                        2007049788

With love and thanks to:

Megan

Mark

Mom & Dad

Contents

Acknowledgments

Writing *PR 2.0* was an amazing experience. I learned so much from the many professionals who contributed to this book. Every chapter of *PR 2.0* has expert commentary from the PR service providers, communications and new media executives, technology gurus, and journalists who took the time to answer all of my questions. These individuals also played an instrumental role in helping me to put together a book that answers many of the questions that communications professionals are asking today about the convergence of public relations and the Internet.

It was a great learning experience hearing the insight from executives at PR Newswire, Business Wire, Market Wire, Harris Interactive, Bulldog Reporter, FAS Research, Lawrence Ragan Communications, Cision, Delahaye, and Tekgroup International. These are the forward-thinking companies leading the PR 2.0 revolution by providing new media services to brands. There were executives who spent hours with me, speaking on the phone and then reviewing the material I prepared. Special thanks goes to Harris Interactive and Humphrey Taylor and his team of executives, Randall Thomas, and John Bremer. Also a special thank you to Rachel Myerson who, every time I write a book, works so hard to find the right PR Newswire executives to interview, and Mary Durkin who pulled together the Cision executives for me.

I also want to thank the many communications executives from companies that were willing to discuss their challenges and successes with PR 2.0. It's a long list: Jeanette Gibson, Cisco, Ynema, Mangum, TalkBMC, Bill Barrett, Deloitte & Touche (set up by Deb Harrington), Dave Walton, JVC, Scott Delea, Adverb Media, Tim Bray, Sun Microsystems, Dan Kurtz, Quality Technology Services, Stephen Johnston, Nokia, Brian Phelan, ASCO, and Jennifer Wilhelmi, Reed Business Information. These executives are all extremely busy and they took the time for telephone interviews and/or participated in my Q&As.

There are several agency professionals and consultants who really put the finishing touches on this book with their insight and examples of PR 2.0 strategies and successes. They include Andrew Foote and Ted

Birkhahn, Peppercom, Brian Solis, Founder of FutureWorks, Brian Cross, Fleishman-Hillard, Bill Southard, Southard Communications, Jane Quigley, DigitalGrit, Phil Gorman, Edelmen, Mark Brooks, Online Personals Watch, Steve Lubetkin, Communications Consultant, Jason Miletsky, PFS Marketwyse, and Michael Schneider of Success Group Communications.

There are a number of people who stand out in my mind and whom I cannot thank enough for their participation in my book. Jimmy Wales, Founder of Wikipedia, was kind enough to meet me in New York City and speak to me about how he brought Wikipedia to life and the best uses of social media. I also want to thank the journalists who gave me their honest, straightforward answers about the relationships between PR pros and them. These professionals include Anne Holland, Jeremy Caplan, Jeffrey Chu, Kate Coe, Andy Teng, and Paul Grzella.

Another very important group in this effort is my Pearson Education Editorial team. Martha Cooley and Russ Hall were excellent editors. I also really appreciate the efforts of the marketing team, including Amy Fandrei (who has since left Pearson), Megan Colvin, Julie Phifer, Amy Neidlinger, and Pamela Boland. This was a great team to work with and I want to thank you all!

Also many thanks to my PFS interns, staff members, and business colleagues for their help in securing interviews with their contacts and for feeding me information and articles that helped me during the writing process.

Finally, a special acknowledgement goes to my family, who always gives me support and strength when I write a book and who understand how much time and effort it takes to complete this type of project.

About the Author

Deirdre K. Breakenridge is President and Director of Communications at PFS Marketwyse, a marketing communications agency in New Jersey. A veteran in the PR industry, Deirdre leads a creative team of PR and marketing executives strategizing to gain brand awareness for their clients through creative and strategic PR campaigns. She counsels senior-level executives at companies including IncentOne, JVC, Michael C. Fina, Quality Technology Services, and RCN Metro Optical Networks.

Deirdre is an adjunct professor at Fairleigh Dickinson University in Madison, New Jersey, where she teaches courses on Public Relations and Interactive Marketing for the Global Business Management program. She is the author of two Financial Times/Prentice Hall business books: *The New PR Toolkit* and *Cyberbranding: Brand Building in the Digital Economy*.

Deirdre has spoken publicly on the topics of PR, digital marketing, and brand building for the Public Relations Society of America (PRSA), The National Association of Broadcasters (NAB), Strategic Research Institute (SRI), Women's Presidents Organization (WPO), Tier1 Research, and at a number of colleges and universities. Deirdre is a member of the PRSA and has served on the Board of NJ/PRSA and the New Jersey Advertising Club.

Foreword: The Road from PR to PR 2.0 to Public Relations

Welcome to what just may be the greatest evolution in the history of PR.

Modern Public Relations was born in the early 1900s, even though history traces the practice back to the 17th century. The term public relations was said to be first documented by U.S. President Thomas Jefferson during his address to Congress in 1807.

It wasn't until World War I that we started to see the industry crystallize and spark the evolution of PR as an official profession.

Ivy Lee and Edward Bernays are credited with creating and defining the art and science of modern-day PR in the early 1900s. That's almost 100 years ago; and yet, in what I believe to be PR's greatest renaissance, many of their early philosophies and contributions can be sourced to further evolve PR today.

Ivy Lee developed the first working press release; you can love him or hate him for it. But, what we can't overlook is that he believed PR was a "two-way street" where communications professionals were responsible for helping companies listen as well as communicate their messages to the people who were important to them.

Edward Bernays, who is often referred to as the father of PR, was most certainly its first theorist. A very interesting bit of history is that Bernays is a nephew of Sigmund Freud. Freud's theories about the irrational, unconscious motives that shape human behavior are the inspiration for how Bernays approached public relations.

What's absolutely astounding to me is that he viewed public relations as an applied social science influenced by psychology, sociology, and other disciplines to scientifically manage and manipulate the thinking and behavior of an irrational and "herdlike" public.

According to Bernays, "Public Relations is a management function which tabulates public attitudes, defines the policies, procedures and interest of an organization followed by executing a program of action to earn public understanding and acceptance."

Why is this astounding to me?

Basically, Bernays is the inspiration for the PR 1.0 publicity and spin machine and the architect of how a majority of companies still approach PR today—even though this is all changing right before our eyes. Many of his thoughts, which fueled his books, *Crystallizing Public Opinion*, *Propaganda*, and *The Engineering of Consent*, were on the cusp of predicting what PR currently is facing in the dawn of Social Media. And, Social Media is reintroducing sociology, anthropology, psychology, and other sciences back into marketing.

If we combined the theories and philosophies of Bernays and Lee with the spirit of the new "social web" aka Social Media, we might have a new outlook on this social science that resembles the new driving principles behind PR 2.0.

But what happened to PR?

It no longer triumphs as a darling among the various marketing disciplines, and in many cases, is regarded as a necessary evil these days.

Somewhere along the way, we, as an industry, lost our vision. We got caught up in hype, spin, hyperbole, and buzzwords, and forgot that PR was about Public Relations.

Unfortunately, these days PR is more aligned with theatrics than value. Enter Social Media and the democratization of the Web.

These are indeed exciting times as Social Media is truly the catalyst for reflection and an opportunity to do PR and amplify value and increase effectiveness in the process.

What is Social Media?

Social Media is anything that uses the Internet to facilitate conversations between people. I say people, because it humanizes the process of communications when you think about conversations instead of companies marketing at audiences.

Social Media refers back to the "two-way" approach of PR that Ivy Lee discussed in his day. It's about listening and, in turn, engaging people on their level. It forces PR to stop broadcasting and start connecting. Monologue has given way to dialog.

Now, enter PR 2.0.

Just so you understand, it's not a trendy term meant to capitalize on the current trend of "everything 2.0." Honestly, it's already ten years in the making, but Social Media is truly advancing the adoption of a new, more significant role for PR.

Here's how I defined it in the 90s (it's dated, but it is still relevant today):

> *PR 2.0 was born through the analysis of how the Web and multimedia was redefining PR and marketing communications, while also building the toolkit to reinvent how companies communicate with influencers and directly with people.*
>
> *It is a chance to not only work with traditional journalists, but also engage directly with a new set of accidental influencers, and, it is also our ability to talk with customers directly (through online forums, groups, communities, BBS, etc.)*

No BS. No hype. It's an understanding of markets, the needs of people, and how to reach them at the street level—without insulting everyone along the way. PR will become a hybrid of communications, evangelism, and Web marketing.

PR 2.0 was actually inspired by Web 1.0 and the new channel for the distribution of information it represented. It changed everything. It forced traditional media to evolve. It created an entirely new set of influencers with a completely different mechanism for collecting and sharing information while also reforming the daily routines of how people searched for news.

PR 2.0 is a philosophy and practice to improve the quality of work, change the game, and participate with people in a more informed and intelligent way. It's not about the new Web tools at all. They are merely tools used to facilitate conversations…but everything, especially intent, knowledge, and enthusiasm, are unique to YOU.

You are the key to new PR.

To be direct, the truth is that PR 2.0 is really what PR should have been all along. Now with the democratization of media, people are becoming the new influencers, complementing the existence of experts and traditional journalists, but still regarded as a source and resource for customers equally.

Understanding new PR to reinvent it is the goal of this book. Deirdre Breakenridge has poured her life's experiences and passion into these pages to inspire and empower you with the ability to change, and ultimately, participate in new media. In doing so, you will learn today's communication methods that will help you engage in meaningful conversations and build stronger trusting relationships—both personally and professionally—with customers, influencers, experts, and traditional media alike.

PR 2.0 is about putting the "public" back in Public Relations.

Brian Solis
Principal of FutureWorks PR, Blogger at PR 2.0
www.briansolis.com

Introduction to PR 2.0

Public relations professionals are news and information hoarders. We have to be up-to-date with our current events. When I taught PR classes as an adjunct professor at Fairleigh Dickinson University, one of the first things I would tell my undergraduate students was they should select one newspaper, *The New York Times* or *The Wall Street Journal,* and find the time every day to stay abreast of world issues. I also explained to them how extremely important it is to read the PR trade publications to stay current with news of the profession. *PR Week* and PRSA's *Public Relations Tactics* are excellent publications. In addition, PR people need to be well informed when it comes to public issues and news that is relevant to their clients and/or respective industries. It's critical for PR professionals to read, be knowledgeable, and stay extremely well versed about the markets their brands try to reach.

Newspapers and PR trade publications are excellent resources for information, but there are many more conversations taking place on the Internet about your brands and their competitors. You need to know about these conversations. Sometimes you need a good, hard kick in the pants that makes you wake up to the ultimate mind expansion—the desire to try new strategies to obtain valuable information, build relationships, and interact in ways that are unfamiliar. If you find it easy to become set in your process or methodology, read on because you're not alone and are probably in very good company. Maybe you've been doing PR for a couple years, 5 years, or 10 years, or perhaps you're approaching 20 years, which is where I am today. No matter what stage you're at, don't freeze up or feel uneasy and threatened when you hear about new ways people are networking and conversing online and ways you need to communicate to them.

These new methods include

- A great deal of social networking, such as blogging and interacting on Web sites, that enables you to meet "friends" and share content

- New ways to reach groups by employing social media tools in news releases

- Really Simple Syndication (RSS) technology for targeted news and information

- Wiki, as in Wikipedia

- Any other intimidating 2.0 terms you're unfamiliar with

On the other hand, you might be very familiar with the new media terms, but just haven't embraced these resources enough to place them into action and have them incorporated into your daily PR regimen. You will discover that there's a time and a place to use PR 2.0, and after you've read this book, you'll let your new frame of reference tell you when it's time. You will also rely on your solid training as a PR professional and skills of the past to guide you to great success.

Are You Ready to Be 2.0 Ready?

I remember having this incredibly uncomfortable feeling during a meeting back in 2004. My Sr. Vice President of Client Relations, Dennis Madej, and I had driven all the way to Long Island for a pitch meeting with a small technology company that had developed a load balancing product. It was the first affordable system used for traffic management on e-commerce Web sites for small to medium size businesses. The CEO and Founder of the company said, "We need you to educate us on new media strategies." At the time, my company, PFS Marketwyse, had been working for a year or so with GLOBIX (Amex: GEX), a leading provider of Internet infrastructure and network services. We also worked for about six years with JVC Professional Products Company to publicize its proprietary technology in a complete line of broadcast and professional equipment, as well as other smaller technology firms, whether they were providers of mobile applications or CRM. We felt fairly confident we would be able to provide this technology company with PR and new media strategies.

Our immediate response to the CEO's inquiry was that PFS was very tapped into new media with the most current, Web-based media list generating tools and online distribution strategies. We had great contacts with technology publications and we utilized PR Newswire's ProfNet service, which brought our client experts together with technology editors who were looking for thought leaders to interview for their articles and feature stories. I mentioned we were familiar with Search Engine Optimization (SEO) that we'd done Webinars, and we would be able to help them with developing blogs. However, this wasn't enough. The CEO looked at us with the same question. He still wanted us to educate him on the *new media strategies*. Have you ever been in this type of situation? When you wished you knew more? We were in desperate need of PR 2.0.

Surprisingly, we won the account because the executives from this small tech firm saw our enthusiasm, knew we were hungry, felt our energy and aggressiveness, and believed our media contacts would propel them to a new level of publicity. They had been "burned in the past," as so many have, "by PR companies that promise the world and deliver very little." However, we won the account as a result of our attitudes and an impressive technology portfolio; so much so, that these executives were willing to take the chance on a small agency that wasn't entirely up to speed on new media strategies, but had a lot of potential. We were honest about our level of understanding when it came to new media strategies and at the same time, as a small PR division of a marketing company, realized we needed a crash course in PR 2.0. There was nothing holding us back except our own sense of complacency. A complacent attitude is dangerous when technology is constantly changing and advancing, and so is your client's competitive landscape. I knew, and so did my Sr. VP, that it was time to raise the bar. That's when it hit us; there was so much more to learn, and we had touched only the tip of the iceberg for our own company and our clients.

That's why this book is so important to all you PR professionals who have had a taste of new media and really want to dig into the latest PR strategies on the Internet. Is this an easy task for the average professional? I'm not so sure about that. It depends on your educational background, work experience, training; and I hate to say this—for some, your age. In my last book, *The New PR Toolkit*, Chapter 1 discussed the rate at which people accept technology. The group known as the Innovators are "Often young and mobile, the members of this group embrace technology early on and were right there at the birth of the commercial Internet, jumping on the bandwagon with creative ideas." It's no surprise that today the Innovators are the first to enjoy MySpace.com, Facebook.com, and the self-made videos YouTube.com offers. Where else can you see a man's face change every day over a seven-year period and watch a three-minute video on Christmas decorations (specifically a house that lights up rhythmically to music)? *The New PR Toolkit* maps out the other stages of accepting technology, including the Early Adopters who are less prone to taking risks, but certainly are helping to fuel the growth of new media strategies; the Early Majority—the large group that uses the Internet mostly for e-mail, research, and news; the Late Majority who are very suspect of what the Internet has to offer; and finally, the Laggards, who just as they sound, would rather not be bothered with technology. As a group, the Laggards are extremely concerned with privacy issues and are "lagging" behind. As professionals, we are all different. It's up to you to determine where you fall on the technology acceptance spectrum and what type of PR you feel you need to offer to the brands you work with.

As you read this book, there are some very different and unfamiliar examples of what brands are doing online and how PR 2.0 has been tremendously successful. There are other examples of brands that backfire with their 2.0 strategies and have a miserable failure on their hands and reputation issues to deal with. I would like you to keep one very important notion in mind during your cruise through the new PR 2.0 strategies: The responsibility of the PR professional is always to communicate with facts, accuracy, and integrity for the brand(s) you represent. If you can abide by this rule and expand your frame of reference to accept the momentous changes in technology and all the Internet has to offer in terms of social media strategies, then you will benefit from this book. Let's dig deeper into the concept of expanding your frame of reference.

The Big Bang

There's an excellent book that complements the theory of opening up your frame of reference to embrace PR 2.0. It's called *Bang,* and was written in 2003 by Linda Kaplan Thaler and Robin Koval. It's a fast read that discusses what it takes for an agency to create a Big Bang campaign. Just as it sounds, a Big Bang campaign is as great and colossal as the creation of the universe billions of years ago. Although *Bang* never touches on Web 2.0 or PR 2.0, it does provide some very good tips on how to open up your frame of reference so that you are not too bogged down with the marketing information you know about a brand. As a matter of fact, Chapter 2 in Thaler and Koval's book, *Lose the Rules*, impresses upon readers that you need to forget about your fears and you shouldn't over-analyze the information at hand, which all too often will impede the creative brainstorming process. Why is this theory important to you as you read *PR 2.0?* Mostly because as PR professionals (and I don't want to generalize) you have the incredible responsibility and sometimes daunting task to completely understand and over-analyze information to protect the reputations of the companies they represent. There's a very fine line here you don't want to cross. *PR 2.0* shows you there's a way to protect and preserve the brand reputation so that you can communicate creatively with social media strategies, and at the same time use your knowledge and the power of the Internet to create new successes in your campaigns.

About This Book

So, now you're geared up to journey into *PR 2.0*. The first section of the book should be somewhat familiar territory, providing discussion on how PR professionals are moving forward and learning the best skills to work and thrive in the Web 2.0 World. Chapter 1, "PR 2.0 is Here," highlights several strategies in campaigns that worked in the PR 1.0 landscape, including viral marketing, online newsletters, and e-blasts news releases. The chapter's real-world stories should make you feel comfortable reviewing strategies with impact that have caught on quickly for brands wanting to create greater awareness online. Chapter 2, "Getting Started with 2.0 Research," is a thorough review of new research techniques, which is always dear to the PR professional's heart. You know through your past experiences that continuous research can be the anchor in a campaign and lends tremendous credibility to a brand when working with third-party research firms. And, you also know how much the media looks to PR professionals for solid statistics resulting from opinion polls they believe might be of interest or influence to their readers or viewers. When you're finished with an introduction to research, Chapter 3,

"Research with Expert Resources," drives home how to work with the online research experts. Here, you learn how easy it is to move your research and campaign tracking efforts online or at least be able to find a good balance between traditional research strategies and what the Internet has to offer.

Chapter 4, "Reaching the Wired Media for Better Coverage," is your chance to hear what the media thinks about building relationships with them and the best way to communicate on a regular basis. It's always important to know how journalists want to receive information and PR 2.0 is no exception to the rule. This chapter talks about reaching the wired media for better coverage. I didn't run across many journalists who are enthusiastic if you try to pitch them through their blogs. E-mail and IM is a better way to proceed. There always will be those members of the media who prefer the accepted PR 1.0 methods. As stated in *Bulldog Reporter's* December 11, 2006 e-mail newsletter to PR pros, "In this day of bold new PR technology...pitching journalists is still all about people and personal relationships." Good old e-mail or sometimes an old-fashioned telephone call works really well. Chapter 5, "Better Monitoring for PR 2.0," is critical to achieving campaign success. Now you're not only monitoring your influencers, such as the media, but also citizen journalists who are blogging daily. Loss of control of communication is certainly a concern and on the minds of many professionals. Chapter 5 digs into the best services and how expert PR service providers use new monitoring strategies to help brands uncover important Internet conversations. If brands, under the guidance of their PR professionals, have the detailed means to monitor communication as it unfolds, there's a greater chance to get more brands involved in social networking and sharing content with audiences across the Web.

Section I, "The Transition to PR 2.0," is the briefing part of the book that bridges the gap between the PR of the past and the PR that's to come. Its purpose is to prepare you for the journey through uncharted waters. Section II, "A New Direction in PR," leads you in a new direction so that you understand in Chapter 6, "Interactive Newsrooms: How to Attract the Media," why it's so important to have your online newsroom interactive with many different resources and outside links for the media to pursue. Newsrooms today should be filled with video, podcasts, RSS feeds, downloadable images, presentations, and even sources beyond what your brand can offer on a topic of interest. Chapter 7, "The Social Media News Release: An Overdue Facelift," allows you to hear firsthand from professionals about the use of social media in news releases, when they think it's necessary to use these tactics, and what types of brands benefit the most. This chapter enables you to become more comfortable with the social media template. It was only in 2006 that Shift Communications unveiled its news release template, which has received a tremendous amount of attention and has prompted PR service providers to offer new media tools for the PR 2.0 releases.

As a follow-up to social media in news announcements, Chapter 8, "Social Networking: A Revolution Has Begun," discusses some the most popular social networking forums, including MySpace, Facebook, and LinkedIn, and how people are conversing in their communities. Chapter 9, "RSS Technology: A Really Simple Tool to Broaden Your Reach," details how PR professionals use Really Simple Syndication (RSS) technology for wider distribution. RSS feeds serve two very important functions. The first is to provide you and the brands you work with customized news and information that occurs daily. You can use RSS as a means to monitor the market, the competitive landscape, or to stay abreast of current events. The other significant purpose of RSS is to enable your brands to feed targeted news announcements to people who want to receive customized information via their homepages or popular news Web sites. Chapter 10, "Video and Audio for Enhanced Web Communications," tours you through new and effective video methods as well as the use of audio files or podcasts downloaded to your customers' computer or handheld devices. Podcasts are the Webcasts of PR 1.0. Professionals are finding that podcasts are extremely popular for use with interviews and roundtable discussions. Also provided in this chapter is the discussion about the PR value of sharing video content on the Internet, which is growing in popularity. YouTube.com, purchased by Google for a sizeable sum, has garnered consumer and media attention. Growing immensely in popularity, it should capture your attention, too.

With the fundamentals of PR 2.0 embedded in your brain and a presentation of the strategies available, one question arises: Where do we go from here? This question is answered in Section III, "Embracing PR 2.0."

Chapter 11 focuses on how to immerse yourself and your brand in social media. You are trained as a PR professional to listen to the market, to know what customers want, and to monitor how they behave. This is your chance to find out what 21st Century consumers are reacting to positively and how they have negative reactions when PR 2.0 strategies go awry. Chapters 12, "The Pro's Use of PR 2.0," and 13, "The Mindset of the PR 2.0 Journalist," although opinion driven, provides you with firsthand insights from PR professionals and media representatives interviewed from a variety of sources across the nation. Several technology innovators, such as Jimmy Wales, Founder of Wikipedia, share their thoughts on social media.

These opinions and the information presented are the perfect segue into Chapter 14, "A PR 2.0 Plan," which is a closer look at how all the PR 2.0 strategies come together in a PR 2.0 plan that is representative of the true 21st Century company. Several companies discuss how they are moving forward with technology to reach desired groups. Like any PR plan, the PR 2.0 plan is stocked with the required plan elements, including a situation analysis, clearly set objectives, a well-planned strategic direction, implementation of the tactics, and of course, measurement, measurement, and more measurement.

As the book comes to a close, Section IV, "The Future of PR 2.0," is the wrap-up with conclusions that support the text's overarching main idea. PR 2.0 is the path to great PR and more engaging conversations through the use of social media applications that enhance the communication and extend the brand's reach in Web communities. Chapter 15, "The Path to Great PR," offers a discussion on the "Future of PR 2.0." PR 2.0 is here to stay, and the role of the PR professional is very different. As a matter of fact, the dialog turns to "What will it look like in the year's ahead?"

In *The New PR Toolkit*, I provided a glossary of "new" terms for PR professionals. It's amazing how these terms are now common everyday language. I would be very surprised if words such as "archive," "bandwidth," "firewall," "hits," "server," unique users," and "URL," were not used by you on a daily basis. If by chance you are not proficient in Web 1.0 terms, please feel free to peruse the book and its glossary to get up to speed. With that said, after reading *PR 2.0* you will have a new PR vocabulary with terms that include "blogosphere," "micro blogging," "social networking," "RSS," "SEO," "social tagging," "wiki," and "vlogs." This technology jargon has to find its way into your everyday vocabulary in order for you to truly feel comfortable in a PR 2.0 world.

With insight from PR 2.0 experts such as Brian Solis, one of the Founding Fathers of PR 2.0, and Brian Cross, another PR 2.0 communications expert, Chapter 15 guides you on how to move forward in a PR 2.0 world, personally and professionally in your everyday PR regimen. The question, "How should I move forward as a PR 2.0 professional?" is answered in increments throughout each chapter of this book. *PR 2.0* prepares you to take that susequent step toward what could be your next greatest PR campaign in a fast-paced, wired, social media-driven, and content-sharing PR 2.0 world. Good luck and enjoy the ride.

S E C T I O N I

The Transition to PR 2.0

Chapter 1

PR 2.0 Is Here

Public relations is an evolving profession. As a communications professional, you work very hard every day to build relationships, maintain existing ones, craft targeted messages, and deliver news that's timely on behalf of your brand. Prior to the advancement of technology, increased bandwidth, and a Web 2.0 platform, PR pros relied heavily on third-party influencers, such as the media, to endorse their brands. The power of the pen and editorial coverage goes a long way in terms of credibility. That's the nature of PR—to build solid relationships and have someone else talk about the benefits of your brand, rather than your brand talking about itself through advertising or other marketing strategies.

If you've practiced good public relations in the past, then you've probably focused your strategic communications on carefully developed messages and you know the value of the third-party endorsement. PR professionals have always prided themselves on being strategic counselors. They strive to achieve successful campaigns through the delivery of strong communication programs, whether that's a program to change an opinion, build a reputation, maintain a brand's image, develop relationships, launch a product, deploy crisis communications, or use the power of a third party to endorse their product or service.

But now, the Internet changes everything: how you view your role as a PR professional, your delivery of effective communication, and the way your brand interacts with its customers. Everything you do, from the research phase and monitoring of brand communication to the way you reach out to people in their Web communities and use new social media tools to create compelling information, is changing. The Internet enables you to extend your communications in ways you never could have imagined and to connect with groups you probably never thought you could reach.

As you read *PR 2.0*, keep in mind that whether it's 1.0, 2.0, or any .0, you must set your mind to delivering great PR. That means creating and disseminating excellent communication with meaning and value. You not only provide important information that is useful, but you also give your customers a means to communicate in two-way conversations with you at all times. Welcome to your new and improved industry. It's the Public Relations of PR 2.0, where you learn, embrace, and engage in the true convergence of the Internet and the public relations profession.

The Web has evolved from thousands of separate Web sites into thousands of communities. People within these communities all want to share information to make informed decisions. PR 2.0 is the greatest means to provide different groups with the communication they need. It gives you the ability to use new social media applications—including blogs, wikis, social networking, Really Simple Syndication (RSS) technology, streaming video, and podcasts—to reach consumers in ways PR pros have not experienced before. Social media applications enable you to go directly to the consumer. Although brands always have their top influencers, such as the media for editorial coverage, they also use the Internet to engage in direct communication with their customers. It's exciting to realize that through social media you have the ability to have a 24/7 focus panel (just by listening to what your customers are saying) on your brand's Web site. This type of communication is invaluable!

There are many exciting facets of PR 2.0, from how it evolved to all the many intricacies of its usage today. Brian Solis, Founder of FutureWorks (www.future-works.com), who is also interviewed in the last chapter of this book, "The Path to Great PR," started promoting the PR 2.0 concept in the 90s. He was a founding father of the PR 2.0 concept and realized early on how PR, multimedia, and the Web would intersect and create a new breed of PR/Web marketers. Although you might not know it, Solis has been talking about PR 2.0 for almost ten years.[1]

PR 2.0, as exciting as it appears, also is creating controversy over the new ways a brand needs to communicate. Frankly, it makes brand executives and their communications professionals nervous. Does communicating direct to the consumer and not following the general rule of the credible third-party endorsement through an influencer lead to loss of control of communication? Face it—communicating direct to consumers on the Web might not always lead to a "credible" third-party endorsement (especially when a greater number of citizen journalists get their hands on information and want to publish it). However, that's not a reason to avoid PR 2.0 or be hesitant of social media applications that ultimately enhance your brand communications. With PR 2.0 comes the incredible ability to monitor the communication of citizen journalists and your influencers (and, yes, now many of them are bloggers).

To digest all this information about PR 2.0, embrace the new ways to communicate to audiences in the chapters ahead, and to visualize how the PR profession is moving toward the best PR ever practiced, it's important to know where you've been and how you got to this crucial point. You need to understand what has worked in the past so that you can incorporate some of the greatest PR practices as you propel forward. There are many strategies on the Internet that have worked for years and now, coupled with new social media applications, the result is powerful and meaningful communication with consumers who demand information and want to gather, organize, and share content within their online communities.

You Can Discover a Better Way

You've probably figured out by now that the Web in its infancy was a crazy time; that craziness had to end somewhere. But, despite the turmoil of the dot-com explosion, which eventually led to the dot-com implosion, it wasn't a completely negative experience. Many professionals walked (okay, maybe they limped away if they invested in e-brands that met an early demise). with some real and valuable lessons learned. Hopefully, you and the brands you supported were not "burned" too badly, and, with any luck are still in existence today. However, every experience is an opportunity to do it better the next time around, to make wiser choices in the next phase, and to rise above each and every communications challenge you face.

When you left the Web infancy phase behind, you should have gained new insight and managed to salvage many innovative Web-based PR resources and functional tools that still serve you well and still deliver successfully for you today. The short list of these Web-based tools include

- Online media databases that offer quick and targeted list genera-
  tion as well as editor pitching techniques and strategies (Cision
  MediaSource Database is discussed in more detail in Chapter 2,
  "Getting Started with 2.0 Research")

- A customized method to e-blast news releases to hundreds of news
  outlets just by pressing a key on your computer

- The use of online media kits or Cyber newsrooms with easily accessible company news and information (some good examples include
  Ford Motor Company, AT&T, and Dell's online media
  centers/newsroom)

- Many more opportunities to get brand coverage in publications
  that have cyber versions (with a separate online editorial department in desperate need of updating content daily)

- Internet wire distribution services for wider yet more targeted
  distribution, such as PR Newswire or Business Wire

- Video news releases (VNRs) for products and services that deserve
  visual PR

- Video on demand (VOD), which is the ability to archive video
  footage for easy download and review on the Internet

- An e-based tracking program to monitor promotional coverage
  with the capability to analyze how intended messages are received

That's only a partial list. So, despite the tragedy and trauma experienced by many companies, their executives, and business owners/entre-
preneurs, the Internet implosion made PR pros more watchful, a little
more selective, better prepared, and definitely more experienced in the
proper use and management of Internet technology for brands. In addition, survival of the fittest dictated that you quickly learn how to use the
Internet to work smarter—fast tool, less paper! The transition from Web
Infancy to PR 1.0 showed you how to be a vital communicator, more than
a paper pusher. With less paper to push and more time and energy, you
focused on being a strategist and planner. More importantly, professionals
found it easier to communicate at speeds never achieved before in the
history of the PR profession (both for publicity programs and to employ

crisis communications or damage control, when necessary). You entered into PR 1.0 ready to use the errors of the past as a springboard to a better PR future for the brands you represented.

Go Ahead, Let the Good Times Roll

One way to sum up PR 1.0 is to say that it was a time of good, solid functional Internet capabilities. The Internet is a tremendous communications channel with greater speed, flexibility, and customization than any other channel I know. Communicating via the Internet hopefully made your job easier, helped you to control information to some degree (as long as you were using the proper brand tracking and monitoring strategies, which are discussed in Chapter 5, "Better Monitoring for PR 2.0"), and provided you with simple technological advancements that were not entirely confusing. You didn't have to study IT or Web programming to understand the practical and creative benefits of utilizing e-newsletters, viral marketing, e-blast communications, Webcasts, Webinars, and so on. Most would agree that the gradual acceptance of PR 1.0 was so much easier than the struggle you might have encountered when the Web was in its infancy stage. Luckily, after the dot-com bubble burst, PR 1.0 was a period of stabilization. When PR 1.0 evolved, it wasn't threatening. The days of PR 1.0 should have made you feel good about your role as a professional. Many professionals were able to grasp the PR 1.0 concepts and carry them forward—with excellent tools, skills, and lessons learned.

There are so many reasons PR 1.0 made you feel at ease, and even more reasons you would want to hold onto many of the strategies as you journey into the unfamiliar PR 2.0 territory of today. Let's touch upon three main reasons why PR 1.0 was so good to the PR professional.

Reason #1: A Two-Way Highway

The best communication is a two-way communication highway. Every time you send an e-mail correspondence, e-newsletter, an HTML e-blast, participate in a chat session, forum, or newsgroup, and partake in a Webinar (Web seminar), you are able to immediately talk back. You can give your opinion and you don't have to wonder how your audience feels, or guess if they like or dislike something. They tell you what's good or bad in an instant. Remember, it's the PR professional's job to understand the wants and needs of the audience and to listen carefully at all times.

Reason #2: Easier Editorial Coverage

You could provide audiences with more information than they could have ever imagined. For example, the concept of the online media kit or Cyber newsroom became very popular. Not every brand had a fancy newsroom with bells and whistles. However, many brands learned that the best way to be included in a journalist's story was to make sure up-to-date company news and information was available at all times—with or without the help of a PR professional. Journalists found it extremely easy to log on to a brand's Web site, navigate to the media center, and access news releases (in some cases up to five years of archived announcements), executive bios of the management team, high resolution images and logos for download, event calendars, speeches and presentations, past publicity, and white papers. Most of all, they wanted to find the PR person's contact information to set up an interview. With all the information in one centralized area, the chances of the brand being included in a story were far greater than that of the company that didn't have easy access for the media person to a newsroom or media center.

Reason #3: Longer, Stronger Relationships

The ability to build better relationships through targeted communication is the key to brand success. The Internet gives you the capability to review Web sites of news organizations that tell you what they want to cover, online media guides that replace their paper ancestors, and newsletters and other resources that help you to refine your approach. Relationships with journalists, for example, can be built and nurtured more quickly through research on the Internet. You know that the PR pro who demonstrates a clear understanding of a media outlet and the journalist's area of interest is taken much more seriously than someone who hasn't done his homework. Not only is the Internet an excellent channel to build relationships with media, but it's also a vehicle that provides information on a brand's market and competitors. With an abundance of information at your fingertips, it is so much easier to learn about your audiences and customize communication to suit a variety of their needs.

Your Best and Most Remembered Communications Resources

In my experience, some brands were communicating quickly and regularly via the Internet, and others took a little longer to embrace the PR 1.0 strategies. There are so many recognizable and effective strategies. However, three of the most popular early Internet communications strategies that are still prominent today include e-newsletters, viral marketing, and news release e-blasts. These are discussed in the sections that follow.

E-Newsletters

There are obvious reasons why a communications professional would want to develop an e-newsletter outreach program. E-newsletters are versatile and can be used to inform and educate a number of audiences: potential prospects, current clients, employees, the media, stockholders, and the like. Remember, when it comes to newsletters as a form of communication (print or online), the optimum word is "educate." Think about how much e-correspondence you receive daily, and how many brands are deleted from your inbox. Your time is limited, so it's important to stick with the communication that informs, teaches, and provides you with the best tips on a subject matter or perhaps some type of industry information. That's the best kind of e-newsletter.

Sure, I'd like to know what's new at every company that sends me correspondence, but I only have time for the brands that send information that helps me get through my crazy day, and even better, the ones that can provide advice on how to make my day a little easier. That's why I take the time to look at e-newsletters from only PRSA, Bull Dog Reporter, Ragan Communications, TEC Papers, *BrandWeek*, *Adweek*, and *Information Week*. Although there are many more, these are a few good examples that come to mind. They enable me to know what's going on in the industry, from Webinars and events to which brands and executives are making important moves and have found campaign success.

The benefit of using e-newsletters continues. With an e-newsletter you're not limited to a set number of pages. The easiest way to create an e-newsletter is by designing a template. The number of pages in the template is not restricted. It's the exact opposite to a printed newsletter publication, which is usually developed for four- or eight-page spreads. You can't have a five-page printed newsletter, but you can with an e-newsletter. Each month or quarter (depending on how often you distribute your newsletter), you need to decide on the amount of news and information you want to share with your audience and then drop the contents—which can include articles, news briefs, Q&A's, Quick Tips, and so forth—into the template. Some companies don't like to commit to a printed newsletter because at certain times of the year they feel they might not have enough news for even a four-page newsletter. When you begin your newsletter program, it's a commitment to your audience. You can't send one issue as a monthly publication and then wait another three months to send out your next issue. Communication has to be regular and consistent to capture your audience's attention.

The use of an HTML cover e-mail introducing the e-newsletter, with links to the actual PDF newsletter, is very effective. When your audience receives the cover letter communication, they are able to pick and choose the articles that are of the most importance to them. By clicking links within the HTML cover e-mail, you can access those specific articles immediately and then review the entire newsletter later at your leisure, if you like. Because you can turn each e-newsletter issue into a PDF, they are easy to archive on a brand's Web site for quick access and referral.

In addition, there are two other very obvious reasons to use e-newsletters. The first is that the e-newsletter is extremely cost effective. There is no print charge for physical pieces. Although you may incur small programming charges for the HTML cover letter with programmed links, it's still much less money than the printing fees. Additionally, the images you use for Web communication in your newsletters do not have to be high resolution, so they are often less expensive than if you had to purchase high-resolution images for a print publication. Web-ready images at 72 dpi are cheaper than 300 dpi print-ready images. It's also inexpensive to track who is viewing newsletters in the PDF format on your Web site.

GotMarketing (gotmarketing.com) and iContact (icontact.com) are both good programs and cost-effective. The former enables you to track your e-mail marketing efforts for approximately $50.00 a month (up to 5,000 emails for that price). There are different monthly packages that you can subscribe to. The software starts tracking the e-newsletter or any e-blast communication immediately (as it lands in recipients' mailboxes). You can know within seconds if your intended audience has opened their e-mail to review your correspondence. The first message you receive after a GotMarketing distribution is: "Your email campaign entitled 'xyz' has been sent and real-time status reports are now available in your account." In addition, a report is sent to your inbox that details the success of your e-blast. It lets you know the number of entries that successfully uploaded and provides you with the e-mail addresses and information on the unsuccessful files that need to be resent. GotMarketing is an extremely useful tool that saves time and money for clients who want an agency to take on an in-house approach to distribution and immediate tracking.

An alternate approach is iContact, which is an entry-level online marketing program for clients who are just getting started with e-mail marketing efforts. The program enables you to create, send, and track your own e-newsletters, surveys, and releases. For example, with the "Sharp" plan you are allowed to have up to 1,000 e-mail addresses in your database for only $14.00 a month.

One final and critical reason a brand uses e-newsletters is if that brand has a technology edge. For example, if your products or services are Web based, then it would be only natural and expected that you would capitalize on the benefits of e-newsletter communication. Michael C. Fina is a great example of a company that has Web-based communications programs. Headquartered in New York, Michael C. Fina is the fastest growing employee recognition company in North America. It's known for exceptional quality products and services that many Fortune 500 companies rely on for their recognition programs. Although Michael C. Fina is also recalled by many for its beautiful retail store on Fifth Avenue, home to exquisite jewelry, china, and silverware, the larger portion of the company's business is dedicated to perfecting the way employee recognition programs are implemented to set them apart from competitors.

The Michael C. Fina e-newsletter clearly follows all the e-newsletter rules. It's branded to represent the company so that when recipients receive the newsletter, they know it's a Michael C. Fina correspondence. The color, design, imagery, tone, voice, and messaging exude the Michael C. Fina brand—so much so that if you removed the company's logo, you would still know it's from Michael C. Fina. Their e-newsletter educates and provides tips. For example, Michael C. Fina launched its very first newsletter in November 2006 with an issue that discussed an educational training seminar series for professionals, the latest trends in employee recognition, what's on the minds of HR decision makers, the latest version of Web-based e-recognition tools, and the hottest employee recognition gifts ("We all Scream for Flat Screens"). Sure, there are subtle hints of news regarding Michael C. Fina's business, such as the company being named with a Platinum Vendor in 2006, and how it won the Hearts on Fire Retailer of the Year Award. But, the company information is not overpowering or too "in your face" so much so that your audience doesn't benefit from the editorial content presented.

Michael C. Fina is happy with the results of using the e-newsletter program. It's an excellent way for the Michael C. Fina brand to remain top of mind for audiences that live in the HR world and need to access good information. The goal of the program is to educate and help audiences when they need to set up or expand an employee recognition program.

Viral Marketing

Viral marketing is a marketing phenomenon that facilitates and encourages people to pass along a marketing message voluntarily. I like to think of viral marketing as the "Word of Mouth" of the Internet. It reminds me of that simple Breck Girl shampoo commercial that aired on television years ago. The Breck Girl appears in a box on the TV screen that continues to multiply with images of her, as she tells her friends about the benefits of using Breck shampoo. Then, those friends tell their friends and so on and so on and so on, until the entire TV screen was filled with small images of the same girl. It's the same principle on the Internet. Marketers are looking for a high pass-along rate from person to person to increase brand awareness through this viral process. You might have heard the term "Astroturfing." According to Wikipedia, that simply means, "fake grassroots support online." Viral marketing is Astroturfing on the Internet.

There have been some great viral marketing campaigns. I remember when the *Blair Witch Project* was being talked about prior to the movie release based on its Web sites, trailers, and promotional information that almost made you believe the movie was a real life story. Sony always did a great job with the launch of its PlayStation products, with the exception of the latest version of Sony PlayStation 3. Sony's viral marketing campaign was uncovered as a sham and caused backlash for the brand (but nonetheless still talked about). It didn't take consumers very long to figure out that Sony's viral marketing campaign was created by an agency, Zipatoni, that created false video and blogs with young people pretending to be Sony PlayStation fans who desperately wanted the Sony PS3 for Christmas.

Smarties candy, the well-known brand you ate as a kid, recently launched a viral marketing campaign. It's a family business that has been around for decades. If you think about the little fruit flavored, colorful, sugar candies, how much marketing (especially online) have you seen from this brand? The answer is very little. In June of 2006, Ce De Candy, the makers of Smarties, wanted to use Web marketing to move their brand to a new level. At that time, Smarties had a simple Web site, the brand's first and only attempt at marketing. The site was designed with children in mind. It's vivid, with blocks of bright colors on the home-page, and very kid-friendly in the games section where children can play the Smarties Word Game, build a Smarties Jigsaw Puzzle, or play Smarties Air Hockey. There's text when it's appropriate (at the Smarties Store to give product descriptions) and there are many enticing images of Smarties' candy. The site is not fancy, and it's not complicated with layer after layer of unnecessary pages.

The company came up with a viral marketing campaign called Stoopid.com. The new concept was drastically different from anything

Smarties' had ever seen or done. Stoopid.com looks different, it reads different, and it's not really meant for little kids. There are no bright colors or kid-friendly pages with games or images. Instead, Stoopid.com is a viral marketing spoof that appeals to young adults and college students with a site set up to joke about the "stoopid" things that people say, including politicians, celebrities, and average individuals who just make stupid comments. The site is viral with a definite pass-along effect where you can nominate or commit someone for his or her stoopidity. The Stoopid site also enables you to find the cure for stoopidity. When you fill out a short survey of ridiculous questions and multiple-choice answers, you are able to sign up to receive the "cure" which is, of course, a jumbo roll of Smarties candy.

News Release e-Blasts

No one really knows how PR professionals survived prior to Internet e-blast programs. There are many available for you to use.

JVC Professional Products Company relies on specific media to receive releases in a timely fashion. Because JVC deals with broadcast equipment, projection systems, and security products, it has to be very careful about targeting lists and tracking each and every news release. At times, releases are sent out over PR Newswire. But, there are so many releases that require an in-house targeted media list. JVC's PR team has found a tremendous amount of success with the GotMarketing program. In a normal month, they send upwards of five news releases to hundreds of media outlets. And, during JVC's busiest season, right before the National Association of Broadcasters (NAB) tradeshow in April, the PR team can be writing and distributing as many as 30 releases.

"One year we were up to 34 announcements! I can't imagine how difficult and time consuming it would be if I didn't have the ability to take my media lists and customize my e-mail blast to each and every editor," stated Candace Vadnais, the senior PR manager who's been on the JVC account for years. She watches each and every release go out and then looks to see if her editors are reading the announcement quickly.

"If a few hours go by and I don't see certain editors opening my e-mails, I'll jump on the phone to let them know that something exciting is going on at JVC." There are two popular ways to blast out your news. JVC uses both ways, depending on the number of announcements. If it's a single announcement, the company uses GotMarketing with a simple e-mail blast that has the news release in the body of the correspondence. JVC avoids sending attachments to editors. This was a lesson learned about five years ago when viruses were forwarded through attachments and no one trusted an attachment that was unsolicited. However, if two or more news releases need to be sent, JVC's PR team crafts an e-mail for the blast and within the body of the e-mail directs the editors to click on a link that takes them over to an online newsroom that has all the releases. JVC can then track the amount of traffic in the newsroom, which should spike post-announcement distribution. Other advantages to using e-blasts include the obvious: speed, ease of communication, the capability to blast to large audiences, and the ability to brand your company with a graphically designed e-blast that captures the look and feel of the brand.

There you have it—three strong communication tools pre-PR 2.0, which are proven communication methods. But, if you think this is good PR, as they say, "You ain't seen nothing yet." Social media applications lead to more information shared among more people, using stronger visual imagery and in a manner that people want (and now demand) to receive in their communities. Although PR professionals can easily administer e-newsletters, viral marketing campaigns, and e-blast programs, social media is just as easy and these new media applications are not expensive (as one might think). The widely recognized PR 1.0 strategies are comfortable, familiar, and not technologically confusing or challenging for most. But, the 2.0 strategies are effective and a powerful means to engage customers in conversations. And, even though communications professionals choose to adopt tried and true strategies and carry them forward from period to period, that doesn't mean you can't be flexible with your communication and deliver information about your brand in new ways that people prefer and practically demand.

If you feel relaxed and at ease about the ideas discussed in Chapter 1, great; you have successfully progressed from the Infant Web through PR 1.0. At this point, you need to remember that comfortable and familiar may feel "good," but they don't push you to the limits of your creative and technological ability. Comfortable and familiar do not open your frame of reference. You have a lot of work to do to achieve effective PR 2.0 communication and to feel content in that realm. That's the ultimate goal. If you drive yourself to want more, to learn more, and to adopt more, you'll get there a lot quicker. And, as you practice with new techniques over and over again, they'll begin to feel comfortable and familiar too. That's when the learning process should start over again.

Remember that you are striving for great PR, which ultimately involves credible, accurate, and timely communications. You will always be communicating, facilitating, and monitoring relationships on behalf of your brand. With that in mind, you're ready for Chapter 2, as you gradually ease into PR 2.0, with the new research methods available to your brands online. You can't stop now. Forge on!

Endnotes

1. Several other early PR 2.0 adopters and influencers along with Solis have carried the PR 2.0 flag forward. They include Tom Foremski and his outcry for the death of the press release; Todd Defren, who offered the first social media template and continues to help PR professionals understand how to engage in the new landscape; Chris Heuer, who helped lead an effort to propose a standard for construction and distribution of Social Media Releases as well as helped define how marketing can and should participate in communities; and Shel Holtz who hosted the original NMRcast (NewMedia Release Cast) and continues to demonstrate the value of Social Media and how to join online conversations.

Chapter *2*

Getting Started with 2.0 Research

I don't think there's enough time in a day to gather, organize, and absorb all the information you can obtain on the Internet. You have the ability to be wired with knowledge from the time you wake up in the morning until the moment you fall asleep at night. There's your home desktop computer, PDA, work computer, wireless laptop, and Apple iPhone—you can log on just about anywhere, anyplace, to find any piece of obscure information you need. Because the Web is an open source channel, and the new way to interact online is through social networking and blogging, you have greater access to more information and opinions that can be captured by brands who want to stay "close" to their customers and watch their every move.

One of the first lessons you should have learned early in your career is that most of the time you're looking for very targeted information—the more targeted, the better. The key to a successful public relations program is reaching the right groups and avoiding the mass communications effort. When it comes to the type of intelligence you need, take a moment to reflect on your average busy day. How much targeted information (daily) do you need to be successful? There's intelligence that helps you to create new business, keep up-to-date on your brand's marketplace and competitors, understand your key influencers such as the media, research audiences' behavioral patterns, and monitor and analyze tracking information to determine whether your brand is well received in the market. The answer is—you need a tremendous amount of specific information.

At first, you might think it would be extremely easy to pull an abundance of statistics and facts in the least amount of time because the Internet is rich with information. Well, that all depends on the type of resources available, time constraints you might have, and the research methods you employ. If yours is a smaller company on a restricted budget, you might be attempting to gather the research online, on your own without the help of an outside firm. I definitely don't discourage the creative, "home grown" kind of research—defined as research you do on your own, without the help of an outside research vendor or paid software programs. Or, perhaps you're in a larger company and you have the resources to contract with a third-party vendor to assist you. No matter what size company or the options you choose, chances are you will still want more time in the day to soak up the abundance of information available. Certainly, there are far worse problems for a professional to have.

The Best Commitment You'll Ever Make

One thing to keep in mind: In a Web 2.0 world, you need to do your research. It's not a question of whether you should research; the question is, what approach are you going to take and why didn't you start the program a long time ago. Your brand deserves constant research, at many different intervals. Some brands research at inception, thinking it's acceptable to strike the market hard at launch and not at any other time—or other times when the brand feels threatened and it's a matter of survival, perhaps as a result of a significant change in the brand's competitive landscape (due to social, technological, legal, or economic changes). Then, some brands research constantly for growth opportunity, and yet others research simply to maintain their position in the market.

It doesn't matter how big or how small you are, if your brand is known or just starting to become recognized. You can never sit back and watch the world change without keeping yourself well informed and your company loaded with intelligence. And sharing the intelligence is just as important—not only with your entire public relations team, but also other areas of the company, which could include senior management, other marketing professionals, and those in charge of new business development.

Your research also depends on your customers' technological acceptance rates. Are they a "wired" group and are most of your marketing programs online? Also, what resources (time and employees) will you devote to a research program and when are they available to you? I always try to keep in mind the varying levels of acceptance of technology. If your customers are spending a great deal of time on the Internet, interacting in new ways on blogs, social networks, and wikis (that is, the innovators, the early adopters, or the early majority) and you use online programs to reach these groups, then the newer research methods are an absolute must. Remember that the percentages of groups online have changed considerably.

According to PEW Internet's December 2005 study on Generations Online, "Internet users ages 12–28 are more likely to Instant Message (IM), play online games, and create blogs. Internet users over age 28 (but younger than 70) are more likely to make travel arrangements and bank online." Online research strategies capture the different groups and help you listen carefully to what these consumers are saying much more quickly than traditional research methods.

Today, research strategies provide instant access to real-time data and detailed transcripts of communication that used to take weeks to collect, analyze, and compile in a report. With instant access to information, you can listen carefully, react quickly, and then improve your brand's product/ service by placing the research back into the product development cycle. JVC Professional Products Company is a great example of how a company is actively listening on user groups and forums. JVC executives spend a significant portion of their day listening to the positive and/or negative feedback on their broadcast equipment on these forums. JVC uses online strategies by tracking the user group comments and placing the information right back into the product development cycle. They use the information to enhance their broadcast quality camcorders and broadcast equipment.

Online research strategies enable you to clear up issues before they escalate out of control. However, beware as you are obtaining your intelligence. When you join a forum or user group, or a group within a social network, you need to be transparent. It appears very obvious to other forum participants if you are from a company monitoring conversations, or a marketer, planting information and steering the conversation to promote your brand. Years ago, you would need to have your ears pinned to the ground to hear what the market was saying to understand brand expectations. Of course, now you should have your eyes and ears glued to your computer screen, PDA, or other wired devices, to make sure you listen to everything your customers say.

JVC is a good example of a brand that listens to the market and as a result, the company has successfully created high quality, affordable products for end-users who want to transition from standard definition (SD) camcorders to camcorders that capture the finest quality video footage in high definition (HD). Similar to JVC, with immediate access to intelligence, you can formulate your strategy quickly and respond to those needs appropriately. The only way to actually listen is to have some sort of ongoing research or monitoring program in place (24/7, if possible, because the Internet never sleeps). Today's online research methods enable you to have the most sophisticated tools to do the job.

Are You Ready for Research?

You're not ready for 2.0 research unless you have thoroughly evaluated the resources you have available, including the people who can review and analyze the information, and the money you need to invest in your research program. You might have only one in-house marketing person who can spend a couple hours a day on research, or perhaps you have a small team of researchers who can devote their entire day to research. Then again, maybe you're part of a huge multinational company with a large department focused on intelligence gathering. The commitment to research means knowing who is best suited to run and manage the research program; these are the professionals charged to gather the information, analyze, and report on the findings. Even if you have the budget to invest in a large research program (such as a third-party research firm for primary research through web surveys, polls, or online focus groups), it's important to recognize that if you outsource to such a firm, there still needs to be a person from your team who is the liaison between the brand and the third-party vendor. It is this professional's responsibility to manage the research process and then share the information for the purpose of integrating the results into new programs moving forward.

So many levels of research can be applied in a Web 2.0 world. For example, the levels vary for small, medium, and large companies and for start-ups versus the company that has been in business for 100 years. Keep in mind that research for the start-up or small company is definitely different from research that you might employ for the more established company (a mid-to-large size company) that makes a considerable investment and has deep pockets for research strategies. Obviously, the more time and money you invest, the more you expect in ROI. Colleagues of mine, from small start-ups to larger firms, have asked me the same questions, "How do I begin a research program for my brand, and what do I need to start?"

A research program needs to be part of a yearly or six-month planning process. Most companies do their budgeting in the 4th quarter of the year and know exactly what type of investment they are going to make in research for the year ahead. For the start-up or small company, beginning a research program usually means more of a commitment in terms of a person's time. The dollar investment is small at the onset and as research proves valuable, more time and money is invested. Mid-to-large size companies conduct strategy and planning upfront and then charge either their marketing communications department or the PR/marketing agency with the responsibility to scope out the research options.

When beginning a research program, it's important to determine the following: the type of research necessary for a campaign (market research, competitive intelligence, audience opinion research, media research, and monitoring of communication and editorial coverage), if the research is within budget (see the following list broken into small cost effective and more extensive resources for larger companies), and what firm (if outsourcing) is the right partner for the job. The selection of the right research partner is critical. Although technology provides you with incredible, interactive, and visual research tools, if you don't have the right partner, you will not be able to achieve your desired results. The right partner will lead you through the research process and help you every step of the way to interpret the data accurately. A few best-pick, no-cost, or very cost-effective resources for the small or medium to the large size company that's looking for effective research tools are as follows:

- Start-up or small company resources
  www.news.google.com, www.highbeam.com,
  www.cornerbarpr.com, www.websurveyor.com,
  www.surveymonkey, www.surveygold.com, www.mediamap.com,
  www.usprwire.com, www.clickpress.com, www.sbwire.com,
  www.marketwire.com

- Mid-to-large size company resources

  www.hoovers.com, www.cision.com, www.vocus.com,
  www.prnewswire.com, www.mediaatlas.com,
  www.businesswire.com, www.delahaye.com, www.lexisnexis.com,
  www.burrellesluce.com, www.harrisinteractive.com

New Research Methods to Reach the Influencers

The media is one of our most important and powerful groups. In the case of the small company needing media research for a campaign, it might take only one person using a free search engine, such as Google, Yahoo!, or MSN, for news searches. There are also Web sites, such as HighBeam (www.highbeam.com), to access articles written by journalists. Any editor who you pitch will appreciate that you take the time to research and learn more about his or her area of interest. HighBeam is an easy research tool that I discovered a few years ago by doing a quick search on the Internet. If you go to www.highbeam.com, you can sign up for the free basic membership. The free basic membership enables you to search parts of the HighBeam library, use the HighBeam BlogEnhancer, use HighBeam RSS feeds, and search the HighBeam Web (but up to only five sources). Of course, you can also receive full access to HighBeam's award-winning library for less than $200.00 per year.

At a larger company you might tap into Vocus (www.vocus.com) or Cision (www.cision.com) media resources. Vocus provides a web-based software suite to help organizations manage local and global relationships and communications with key groups including journalists, analysts, and public officials. Cision has an excellent media information-gathering software program called Cision MediaSource. Sure, Cision's MediaSource enables professionals to compile general and targeted media lists online (more than 300,000 media representatives with 5,000 new updates daily), but it also enables you to dig deep into pitching strategies, which is valuable knowledge about your audience. The ability to know exactly what editors want and the best ways to reach them saves time and energy. For a smaller boutique, the subscription is approximately $3,000 for the year.

Of course, the yearly fee increases with more users. With the licensed soft-ware, research assistants or PR account managers are able to log on to the Internet (even remotely when they are on the road) to access information on journalists. Regardless of the type of effort, free search engine, or paid for online database subscription, you want to be able to find your key media, learn the best ways to reach them, and discover what topics are of the most interest to them.

An Interview with the Cision Experts

Peter Granat, Executive Vice President of Cision, and Vanessa Bugasch, Director of Product Marketing, discussed in detail how Cision has become a trusted source for PR research. Over the last several years, a company called The Observer Group out of Stockholm, Sweden acquired Cision, formerly Bacon's Information. The Observer Group is a consolida-tion of the largest print monitoring clipping companies around the world, as well as the largest media research and analytic companies. The Cision brand, under the new parent company, will move forward with a much larger portfolio of services. In North America alone, Cision acquired a company called MediaMap about five years ago, and then bought Delahaye, which specializes in brand measuring and analysis. Cision also entered the broadcast monitoring space last year with the acquisition of Multivision, becoming the number-two spot in North America against Video Monitoring Services (VMS) in broadcast TV and radio monitoring. A number of smaller acquisitions, both in Canada and then also in Europe, are rounding out Cision's overall portfolio of services. According to Granat, "It's actually a really exciting time. I joined Cision through an acquisition of MediaMap. We competed with Bacon's for a number of years in the same directory space, but more focused on technol-ogy and financial services, and that was about three years. I now run the Marketing, Product Marketing, Sales, and Services for the Company."

Granat and Bugasch agree that PR professionals need to closely moni-tor brand communications and analyze how the brand is being received in the marketplace. Many of the tools that are out there support this idea.

One of the things Cision does through Delahaye is a Brand Audit. They recommend that you start with a baseline program. You have the ability to capture traditional media research as well as social media and consumer generated media in the form of an audit. You can also do some survey research to understand what the perceptions are about the brand in the marketplace today and what consumers are saying. The larger brands focus primarily on the consumer space and the social media, but that's a good way to kick off any type of a project to understand where you are, and then be able to measure against that over time. Cision typically recommends this as a starting point to really understand what is being said about your brand in the market place, online, offline, through traditional media, and through consumer generated media. This is not just blogs: it's discussion groups, and even review sites.

Another interesting point made by Granat and Bugasch is that it's very hard to get that aggregated today. Today's challenges are similar to the challenges people had with traditional media: Do you use a clipping service? Do you use Factiva? Where do you go to get everything that's being said about your brand, online and offline? The same thing is happening in blogosphere space. Granat stated, "I think that's going to work itself out over time, but I don't think there's an easy answer, so what we tend to do is focus on the influencers that matter, similar to how we handled traditional media. In the truthful media space, usually the marketers know the core media list, their top tier media that really has an influence on their buyers. That's typically a place that we start with, both for traditional media, but then there are some things that we can do now with social media to look at even the influencers that matter there." Granat explained that there are some tools that are being developed in that space. In traditional media space it's usually your top-tier trades and it really depends on the brand.

On the analysis and the monitoring side, with a combination of the Delahaye services, Cision goes out and basically looks at how your messages are being portrayed within the traditional media. Against your competitors you can look for issue development—there are many different tools put in place that can measure this over time. One of the things Cision tries to do is simplify measurement for all the different types of practitioners with a model called the communications cycle. It really starts with the research process, and not just researching your media, but identifying the baseline of what's being said about you today in the marketplace. Then you can use the online directory tools and databases, such as Cision's MediaSource portal, to go out and build your key constituent list you want to target with your messages. The tools today have really evolved from the directories, which used to take days to pull together. Now, in a single morning, you can sit down and build a very targeted media list with the Media Source platform.

With respect to targeted research on the media and reaching the media through blogs, Cision gets very detailed. Granat and Bugasch stressed, "There are bloggers that matter, and we've tried to focus on the top tiered reporters by industry. For instance, a couple of years ago blogs were very big in the technology industry. eWeek and *PC Magazine* went off on their own and set up their own blogs as well. We've actually created those as separate sites within the MediaSource platform and you can read about the focus of their blogs, which might be a different subject than what journalists write about in eWeek. We can even answer questions about whether they accept pitches at their blogs, and how they like to be contacted. We built up profiles on thousands of reporters that are focused on blogging outside of their traditional media outlets. That's relatively new in the last two years."

Granat and Bugasch touched on how the media went through a couple stages with a lot of different fragmentation of the outlets, with very small niche publications. What had died off before seems to be coming back again. They've been following that trend and continue to see electronic publications appear, whether they are blogs or publications that need to be added. If you get into a vertical or a niche that you're not familiar with, you can quickly identify the key publications that are important to that industry sector. Cision has taxonomy or a topical index that's built inside MediaSource for you to look through and become educated in the various media categories. This is extremely valuable if you're on the agency side, where you're juggling a couple different clients and you have to come up with key media contacts very quickly. With more and more online media outlets and bloggers, there is a continued fragmentation of the media.

Granat, who has been in the business for 15 years, stated, "I think that's one of the things that's very core to Cision. It's a proprietary methodology that we use: the content collection process, and how we reach out to the media. I would say that's one of the reasons that customers come back to us over and over again. From a competitive standpoint, a core differentiation for us is our collection process and how we keep it up to date. We've built a core team who really knows how to work with the media. I've heard things like, if you call the *NY Times* voicemail system and get into their editorial department, they actually refer back to Cision for contact information. Part of it is definitely just the brand we've built up, but definitely the way that we approach the collection process; even by using our customer base as an asset because we do hear about a lot of changes through our customers directly as well. It's a combination of all of these things. The way that we've automated the research process, collecting the information, verifying it, and then working with our customers to get it accurate."

Looking ahead, Granat and Bugasch offered their outlook for PR pros. They think there will be an expansion in the way we look at communications for global and local campaigns over the next ten years. A similar set of tools will be available to have both consistent messages but also targeted messages based on the audiences you're trying to reach on both a local and global basis. The new type of media they've seen emerge in the last two to three years, and that's really the social media area, is going to play a bigger role. There's going to be a shakeout in this area. You get numbers thrown around in the media, about 55 million blogs. It'll be similar to the traditional media in the sense that you have to go back and focus on the influencers that matter, whether they're bloggers or traditional media. If someone has a large audience and they're influencing and they're reaching out to your key constituents, those are the individuals you want to contact. There's a basic way of tracking these newcomers, and there will be much more sophisticated ways of doing it through survey research as well as through the tracking of threads through the Internet, which really hasn't taken hold yet. The Cision executives thought we'd see more of that through social media. This 55 million number that gets thrown around on Technorati and the other services is going to become less important for PR professionals over time—similar to the user groups in the early days of technology, back in the late 80s and 90s, and how they were so influential. There's always going to be a core group online who are passionate about your brand and who you need to communicate with over the next 10 years.

2.0 Changes for the Better

There have been so many changes over the last couple years. If you think back to just a few years ago about the data collection process, it really has changed dramatically. The data collection process has really changed the way PR people work. People are much more comfortable working from home. Many doors are open in terms of flexibility. You can do your job and be extremely efficient, too. I agree with the Cision executives when they said that change and efficiency has occurred in several industries, but more so in the PR industry where information is critical to the success of the job. Having access to all this information 24/7 from anywhere makes it much more successful today than any other period of time. With this comes many challenges. As you know, it's no longer a 9–5 job. But, then again, has it ever been? Because the news never stops, you need to be available and have access to these kinds of tools—not just Cision, but also everything from Google News Alert to other resources on the Internet. Trying to manage and sort through all this information has definitely changed the nature of your job but at the same time has made it the most exciting time to be a communications professional with powerful knowledge to leverage at any time.

The many PR pros coming out of universities today into an environment where the bar has been raised are expecting better tools to reach every single media outlet and journalist, traditional or Cyber-based. However, there are still regional newspapers and newsletters that aren't online, and even the most sophisticated service providers have to collect that information manually. Part of the challenge is making sure professionals understand what's possible and what's not. Just as the bar is raised for you, the bar has also been raised for all the providers in the industry that will serve your brands in the Web 2.0 world. The needs are real time, 24/7, with constant access and the desire to have speed of delivery. The way news moves around the globe, collecting information is a challenge. But the best providers in this market are forging ahead with new technology and platforms to give you the intelligence for successful brand communication.

Research will make or break your brand. It's not clichè, it's fact. If you were to ask any of your peers who have practiced public relations whether they are pre-Internet or work in the Web 2.0 world, they will tell you that your brand's survival is only as good as the research you feed into its lifecycle. So, from the time you have a concept in your head to the time you launch the concept in the market, it's your constant, targeted intelligence that gives you an edge over your competitor. You should never skimp on research, and your research needs to be steady during the life of your brand. You should keep several key points in mind as you embrace research in a 2.0 world.

- Take advantage of the intelligence that's available on the Internet. There are research tools that can help you create new business, keep up-to-date on your brand's marketplace and competitors, understand your key influencers such as the media, research customer behavioral patterns, and monitor and analyze tracking information to determine if your brand is well received in the market.

- Don't just sit back and watch the world change. You must keep yourself well informed and your company loaded with intelligence. Of course, you should also practice sharing the intelligence, not only with your entire public relations team, but also other groups in your company.

- Make sure you have thoroughly evaluated the resources you have available (in terms of people and the hours they can spend a day reviewing the information and using it for continuing marketing efforts) and the money you have to invest in your research program.

- Although PR 2.0 changes the way we communicate and has a heavy focus on direct-to-consumer communication, the media is still a powerful group (in traditional and online publications and in the blogosphere). Take the time to find out the most you can about your key influencers. You should use online research to learn exactly what editors want and the best ways to reach them, which saves time and energy in your approach.

■ Realize that the new type of media that's emerged in the social media area is going to play a bigger role in research 2.0. There's going to be a shakeout in this area. Although the numbers in the media are about 55 million blogs, the situation is similar to traditional media in the sense that you have to go back and focus on the key influencers that matter.

■ Use the flexible 2.0 research that's available on the Internet—from the free search engines to the paid service providers with amazing technological advances—to allow your brands to more than just survive, but to thrive in a fast-moving, highly competitive, and constantly changing environment.

Chapter 3

Research with Expert Resources

Brands are using the Internet to find the best PR research strategies for market and media intelligence, with the right partners to assist them. When budgets are tight, organizations keep research strategies in-house and use Internet searches for secondary (previously published) research. There are also "free to inexpensively priced" tools to construct polls and questionnaires in-house for primary (first-hand) research. Then, when funding is available, more formal research services can be contracted. Either way, you can rely on the Internet. It has the reach and the expert resources needed for your research program—whether you conduct the research yourself or you hire the pros to handle a program for you.

The Internet Meets Your Budgetary Requirements

Luckily, even when you're on a restricted budget, you can work with PR service providers who make it extremely easy and cost effective to use 2.0 research tools. Today, smaller companies are able to invest in a research program, sooner rather than later. Ted Skinner, Vice President of Public Relations Products at PR Newswire (www.prnewswire.com), explained that PR Newswire has spent years researching and probing PR professionals. Yes, even the research providers do their own research, which leads to more affordable products for brands. One such product is MediaSense, which offers a brand the ability to track and evaluate messaging and market perception, and also enables you to have more control over brand communication. The notion of having tighter control over communication in a PR 2.0 environment is appealing. The service works with a linguistic model that is able to analyze content electronically through artificial intelligence, which enables it to know the different meanings of the same word. As an example, the computer can distinguish from the words surrounding a keyword the difference between the bat of an eye, a baseball bat, or the animal. The computer reads information like a human being can and, through a natural language process, is able to decipher a wide range of words and terms; the computer can even determine the tonality of a story, whether it's positive, negative, or neutral.

You also need a research program that gives you the ability to research and analyze market intelligence. For example, it's in your brand's best interest to identify, track, and evaluate its top five competitors. You need to know how these companies are performing in the marketplace and whether your brand surpasses their performance or pales in comparison. According to PR Newswire's Skinner, MediaSense is used by many different organizations, from nonprofits, universities, and lobbying groups to high-end multinational corporations. One of Skinner's favorite success stories is about a PR agency that asked PR Newswire to assist them in a new business effort. The agency needed to get its hands on information, approximately 12 months worth of reporting on a tough challenger they competed against for a new business opportunity. Their intention was to use this high-quality report as a part of their presentation to win the new account. The information, available from MediaSense, enabled the PR agency to undermine the incumbent's position by obtaining a detailed report from a neutral third party on that agency's performance over the past year. The PR agency used this valuable intelligence to uncover its competitor's weaknesses, and won the new business account. Although MediaSense is an annual investment of $10,000, it's a considerably small investment if you break it down over the course of the year. Skinner goes into more detail on monitoring brand communication programs (especially how PR 2.0 needs to be monitored through blogs) in Chapter 5, "Better Monitoring for PR 2.0."

Gurus Need Not Apply Here

There are also inexpensive software programs for license or purchase to aid you in your media intelligence. You learn more about media intelligence and the importance of building relationships with the media in Chapter 4, "Reaching the Wired Media for Better Coverage." Among the interesting examples of less expensive and easy-to-use resources (as compared to the well-known service providers, such as Cision or Vocus) are

CornerBarPR and Bulldog Reporters Media List Builder. CornerBarPR has been in business for about five years. Don't let the name fool you. They have a serious online tool that is simple and boasts approximately 60,000, and growing, media contacts for PR pros to generate their targeted media lists. CornerBarPR does not claim to provide the advanced features of the more widely recognized media databases. According to Richard Barger, who goes by the title of Chief Curmudgeon, "Our service is a cost effective resource for the entrepreneur or small start-up that needs to develop that targeted media list." CornerBarPR is not a fancy solution and the Web site isn't flash enabled, but the free demo alone is a good indication of how easy it is to use this media-generating tool.

Bulldog Reporter's Media List Builder is another quick and efficient tool that enables you to create highly accurate and targeted media lists. Because the program is online, you're able to develop your list in minutes without any training or complicated instructions. The service also provides you with exclusive pitching tips with each list you generate. Short blurbs offer you advice on different media contacts and the types of material they prefer to receive. Other tips from Media List Builder include when to follow up with an editor (the best time to call or e-mail), pitching pet peeves, quirks and editorial topics, and "hot buttons." Media List Builder has no membership or licensing fees. It's a pay-per-use service that's based on the number of editorial contacts you generate. According to Mike Billings, research manager at Bulldog Reporter, "The service is designed for small practitioners. You pay only $2.00 per editorial contact. Bulldog is currently working on a subscription service. This program is PR 2.0 friendly and will even include a wiki feature for PR professionals." Another excellent feature of Media List Builder is that there's no charge for building the list. You can review your list first and then decide if you want to purchase, receive, and archive it for future use.

If you are in a position to use media-gathering intelligence tools, you'll quickly experience how easy they are to use. Most of these tools don't require much more than a brief review of media outlet criteria and then the selection of the types of media outlets/editors you need to reach. Everything is accomplished online. And, you definitely don't need to be a 2.0 guru to manage the media list building process. A long checklist asks you to narrow down your criteria for the most effective search. You can search by interest/category, editor's title, circulation, regional or national outlet, type of information accepted, and if it's a paid versus unpaid subscription. The same types of criteria exist for online publications. In the case of a broadcast search, the criterion is, of course, different. For broadcast, you're looking for a specific program format, whether or not the station accepts interviews, and the program's reach. As long as the person or group in your organization has access to the Internet, you're ready to explore the research tools for today's communications professionals.

It's important to conduct continuous research for your brand. I believe you need to do research at intervals. Your audiences' habits and behaviors can change in an instance or eventually change over time. Primary online research—including polls, surveys, and focus panels—can be quarterly efforts for some companies and for others, monthly. Of course, that ties directly to your budget. Some companies prefer to do more research throughout the year in-house, and then use outside resources for one large study to complement their efforts.

Find the Right Research Partner

The Pharmaceutical Safety Institute (The Institute) is an independent, service-providing organization formed to restore and maintain consumer confidence in medicines worldwide. The Institute kicked off its research program with a prominent third-party research provider, Harris Interactive™. Harris Interactive (www.harrisinteractive.com) is a partner that provides not only the technology for online research, but also guides you through the process every step of the way.

Harris Interactive is the 12th largest and fastest-growing market research firm in the world. The company provides innovative research, insights, and strategic advice to help its clients make more confident decisions, which lead to measurable and enduring improvements in performance. Harris Interactive is widely known for *The Harris Poll,* one of the longest running, independent opinion polls, and for pioneering online market research methods. The company has built one of the world's largest panels of survey respondents, the Harris Poll Online[SM].

Although The Institute gathers a great deal of in-house research, it still needed to use an outside source to validate and add credibility to its research efforts, in the eyes of the media and the public. The Institute researched several different research providers, but really wanted a partner that would help them to build trustworthiness in the market among the Life Sciences sector, healthcare professionals, and consumers who were all concerned with drug recalls and what's been labeled a "crisis" of safety in the U.S. and worldwide. By commissioning Harris Interactive to complete an online research study on Consumer Perceptions of Drug Safety, the Institute was able to gain the recognition and credibility it desired, with the Harris Interactive name behind some very interesting survey research findings.

It wasn't a difficult decision for Dr. Axel Olsen, President of The Institute, to invest in the online research program with Harris Interactive. In fact, Dr. Olsen knew an online survey would be an effective tool to reach the 21st Century consumer. Prior to selecting Harris Interactive to conduct the survey, The Institute screened many other research organizations. Most research providers were in the $10,000 to $20,000 range and offered to provide a research program with several research components: the development of an online quantitative survey instrument (15 to 20 minutes in length), a panel of respondents representative of the desired targeted population, 1,000 online completed responses, a tabular report and an SPSS data file, and a summary of key findings.

Although there were less expensive options, The Institute chose Harris Interactive as a partner because they wanted an experienced provider, one whose name they could leverage in marketing efforts. (You learn more about Harris Interactive in an interview with Humphrey Taylor, the Chairman of *The Harris Poll* at Harris Interactive, and two key methodologists for the company, John Bremer and Randall Thomas, at the end of this chapter). The choice to use Harris Interactive was also based on the fact that the organization is known to be a leader in conducting online market research. As the survey contract negotiations went back and forth between the two parties, Harris Interactive provided concrete evidence on successful web-based research that really helped Dr. Olsen and his team feel comfortable about the effectiveness of online surveys. One of the first questions to arise was whether the media would see an online survey as a valid instrument to gather information on consumer opinions. Would some of the medical journals and healthcare publications they were trying to reach accept online research, or did they include only telephone survey research in their publications? The Institute wanted to be certain that the *Journal of the American Medical Association* (*JAMA*), which is a well-respected medical journal, would accept online survey research. A quick call to *JAMA* informed Dr. Olsen that even the hardcore research publications accept online statistics as valid research, as long as the sample size was large enough. Harris Interactive proved that online research was an effective means to collect data on consumer drug safety perceptions.

What the Experts Have to Say

According to one article in *American Psychologist*, there are several pre-conceptions about Internet data.[1] Some of these include

1. "Internet samples are not demographically diverse."

2. "Internet data are compromised by the anonymity of participants."

3. "Internet-based findings differ from those obtained by other methods."

An informal interview with the Harris Interactive executives helps to clear up these three misconceptions and really provides an in-depth look at why you should incorporate online research into your program. The professionals who participated in the interview were:

- Humphrey Taylor, Chairman of *The Harris Poll,* Harris Interactive

- John Bremer, VP, Global Representative, Harris Interactive

- Randall K. Thomas, Director of Internet Research and Senior Research Scientist, Harris Interactive

Q: What are the biggest differences among research methods today, as compared to the tools we used years ago?

Humphrey: I think the biggest difference, obviously, is that 10 to 15 years ago there was virtually no online research. Now, out of the worldwide spending on market research, a big and rapidly growing chunk of it is in fact done online. Telephone research, which was a substantial part at one time, has not only been on the decline, but has, in some ways, been getting worse because of the weakening penetration of traditional land lines. Many countries now have more people online, and there are fewer landlines because of cell phones. Also there is the increasing difficulty of getting people to actually talk to interviewers on the telephone. That's one big difference.

John: Yes, I think even though the research industry has always been at the forefront of using fantastic analytical tools, I also think there's a convergence of academic and some heavy hitters from the statistical, economic, and the psychological worlds. The tools we are using now are even more advanced than they were 10 to 15 years ago.

Randall: The research tools have changed fairly dramatically. A couple things we can see, going along with that visual theme, is that we've developed many tools which enable us to measure reactions using visual presentations, and some of those are ad concept testing and package testing. There's also discreet choice modeling. You can see many elements simultaneously that would be hard to do in any other modality. People are presented with more realistic choices using multiple variables and they make decisions very much resembling those that occur in real life. From that, we can find out how important various features are. So, we can get more complex information from the new types of tools we're developing. I work on new research tool development, so part of my job is to review tools as we develop them. We're developing new kinds of scales. When we think about visual analog scales, we can create scales of any visual form that we want to map out the human mind, and as long as people see them as meaningful, we can more accurately measure ideas involving how people feel, think, and what they're going to do. In other modes of research, you often have to simplify the scales, present them in very practiced ways, and as a result, might not be able to explore novel ways of thinking or reacting. For instance, for car interiors, we can actually show respondents a different lighting format within a car interior and ask them to pick the lighting formats they like. On the Internet, they can actually click on different buttons and see an overhead light come on within the car interior. Or you can see a side light come on, and you can ask, well what kind of combinations of lights or what types of lights do you like in the car interior? This can't be done very easily in other modalities. It's also very interactive, it goes with Web 2.0, so many tools we're developing are going after the interactivity of the Web, portraying events in a much more complex fashion, resembling real life.

Humphrey: Additionally, not only has the Internet enabled us to do many more interactive interviews, they are much faster, across many more countries, and in many more languages than previously.

Q: Do you think that the combination of the traditional and the online research provides really solid information and data?

John: I think it depends. There are a lot of things going on when you consider the research methodology. Can you reach the population or a proportion of the population you want to online? Is there some form of a social desirability bias? Humphrey and Randall wrote a paper on social desirability bias which talked about if you are doing studies online, you can sometimes get more truthful answers. So there are times when doing the research online by itself gives you better answers—more reliable answers.

Humphrey: Let me give you an example. When we ask people at the end of a telephone survey about their sexual orientation, we get up to two percent who identify themselves as gay, lesbian, or bisexual. When we ask the same question at the end of an online survey the number is at or close to six percent. When we ask about going to church, the numbers are different. When we ask about believing in God, the numbers are different. When we ask about drinking alcohol, the numbers are different. So, anything where there is embarrassment to telling a human being you drink or don't go to church or don't give to charity or whatever it is that makes you feel uncomfortable, then the numbers, we think, are much better with the online surveys.

John: There are times when doing mixed mode studies, in certain countries, is really to a brand's advantage. One of the things you'll hear a lot about is convenience. Convenience is an important factor in survey research. When somebody doesn't want to talk to a telephone interviewer, they can for the most part avoid him or her. You have the option of saying, "Look, I don't have to talk to you now." You can take a survey online, or you can take a survey via telephone. For physicians, we often give them the option of taking it via paper, via Internet, via telephone, anything that is convenient for them and enables them to take the survey and give us the most thoughtful answers they can. That's really the result we want.

Humphrey: That's particularly true, as John implied, in terms of professionals and business people, some of whom will do a survey online and not on the telephone and vice versa.

John: So, that's our mixed mode methodology. When you use a mixed mode approach, it helps to reach certain populations, particularly internationally. In certain countries, the Internet penetration isn't high enough to enable us to do a full online approach, but it is high enough for us to get some of our interviews online and the rest through more traditional modes such as face-to-face or telephone methodology.

Q: Just stepping back for one moment and thinking about your populations, are you finding that certain demographics are more apt to participate online?

John: I'm a statistician, so understand I'll always say it depends on a lot of things. It's not as though you can say men prefer to do surveys online and women prefer to do surveys on the telephone. There are certain types of people who have definite preferences and it gets back to what I was talking about before, which is convenience. We tend to see that professionals will take surveys online more than they'll take surveys on the telephone. For certain income groups, they might choose to take surveys online more. I haven't really found that the gender has played any role. I have found that the younger age groups do tend to be more comfortable online, so they do have a preference, making it difficult to get them in many survey modes at this point. Even though I have an inclination that they have an easier time, or a better time taking it online, they're still not the easiest to reach.

Humphrey: I think that in America, more college students are online than have landlines and can be reached by a telephone survey.

John: That's absolutely true. We know that, even in the 18- to 24-year-old age group, 24 percent have given up their landline at this point and traditional telephone interviews do not call cell phones just because there's an additional cost, and there's an inconvenience factor to the person taking the survey. So we're getting less data from telephone research.

Randall: We're able to present a lot more visual stimuli, whether its video or visual images for people to view. And, the thinking and answers we get are more visually based rather than orally based, as might be obtained in telephone or face-to-face interviews. It's a different way of thinking about research. It requires more interaction with the visual environment as well.

Humphrey: One important difference is that we can test television commercials or movie trailers online in people's homes, which we couldn't do before. We had to bring people to theaters to have them look at trailers or commercials.

Q: What do you feel are the benefits of 2.0 research?

John: I'm one of the biggest cheerleaders for online research. I think there are a lot of benefits out there. There are several benefits such as what Randall was just talking about, which is the ability to get more information. Again, it has to be appropriately analyzed. The fundamentals of market research and survey research haven't changed. Even though we have great technology and better ways of doing things, the fundamentals are still there. But you can collect more data from more people, so you have the ability to take that and get bigger sample sizes with more in-depth analysis of your population of interest. We've talked a lot about doing things better. There are analytic techniques that were out there but we weren't able to use them quite as easily as we use them now. We have the ability to get a very particular population of interest.

Humphrey: A specific example is the number of people who say they have been diagnosed with depression. It's much higher online than it is on the telephone. And, we can go back to the same people much more easily, quickly, and less expensively than you could if you did it by telephone.

Q: Do you feel that PR professionals have been skeptical of online research, or as a group have they really embraced new research methods?

Randall: From what we see, PR firms are embracing online because the results we obtain from online research are quite comparable to those obtained from phone research.

John: To address the skepticism issue, the one point I do want to make is that we're using the phrase "online research" but not all online research is created equal. One of the things that I'm very proud of is the work that we've done here at Harris. There are certainly some other really good firms that have taken the time to look into what produces a representative result online. Part of the problem is that there are some firms that are very quick and dirty. They provide a sample and you're not entirely sure where the sample is from. As a result, there are times when people do get burned.

Online research, when it's done well, is a fantastic tool. Online research when it's not done well can leave people with distaste for doing Internet based research. I think that many PR firms are savvy enough to understand now that you need a combination of looking at survey designs, sampling, and weighting together to figure out what really does constitute a good survey. And that's not only true for online; that's true for telephone and for face-to-face. The fundamentals of survey research have not changed. At one point people thought the fundamentals *had* changed. They really haven't. So I think there was some skepticism a while back when people were getting burned with some data that really was not representative of the populations they were trying to project to. I think many PR firms are much more knowledgeable and understand that the fundamentals haven't changed as long as they look at the research they're getting with regard to those fundamentals. Then they understand that well-done online research can be such an incredible thing.

Q: Tell me one of your favorite online research success stories.

Humphrey: This is my chance to tell you my favorite story! A few years ago we were pitching to a small pharmaceutical company, and they were very happy with their existing research providers and they more or less said, "Thanks, but no thanks." As we were leaving we said what sales-people sometimes say stupidly, "Well, if you have a really difficult prob-lem, why don't you come back to us." A few weeks later the phone rang and they said, "We have a really difficult problem."

It was Friday morning. They said, "Next Wednesday we have a Board meeting and our CEO wants to go into the Board meeting with data about how patients taking our drug compare with patients taking two other competitive drugs." We wrote a questionnaire, got it approved by 3:00 in the afternoon on Friday, and sent it out into the field that same day. By Sunday morning we had several thousand responses including more than 500 taking drug "A," drug "B," and drug "C." We wrote a report and when the CEO came in on Monday morning, the next working day (after the day they called us), there were results from a survey compar-ing the three different samples taking the three competitive drugs. He looked at that and said, "That's terrific, but if I had known these were the answers they were going to give, I would've liked to ask them two more questions." That was fine. We wrote the two additional questions. We went back to them on Monday afternoon. We had data in on Tuesday, and we wrote it up on Tuesday. The CEO went back into his Board meeting on Wednesday with two waves of interviewing with very large numbers of very hard to reach people. As a result, we gained a new, happy client.

One other example is also worth mentioning. The biggest survey we ever did involved 1.2 million people in over 90 countries around the world in maybe eight different languages. We were able to do that in about 10 days, which is sort of mind-boggling.

Q: Where do you see online research going in the future?

Randall: I think there's always a creative and economic tension there that some companies start to recruit market research professionals inter-nally to help them figure out information and then they go through downsizing cycles, which then causes them to look to the outside. I think the market research field in general has seen companies try to have this internalized specialty, and then outsource it...and then try to have the internalized specialty again. I think it goes back and forth. I see it as cyclical, not necessarily as a growth concept for the next 10 years.

Humphrey: I've found there are two cycles that go on. I'm extremely old. I've been around much longer than young John and Randall here. I have seen many clients go back and forth between downsizing where they outsource research and then hire in people because they think it's too expensive to outsource it. Usually every time a new CEO comes along he will reverse what his predecessor did. You downsize, you hire in, you downsize, you hire in.

The second trend is what I call the decentralization and the centralization trend. In the '70s and '80s I was doing an enormous amount of work for a large financial institution, and every few years they would centralize everything into one big marketing research department for all their different divisions. Then they would have a new CEO or head of marketing and they would decentralize everything. Each team in every division had its own marketing research department. Then, another CEO or some manager would come along and they would centralize it all again. I think you can make a strong case for all these things but new managers like to make changes, so these two trends go on forever.

Randall: Now, in terms of online research growth, I see the tools getting increasingly visual. I see interfaces being more intuitive and potentially getting into peoples' brains a lot more effectively. In ten years, I predict that we will measure things a little more accurately than we can today. We'll be able to render decisions that people have to go through, or simulate them more adequately, so that we understand and arrive at better predictions. This is something that's been going on for the past ten years, but I see it continuing onward. I think that tools will get increasingly visual and orally presented as well, but through the computer.

John: The discussion of where research is going in the future always goes in a few directions. The first direction is technology: What advancing technologies are we going to see. The second direction is the respondent experience. Even the technology discussion goes in two directions.

One, the computer itself is changing. I think today is actually the release of Windows Vista, the new software that's supposed to incorporate a lot more things in it. It's supposed to become part of your living room. Some would claim that Mac has already done this, but I'm not going to get into that argument. Really it's the advancement of technology. There have been some advances in cell phone technology that might lead to more people using different tools to do what we'll call "online research." We also talked about some things earlier, which is what sort of technology is going to enable the client and the respondent to see more information and have more convenience in the way that they respond.

I think the real benefit of a market research company is not just data; it's analysis of that data to provide better understanding and insight. I think the client is more involved now to some degree. We bring them more into the process. But it's still through the guidance of the market research community that gives them the right answers. There are some who just want to do it on their own, but as Randall and Humphrey have said, that's more statistical in nature. So you've got the application of being able to see the data in real time and then you've got the respondent experience, which is what Randall has just gone through. I see qualitative moves going back to being what we call face-to-face in virtual settings—with an ability to see everyone in the room. One criticism of online focus groups is that although they might provide excellent information, you're not really getting the emotion or the body language. As we can move to the visual video aspect; we are going to get to see emotion and things of that nature.

The analytic methodology is being used better with online research and will just continue to get better. This sounds sort of geeky, but at the major survey research organizations, we're just getting more capable statistically and better at what we're doing. We're getting better at taking advantage of all these powerful resources you can utilize online. That's going to really contribute in the next ten years. Even with the coming advances, I think the fundamentals of market research will remain the same—thoughtful consideration of sample, well-designed questions and responses, and appropriate analyses.

As you explore research with Internet resources, there are several key points you need to remember:

- If you haven't started your research program, get started. The Internet is the best place to start—it has everything you need.

- Your brand is never too small or too big to do research at different intervals.

- The Internet has incredible, interactive tools to research the 21st Century customer, from your in-house intelligence gathering to formal research with a third-party service provider.

- If you outsource your research program, make sure you take the time to select the right partner—one who guides you through the process.

- Take advantage of new 2.0 research strategies that will provide you with accurate and instantaneous intelligence.

- Online research enables you to collect more data from more people, and you have the ability to get bigger sample sizes. Be more interactive and do more in-depth analysis of your population.

- Online research enables you to test audiences visually in ways that were never possible before the Web.

- New research strategies are continually improving, and in the future you'll see interfaces being more intuitive and tapping into audiences' brains much more effectively.

Endnotes

1. Gosling, Samuel D. and Simine Vazir of The University of Texas at Austin, Sanjay Srivastava of Stanford University and Oliver P. John of University of California, Berkeley, "Should We Trust Web Based Studies?" Feb/Mar (2004), *American Psychologist*.

Chapter 4

Reaching the Wired Media for Better Coverage

Where does the editor/journalist fit into PR 2.0? Even though PR 2.0 breeds citizen journalists who have a passion for publishing their opinions on blogs and social networks, the media will always be a powerful influencer. Remember that the media triggers and feeds into today's web conversations. Today, most journalists are wired for the Internet, on the go, and ready to converse with the professionals who know their communication preferences. Whether you intend to prepare a general PR release or are responding to a specific request from a journalist for information about your company's products or services, the Internet has become a valuable two-way conduit for researching as well as disseminating information. If you focus your time and energy into gathering targeted research—especially investigating information about your brand's key media influencers—getting them interested in your communication will be easy.

When you reach out to your media influencer, you should know as much as you can about that person—whether she is singled out and communicated to as a part of a campaign, or she appears on your news release distribution list and receive announcements on a regular basis. Work hard to build relationships with journalists because the influence of the journalist's pen (or keyboard) is extremely powerful. A solid list of good media contacts might be the key to securing your next big feature story for your brand, or maybe your exceptional relationships with media contacts can land you your next job or your next big promotion. In some cases, it's your elaborate list of media contacts and your editorial portfolio that might win you a large piece of business.

You've heard the expression "It's who you know." Well, in the PR world, the same applies, and even more so. When you first begin in PR, if you are in a smaller company, you might not have outside resources to help you develop your media "House List." But, with the reach of the Internet, it's not terribly difficult to find the right contacts, whether it's a national newspaper business editor or key journalist per vertical market. PR is moving at a fast pace, so you need to keep in mind two challenges. Journalist turnover will always be an issue. If you keep up with your editors, you can follow their careers from one media venue to another. The other challenge you might face is that building a relationship with anyone takes time and a great deal of trust between both parties. The Internet can help you with both challenges, especially when it comes to finding and keeping in touch with those key influencers who help you share information. There are no excuses for not taking advantage of research 2.0— Internet style. Because the news, media commentary and coverage fuel the conversations in the blogosphere, you need to keep your influencers close. Your media outreach program should aim to build strong relationships, and, as a result, you'll secure excellent media coverage that leads to more positive conversations among your customers.

How Far You Go for the Relationship

Although the Internet makes it easier for you to find the right information, build stronger relationships, and do this in so much less time, can you ever have too much information on a journalist? Is there anything wrong with knowing everything about his or her writing style and career history? What about likes and dislikes? Should you make it your business to know about your "A" list or top-tier journalists' general hobbies and interests? What about their overall writing backgrounds? (Should you go as far back as college?) The Internet has this information. You'll come to find as you expand your media database that as long as you don't come off "stalkerish" in the eyes of your media contacts, there's no reason why you can't take full advantage of what the Internet has to offer in terms of intelligence. But you should employ the same respect and etiquette you would use in any relationship.

Anna Maria Virzi of Ziff Davis' *Baseline* magazine cautioned PR people who are too proficient at gathering information on the media that they need to be careful of occasional backlash. Some reporters prefer to remain private people, and they don't necessarily want the spotlight turned on them. In an interview, Lisa DiCarlo, a senior editor from Forbes.com, mentioned that she felt uncomfortable with some of the information PR people had collected on her. The details went far beyond what she thought was normal intelligence gathering. Some of the information included how she "doesn't divert her eyes from the executive to write on the notepad," which the person being interviewed felt was "an intimidation tactic." DiCarlo explained that research on what she covers and how she covers it is acceptable, but she said, "Examining the personal interviewing styles was creepy." Both Virzi's and DiCarlo's comments were shared back in 2002. You can only imagine the type of information you can obtain on journalists today if you connect with them on Facebook.com or LinkedIn.com.

In general, editors tend to build relationships with you if you work for a newsworthy company because they need your help daily with their stories and deadlines. They usually call upon you with one straightforward request. If you offer information on your own for dissemination, it is incumbent upon you to make sure the content of what you share meets the same criteria.

Give Your Influencers What They Want

Because the journalist's request is so important, let's break it down, piece by piece, to understand how to give the influencers what they want.

Give timely information. Timely information refers to something relevant about your brand. Perhaps there's a hot topic in the news that surrounds your products or services that you must address immediately. In a 2.0 world, an editor really can't wait for you to take a week to schedule an interview with a source. He or she has Really Simple Syndication (RSS) feeds (the whole family of Web feed formats used to publish frequently updated digital content), blogs, and uses different tags to find as much credible information as possible to enhance his or her story.

When called upon, you need to have your executive prepped and interviewable on a moment's notice; or you can step up to the plate and become the key company spokesperson. When there's breaking news, an interview can take place on the spot. Depending on the nature of the story, there are cases when the journalist's sense of urgency is not as immediate. Of course, the Internet plays a huge role in getting information to editors in an instant. Whether it's answering questions via e-mail or instant messaging (IM, which might not be as popular), sending digital files that can be downloaded into stories, or using File Transfer Protocol (FTP) to get graphics to media outlets, rigorous deadlines must be met.

Give accurate information. A #1 rule of thumb is you always need to make sure your information is accurate. Just as an editor has to check facts and have second sources—so do you. You and your executives need to make sure that anything said "on the record" or even "off the record" is accurate. Whether you say it, e-mail it, or IM it, the information will show up in print, or online. If it's discovered that the information is inaccurate, the black mark may stick with your brand (both the brand you represent and your own personal brand as a PR professional).

Give novel information. The media looks for information beyond what they've researched themselves. They need it to be relevant and it should enhance the story they are researching. You might have already experienced those awkward pitches when an editor says, "Okay, now tell me something I don't already know." It's human nature to feel stunned at first by this statement. Even if you felt tongue tied, hopefully you had a contingency plan. Have a backup angle and rehearsed segues ready to go, if the first angle doesn't spark immediate interest. Bull Dog Reporter's e-newsletter reminds its readers to provide substance: "The best PR people have stories I haven't read about before…If you come to me and say, 'My client has a great investing record,' I'll say, 'So what?' What I want are special insights that go beyond conventional wisdom and offer special, unique stories." However, the "so what" factor is very true. As a PR person, you're meaningless to a journalist unless you are a credible resource they can count on for new information that can be obtained only by you and/or your brand.

Give information that can help meet deadlines. It's so important that you, as the PR pro, help the editor to get everything he/she needs to complete a story. If there's one thing you should strive for in your career, it's to position yourself as a PR person who provides valuable information and someone who can get the information at a moment's notice. As a result, you will have many editors in your corner (or in your database). This follows the fundamentals of PR, which have not changed extensively since the days of Edward Bernays (the Founding Father of PR). PR is, and hopefully will always be, based on providing accurate, credible, and timely communication. For instance, you wouldn't approach the media unless your story was relevant and fit into an existing trend or was a part of an emerging story of interest.

Using the Internet is the best way to ensure the relevancy of material you share. You can tap into the Internet every day and night, if you choose. And the many resources at your fingertips—from search engines to paid software programs—enable you to uncover a tremendous amount of information.

Help Is on the Way

Many PR service providers equipped to help you are available. Look for the programs that enable you to do all your PR research at once. For example, Cision has CisionPoint and Vocus provides one-stop "research" shopping. According to the Cision executives Peter Granat and Vanessa Bugasch (who you met in Chapter 2, "Getting Started with 2.0 Research"), the new CisionPoint platform is the latest step in offering a complete research solution. "We bring together the Delahaye analytics service, the broadcast monitoring, and streaming video into the MediaSource platform, as well as our traditional print clipping and research databases," states Granat. Bugasch explains, "When you think about integration, let's say you're looking at the journalist profile you're going to pitch, and you're looking at their pitching tips and how they like to be contacted. Then you can see what coverage they've actually written about your company or your industry into those clips." Then you're able to evaluate, "Are they writing a positive story about me or a negative story about our organization?" before you even contact them. CisionPoint integrates the clippings, the evaluations, and the journalist database all in one.

The Human Element Gives You an Edge

Companies such as Cision and Vocus, and many of the other service providers, have done their homework. These organizations know what resources you require to help you find detailed media information, with platforms that are simple to navigate. But, there's one fine point you need to remember as you use PR 2.0 strategies to gather your intelligence and communicate with journalists: Nothing can ever take the place of human interaction. The Web certainly gets us the closest to face-to-face real time communication. But PR is about people and personal relationships. The human voice and meeting in person, when the situation presents itself, is still the best way to take a relationship to the next level. So, no matter how sophisticated the technology, keep in mind the human element is always the cornerstone of a relationship.

Vocus has a sophisticated core product—a media database with approximately 300,000 U.S. media contacts, or about 400,000 contacts if you include international media. The Vocus program provides more than just simple media profiling and list generation. It's amazing the type of information and reports you can compile. The program provides you with a full cycle of PR research from media profiling through distribution. The interface is friendly and organized so that you can work through your entire process, from idea to polished information you intend to share. It's the type of program that could be open on your desktop all day, an integrated solution that includes news searches, opportunities database with editorial calendars, awards and speaking opportunities, media contact profiling and list building, distribution, and then analytical reports that monitor your brand (such as, was your brand mentioned in the headline and how many times was the brand name mentioned in the article?).

You should look for certain important details in media intelligence resources. Look for a source that includes a good journalist's profile, one that includes a contact schedule (when is the best time to reach this person), and any previous story written so that you're given a sense or flavor of the person's writing style.

One more very pertinent PR 2.0 question that you should keep in mind: Are journalists with blogs included in the database? In other words, are these blogs listed in media profiles or are they a part of the database as a media channel?

Vocus is keeping a close eye on the blog space. Social media is also incorporated into their programs. According to Kye Strance, a Vocus sales representative, "The newsgroups surfaced in 1998 and it was difficult to keep track of them. We managed to figure out what were the most influential. Blogs are a whole different medium. Bloggers are more prominent. Because there are so many of them, Vocus tracks the top bloggers. Currently, there are several thousand of them. Vocus includes the top bloggers in its database for PR people to access and pitch accordingly."

Another great feature to look for in an intelligence-gathering resource is the use of technology to upload and distribute news releases and media alerts to your media outlets (media lists that you've created yourself). With the click of a button, you should be able to blast out to your own list in a flurry of e-mails. Then, with another click you should be able to check off a box that automatically enables you to reach the journalist the way they've requested you reach them. Vocus enables you to accomplish the former and the latter, and also gives you the option to distribute through PR Newswire. (Vocus takes care of the PR Newswire charges upfront and bills you an invoice later.)

You should be aware that not every editor accepts HTML e-mail. However, when you send out your e-mail to a media outlet, it's the computer servers that determine whether the e-mail recipient needs to receive the e-mail correspondence in plain text or in HTML. From intelligence gathering through distribution and analytics, 2.0 resources provide smart technology so you can act smarter and perform the research a lot faster for your brand.

Resources for Relationships and Better Coverage

You can also rely on paid resources for editorial calendars and services that join the media person with the company executive. As a PR expert, you know the value of the editorial calendar. However, you also know that if you have to go online to retrieve an editorial calendar or call each outlet that you want to pitch to request one, this takes a great deal of time. One PR researcher or assistant could take days, even weeks to gather all this information by hand.

PR Newswire's EdCals is a searchable database that makes editorial calendar research easy and streamlines your efforts. The EdCals database has approximately 100,000 U.S. editorial opportunities. The service enables you to find out what editors and reporters from trade and consumer publications are writing about. You can also find information on lead times, issue dates and, of course, editorial contact information. Similar to other PR resources, you can search by name of the media outlet, subject, geographic location, copy deadline date, all in an effort to find the best opportunity for your brand. Because editorial calendars offer story opportunities for the entire year, EdCals has an export function to transfer the information into an Excel spreadsheet for archiving and future use. Editorial calendars give you story opportunities for the entire year.

Another Internet-based service that offers value to PR pros is PR Newswire's ProfNet. It's a quick and easy service that enables you to connect your company's experts with journalists who want to interview them. ProfNet has more than 100 reporters using the service daily. As a PR professional using the service, you're able to respond to inquiries from journalists each day. The editor inquiries are grouped by category and sent to your e-mail inbox, with a deadline for response. Lead times can be as long as a couple weeks, or as short as 24 to 48 hours. Services such as ProfNet are great because they save you time in the pitching process. By signing up your brand expert, you cut out one of the tougher steps, that introductory telephone call to the journalist, and tap right into what could be a very appropriate opportunity for your brand. Using these types of research strategies is quicker and can be more effective; however, you always need to remember that straight pitching and picking up the phone has, for years, been the key to a strong relationship with the media. There has to be a fine balance of both the traditional "pick up the phone and check-in strategy" fused with the sophisticated research tools of today.

Journalists with Individual Preferences Want News

You've heard about the tools and best practices from the PR person's point of view. It's also important to hear straight from journalists how they want to receive information (both from Internet services and directly from the PR person). You might agree that journalists, in general, prefer e-mail; well, that's no surprise. They also appreciate when you use e-mail to provide them with direct links to related information in an online newsroom because they like to access digital content and high-resolution images for their stories.

Journalists will tell you how they don't like to receive attachments. It's an unspoken rule to alert a journalist that an important attachment is on the way. Many journalists prefer information in the body of the correspondence, even if it's a news release (for fear of opening up an attachment with a virus). They especially appreciate if the news release has several interactive features within—whether it's audio, video, informational links, and the like—so it's easier for them to collect information on a topic of interest. However, there are so many different resources and ways to reach out to the media that it's critical to ask, "How do you want to be contacted and what type of resources are you looking for?"

You might expect all journalists these days to say they are using social media, blogs, and RSS technology for information. However, it's important to note that most journalists rely on a knowledgeable PR professional to help complete their stories with novel, timely, and accurate information.

Andy Teng is the editor of *HRO Today*, a national trade publication written for senior business leaders and decision makers who recommend and buy HR outsourcing services for their corporate and public sector organizations. Teng says, "My publication relies on PR directly from the companies in our space because it's such a specialized industry. In addition, we receive e-mail alerts from Business wWire as well as alerts from Web sites and organizations involved with *HRO*." He spends an awful lot of time these days on the Internet because many companies post information that sometimes even the internal PR person isn't aware of, or can't recall quickly.

For Teng, often the fastest way to gain information is through verified Internet sources. Teng finds online newsrooms helpful and noted that "up-to-date information is usually an indicator of a good source. Many companies often let their sites go stale because they don't think it's important to have constantly updated content. While it might be a budgetary constraint, it also shows a lack of polish for that company. Good marketers reflect their savvy with very dynamic sites."

His preferred way to hear from PR professionals is, "A phone call first, followed by details in an e-mail is best. An e-mail out of the blue usually gets ignored unless we have a relationship with that PR person. Also, a call first usually determines if the PR person needs to pursue the publication any further." To date, Teng said that *HRO* did not have a blog and in his opinion he feels they are "way overrated and few people seem to be able to commercialize them successfully." Teng said he doesn't use IM for professional purposes, and probably would not share his IM with anyone he's not familiar with.

Teng discussed what makes a PR person a valuable resource. "They must work in my space, work with well-recognized companies that we cover, and understand the relevance of their pitch to the industry I cover. Often they don't and hope to win coverage with out-of-the-blue e-mails or telephone calls, a strategy that simply is a waste of their time and mine. They really should spend some time on our Web site and try to figure out if their client is relevant to our scope of coverage."

Teng says that while the Internet has facilitated some very strong relationships between the journalist and the PR person, in some cases it enables the editor or reporter to make an end run around the PR person. It works both ways for Teng. If the information is online, he can often save time by cutting the PR person out of the loop. On the other hand, by making the PR person prominent on the site, he at times finds it easier to call the PR contact instead of digging through scores of Web pages for the information he's seeking.

Kate Coe is a blogger for "FishbowlLA," hosted at www.mediabistro. com. Coe has written for the *London Sunday Times*, *The Chronicle of Higher Education*, *The Journal of Folklore Research*, and *My Weekly Reader*. In addition to blogging at mediabistro.com's "FishbowlLA," she is a TV screenwriter and producer whose claims to fame include working with Audrey Hepburn, winning a Peabody, and being canned by "E!" for sticking her nose into other people's business. Coe's insight on how the media wants to work with PR professionals comes from both a TV producer's and a blogger's point of view. As a TV producer, Coe relies on reviewing news sites, some blogs, and some RSS. She does not use podcasts or video online because, "I don't have time." As a blogger, Coe relies heavily on RSS, news sites, and other blogs. As far as the manner in which Coe wants to be contacted by a PR person, she prefers e-mails, and she says, "Then, if I reach out to you, call me back. I'm astounded at how few PR people return calls." She insists, "E-mail, e-mail, and e-mail. Don't ever call me unless I ask you to." She says, "I don't want to be pitched on IM because I don't archive those messages. Once an IM is gone, it's gone for good. I like IM for quick answers to questions, casual exchange, or maybe breaking something that's happening right that second." For Coe, the most valuable PR people are the ones who know their subject matter, have answers easily available, and who don't "dance around."

As a TV producer, Coe spends a tremendous amount of time on the Internet if she's not on deadline. She looks at Lexis Nexis, and various news sites, depending on the story. She stated, "For a show on video games, I spent a lot of time at fan sites. Wikipedia is NOT a source. It's useful for blogging but I won't accept it as a real source. I don't know any journalist who does." When she assumes her blogger role, she doesn't spend a terribly large amount of time on the Internet. She Googles for another story she can link to. Coe feels that Technorati gives her a lot of MySpace pages, and that's not helpful to her. She said, "I think that technology can make the PR person a better resource—especially if they have images or video I can download. But, often the PR person just doesn't have the technical savvy to know what really works—the specs, how long it'll take to download, and how big the jpeg is. Most PR people know a lot about words, but nothing about images. They just don't know. They'll pitch me an interview with their client or expert but they don't have useable B-roll footage to go with it, or they don't have a way for me to shoot some footage. This is really, really, a pain." She says, "If you want me to post, make sure I've got an image I can use. Invite me to your event and make sure I can get photos the next morning—with IDs."

Another journalist, Paul Grzella, managing editor of the news at *Courier News,* handles what his news organization refers to as the "In-Paper" products that are published by the newspaper in print and then distributed. Grzella gets a great deal of his information from his readers and businesses who send direct inquiries and who also publish their own news releases and photos into the newspaper's calendar section. "My editors also rely a great deal on e-mail and telephone interviews. Of course, we all still want to have face-to-face with contacts, if our schedule permits," stated Grzella. The *Courier News* also subscribes to the *Associated Press* (AP) and the *Gannett News Service.* Editors at the newspaper are also tapped into Lexis Nexis and frequently use Google searches for information. As for his contact with PR people, Grzella says, "Six months ago the phone was my most relied-upon communications vehicle, but now I'd say it's e-mail. E-mail is so much easier."

His paper is using some of the new media techniques. For instance, his sports editors now have blogs, and the newspaper intends to add more in the future. "The reporters with blogs are getting great story ideas from PR people. But, there's really no hard-core pitching going on," he said. Journalists at the *Courier News* are not interacting on IM with PR professionals. Every reporter's e-mail address is provided in the articles published in the newspaper or on the Internet, which cuts down on the need to use IM as a communication vehicle. Grzella feels that PR people who "understand the nature of the paper's mission, are direct and strategic, and the ones who really do their homework, are the professionals that are the most valued." Grzella stressed the importance of understanding his newspaper's mission, which is intensely local. He doesn't want his journalists writing about national stories unless it's somehow related directly to the local community. Local is his news service's corporate mission, and any PR person pitching should know this.

Last, Grzella says that although many of his reporters cover local stories and still have the time to knock on doors (now that's the ultimate in face-to-face relationship building), any story with a sense of urgency can get done quickly by using the tools in a company's newsroom. In some cases, he says, journalists rely less on the PR person because the Internet enables you to check it out yourself. However, journalists always want to know that there is a knowledgeable person who's there to help get the story completed.

In summary, it's important to keep the following key points in mind as you forge through PR 2.0 with respect to your wired key influencers:

- Develop a solid database of media contacts that will lead to tremendous opportunities in your career and for the brands you represent.

- Gather as much information as possible on the journalists you target; just know when to draw the line so that you don't invade anyone's privacy.

- Understand that journalists want to work with PR people who can provide them with timely, accurate, and novel information for their stories so that they can reach their deadlines.

- Invest in research tools when you have the resources and take full advantage of the integrated service platforms that enable you to bundle your PR tasks easily and quickly.

- Find out what journalists expect from you and how they want to be contacted. Each individual journalist might have a PR 2.0 preference, whether it's communication through e-mail, IM, or blogs.

Chapter 5

Better Monitoring for PR 2.0

With the responsibility of communicating to your customers comes the *tedious* and very *time-consuming* job of monitoring to evaluate the effects of this communication in the market. However, once you select the right monitoring and measurement tools, it's a lot less difficult of a job. Once again, the Internet is there to help you effectively accomplish what could be a daunting task. Can monitoring be arduous? Sure, but only when you haphazardly gather information, don't organize it properly, and don't know how to evaluate it against your communication efforts. Similar to a research program, you can't let an overabundance of data paralyze you. There are proven ways to gather, analyze, and report on your data. Allow the experts to help you.

When you add to the mix your customers' involvement with social media, there's a whole new dimension to monitoring. Social media encompasses all the online technologies that people collaborate on, including their opinions and experiences as well as sharing different perspectives. Various social media applications include blogs, podcasts, wikis, Really Simple Syndication (RSS) technology, streaming video, and video blogs (vlogs). As a result, social media now enables your customers to drive the communication. They feel empowered as a part of a larger community that shares information and interacts with one another. Compared to the past, several more groups are communicating now. As a result, these groups band together and are able to react to the community ideas and concepts and communication spreads further. The Internet is no longer thousands of separate Web sites but now larger populations all connected. They're all talking! This is the greatest chance to have more conversations, spread positive information or news, and obtain great exposure for your brand—or it's the worst possible scenario when it comes to monitoring and controlling sensitive communication.

Social Media and What/Who to Monitor

A strong focus needs to be placed on your influencers—these very important people who help to frame your information. Unfortunately, when you communicate to the influencers, you can easily lose control of the communication. Communicating with the media is one of the best examples of how this might occur. From your mouth to the journalist ears, you might think you stated your communication clearly. From the journalist's ears to what he or she writes could be entirely different. Why? Because with communication comes perception, preconceived notions, miscommunications, and the like. There's no guarantee that what you do, say, or distribute on behalf of your brand will surface the way you want it to appear in the eyes of your customer. Another demanding and extremely challenging part of the monitoring task is keeping your eyes on every communication, perception, preconceived notion, and miscommunication out there in the market about your brand. The citizen journalists are also talking in their communities (social media is fueling their conversations) and the Internet; as much as it helps you to obtain tremendous exposure and valuable information about your brand, it creates new complexities to prevent you from tighter control of your communication on a daily basis.

Similar to monitoring the communication, measurement is rewarding, but challenging. One easy solution to PR measurement has never existed in all the days of PR. The largest global agencies work on their own proprietary monitoring and measurement methods. Not everyone's company can work with the largest global agencies. You might have experienced clipping services, which now have advanced beyond reading services (yes, there are hundreds of people paid to read magazines, newspapers, trade journals, and other niche publications) to Internet-based programs that scan by keywords for news on your brand. Back in the day, a cut-and-pasted clip book was handed over to the client. "Here's your quarterly clip book." Big and bulky yet valuable, the clip book was tangible proof of the PR person's performance—a measurement that can be judged. However, clients now want digital clip books that take up less space, that don't sit on a shelf gathering dust, and are easier to share with executives, customers, and prospects.

The logical approach for measurement in years past was to provide the client with reports on gross impressions (how many eyes see the coverage, which differs depending upon the type of print or broadcast medium) and how these measurements turn into advertising dollars. For example, an editorial clip that is two columns of a newspaper could cost several thousand dollars if you paid for the advertising space. At least with the conversion to advertising dollars, you can see how the PR is less expensive and that several good pieces of editorial in top-tier publications such as *Time, Business Week*, or *Forbes,* could be half a million dollars in advertising dollars. But, this still isn't enough for brands to truly reap the benefits of monitoring and measurement in a Web 2.0 world and to justify the dollars they spend on public relations and marketing programs. It's critical to approach monitoring and measurement from several levels. Brands want to see the tangible clips, but they also want to know other types of key information, including

- How are they perceived in the market?
- Are their key messages appearing in stories?
- Are key messages prominently placed in story headlines?
- What is the depth of their coverage?
- How many times do they penetrate a particular vertical market?
- How many articles quote the executives as experts?

The same approach must be applied to today's social media forums, blogs, message boards, and news groups. You might be among the many people who have searched for years to find the best methods to show a measurement that reveals a Return on Investment (ROI) for your communications programs. The nature of the game has changed so drastically from the way you monitor to the manner in which you measure because the Internet has altered our mode of communication. With the broadest reach and a vehicle whose engine continues to run 24/7, old monitoring and measuring will give you only a portion of what's really being said (good, bad, or indifferent) about your brand. Do you only want to know a portion of how your communication or the communication of others is affecting the way your customer feels about your brand? It's time for you to adapt to the new ways that are more 2.0 practical for monitoring and measurement.

Your Advanced Tools for Monitoring

There are many Web resources to help you monitor your messaging and editorial coverage in a Web 2.0 world. The tools are advanced, far beyond the days of the clipping service. Service providers realize they need to add new services to assist with online monitoring. For instance, PR Newswire's eWatch, which historically monitored Internet content, now has thousands of blogs (these are the most influential bloggers) that it monitors. eWatch tracks a client's keywords and provides regularly sched-uled reports of where these keywords can be found. Clients can select to receive these reports via e-mail or by visiting the eWatch Web site.

The eWatch reports provide links to recent editorials or mentions in social media forums. According to Ted Skinner (Vice President of Public Relations Products at PR Newswire), "Our service is under constant review depending on what medium needs to be tracked. Now, companies and their representative PR firms or IR firms are very interested in track-ing what's being said out there in more than the traditional areas." For instance, tracking blogs is different. Within the eWatch system, the reporting is tracking keywords the company provides on hundreds of thousands of articles each and every day. Keywords usually are the com-pany's name, a product name or service, and key spokespeople. However, the tracking goes well beyond gross impressions, which was as in-depth as the interest, pre-Web 2.0. The Web universe is now so sophisticated that it requires you to go beyond the pure number of mentions or gross impressions. So PR Newswire signed a deal with Technorati, one of the leaders in blog tracking, to provide more complete monitoring for the company's clients. Technorati provides PR Newswire's customers with the ability to track online conversations triggered by news releases. "One thing PR Newswire has always done is we've delivered the news to the media who can best take advantage of it and write stories and provide the publicity our clients are looking for," Skinner said. "With the blogo-sphere, our clients are now very interested in saying, 'Okay, what has the information in these news releases triggered? We've just launched a new product, we've sent out a news release. Who's talking about it and what are they saying? Is our message resonating or do we need to modify it?'"

For example, PR Newswire sent out a news release about a company's new CEO. The company expressed its interest in seeing how some of the top-tier media outlets viewed the news, specifically how CNBC viewed it and how *The New York Times* reported on it. Because it's a 2.0 world, PR Newswire was able to provide this brand with a service that not only dis-tributed news releases, but also linked the readers to the results hosted by Technorati. "You're then able to see a list of blogs that are discussing that particular news release. It really gives the company or PR firm a very quick read on how the message is being perceived in that particular envi-ronment and make the requisite changes," explained Skinner.

With all new technologies consumers are experiencing, whether it's the Internet and social networking, Bluetooth technology, or High Definition (HD), there are always the Early Adopters. There are also those who will lag behind and wait for the technology to be more mainstream. As a group, PR practitioners have not historically been the most advanced at embracing new media tools. However, there is a greater understanding about the impact of blogs, which has caused a quicker adoption than in years past. It's a clear indication of the importance of monitoring blogs when you see companies such as PR Newswire teaming up with Technorati, you know that the leaders in PR media resources are respond-ing to a greater need in the market. The worst thing for you, as a commu-nications professional, is to have your executives find out about communication in the market before you do. You want to be the first to know what's being said and then share it with them. For this reason, you need to consider the importance of tracking new media sooner, rather than later.

You might have noticed that with all the conversation emanating from the Web, a great deal revolves around the consumer area. The Web is the vehicle with the largest audience and the greatest interest. Skinner said that most brands are realizing that this channel has the most targeted "sound-byte," or word-of-mouth value, with respect to "this product doesn't work properly or my car doesn't start, and whatever that open discussion might be." The wider the consumer area the greater the conversation's going to be. But, that doesn't mean that Web 2.0 excludes general business and B2B audiences. He says, "More business transactions are being done over the Web every day, whether it's a large multinational like IBM, or a consulting company or a trucking company. I think the B2B world has taken to the Web for many concrete business uses, and has been surprisingly comfortable in viewing the Web 2.0 progress as a part of their world and not just belonging to someone else."

More and more brands on both the consumer and B2B side are involved in blog monitoring and measurement. Companies are looking for measurement reports in a two-week timeframe that evaluates whether blog conversations on a topic are increasing or decreasing, and if there are more participants in a particular conversation. Most companies want to see the conversation lessen if it's a negative story. As they monitor, they wait to see the attitude of the conversation's participants in those first couple weeks before they want to respond. Reports that monitor blogs can tell you if the conversation on the negative side increases, which might be the signal to propel damage control into action. Conversely, if it's a positive story, you might want to fuel it. When there is positive buzz around your brand, it's the best time to send out more communication to keep the chatter going. You might want to take the opportunity to send out some news releases and make your brand spokesperson(s) or company officers available for interviews. You can use real-time monitoring of blogs to keep the momentum of a particular story going.

PR Newswire provides a service that measures blogs—MediaSense Blog Measurement—so you can also tell who is part of the conversation. Linguistic models can, with a fair amount of accuracy, tell you whether the speaker is going to be a male or female, and some of the models are going so far as trying to divide the bloggers, and their commentators—who of course are anonymous—into different age groups. Blog measurement is in the infancy stage but will continue to progress and grow to become more and more important. No matter what phase of the Web—1.0, 2.0, or maybe the next significant phase—the more information you can get, the more you want. It's similar to the way you might have started out with clipping services and print measurements. Knowing the number of editorial clips was fine at one time, but if you were like thousands of other PR pros, you wanted to know more, including a deeper analysis of what the print medium was actually saying and how that impacts your brand.

Evaluating the Conversations

You are no different from your peers if you're nervous about controlling brand communication. Luckily, the new 2.0 monitoring tools allow more flexibility to capture messaging as it's being shared about your company and using linguistic models to analyze the content of the story. For example, an electronic company launching a new product might have received 200 mentions in post launch. In years past, the mentions alone might have pleased the CEO of the company. Today, because you can analyze every article, if you found that 190 of them focused on the competitor's technology with only a brief mention of your own product, then your monitoring and measurement mission was successful. However, your mission to create positive exposure as a call to action for customers to purchase your product might not have proved as successful.

New media monitoring tools enable you to evaluate whether the coverage promotes the right information. For instance, are the messages in the market from your CEO's speeches at conferences or his seminars or quotes in news releases? You will be able to answer the question, "Is that message resonating with the media? Are they not only writing about my company, but are they writing about my company in the context I want them to be writing about my company?" Most blog monitoring is done electronically through advanced artificial intelligence, and the key term here is "natural language process." All this really means is that the computer is reading the story more like a human being than a computer. For example, you or I could read a story that talks about the high quality of an airline, but it might never use the words "high quality." If you're using a keyword search for that story, you're going to miss matching the airline name with that. But you can come away from that article saying, "Boy, that's a really high quality airline," or "That's a really innovative airline." So, what natural language process is able to do is place a wide range of words and terms under that high quality umbrella.

Also, measuring the tonality of a story, whether it's positive, negative, or neutral, is important. The computer is going to be scoring the same way day in and day out. It's going to be doing it in an unbiased fashion. It's going to be doing it more quickly than we can do it as human beings. With the natural language process, it can differentiate between a negative subject and a negative tone. For example, there could be a story about an airline strike, and we'll assume it's going to be a negative story. But if we read the story, it might talk about how the strike is going to be three weeks instead of three months, or perhaps how well the CEO is handling the strike. So the actual tone of the story—the way the journalist treats it, which is what you are looking for—might be neutral or even positive, while the subject is negative. Monitoring and measuring the story for tonality is very important and can be accomplished by utilizing the natural language process.

An Expert's Perspective on Blog Monitoring and Measurement

Another well-known analytics service provider for monitoring and measurement is Delahaye, a subsidiary company of Cision. Mark Vangel has been a research manager at Delahaye for more than 15 years. An interview with Vangel shares some of the many challenges and solutions with 2.0 monitoring and measurement.

Q: How do you help a company to determine what they should monitor and measure?

A: It always starts with the company's objectives for the analysis. Some companies want to monitor as much as possible; to evaluate the entries about them on as many blogs as possible, even though it might be very difficult for them to follow up on all this blog activity. And many of the entries that appear might be very peripheral. I call this the shotgun approach, when clients want to monitor as much as possible. Some other clients we've worked with have in mind a very select group of places, both blogs and discussion forums, that are important. They have a specific list already identified that includes the places where the most conversations are taking place. It's almost like a key publication list when you're working with traditional media.

In some cases, it's an investigation from the onset because the client really doesn't know what's out there. In this case, it's an opportunity for us to look at the universe of client mentions and determine which blogs are the most prolific and influential. Prolific blogs and influential blogs are two different things—blogs that write about you the most often might not be the most influential. We investigate whether blogs are highly trafficked, how often they are being linked to and by whom, and whether the media links to the blogs. We start by conducting a search of where the company or where certain brands or products are mentioned. We see which blogs come to the top in terms of number of mentions, and then, after we derive a list of the most prolific blogs, we begin looking at who's linking to whom, and who's linked to the most often. You quickly get a sense of who's most influential.

Using a blog search tool like Technorati, IceRocket, or Blogpulse, you can get a sense of how many other blogs link to a blog in question. A useful feature on Blogpulse, for example, is called Blog Profile, where you'll find a rank for top blogs and some information on who's linking to the blog or how many posts have been written. As far as influence, another indicator is how many people are commenting on the blog. It's one indication of how many people are going to the blog and the blog's level of interactivity. The blog's traffic, how many articles are on the blog, comments, and how frequently other blogs link to the blog, all help answer the question of how influential the blog is and whether it needs to be monitored.

Q: Are you seeing more blog tracking by consumer brands? Are the B2B companies also looking at blogs?

A: We're seeing a bit less with B2B and more with consumer-oriented products. However, even with B2B, whether tracking developers or engineers, we're seeing more interest from clients. I think there's kind of a

sweet spot where certain types of products are talked about most often—
software, technology, gadgets, and automobiles—but basically there are
niche industry blogs to discuss virtually any topic. Many of the most
prominent blogs talk about whatever is in the news, and a lot of bloggers
talk about blogging. Politics is obviously a hot topic, but we don't see
many political candidates or parties as clients. Blogs are different in orientation from discussion forums, but I also see some similarities in that
blogs are a means of interaction for enthusiast communities. They are a
place where individuals can talk about particular products or topics of
interest. Remember, too, that there are many different types of blogs—for
example, individuals' personal blogs might mention Starbucks tens of
thousands of times per month, some of which contain useful feedback
about the company's service and reputation.

Q: Do you think blogs are just one step in a new direction that stems from the forum?

A: I think blogs and discussion forums are in the same ballpark.
Discussion forums obviously have more two-way communication than
blogs, with which an owner directs the conversation. But they both allow
interaction between people who have similar interests. Interaction takes
place not only in the form of comments, but also in linking between
blogs. Blogs represent more of a wide ranging net of discussions, where
individuals might be exposed to information on many different blogs
through links, whereas forum discussion typically takes place right there
on the site. Early on at Delahaye, in the mid-1990s when we deliberated
how and what to measure on the Web, I remember seeing personal Web
sites—Web sites where people described themselves and their interests.
In some ways the personal journal type of blog is really similar to those
personal Web sites. However, a major difference is the new technology
behind it; technologies to better facilitate quick and easy communication.
You don't have to program your Web site—you just post a new blog
entry.

With blogs, you're connecting many separate sites, whether individuals' sites or businesses' sites. Suddenly, there are scores of new communities that can all become connected. Blogs make connecting easier than in

the past. This is a big component of blogs and the whole Web 2.0 world—the linking and collaboration. Transparency is so critical, as well—in the Web 2.0 world you're not holding onto the information, you're putting everything out there not only because it's the right thing to do, but also because someone is going to find out if you don't.

Q: As far as Delahaye's products or services, how has your company made it easier for PR professionals to monitor communication?

A: My short answer is that we do it for them, in terms of cutting through all the information out there and making it more easily digestible. If you're Starbucks, good luck trying to measure all the references to Starbucks on the Internet. There are tens of thousands of posts every month, some of which are more important than others.

So, does a company like Starbucks care about every single post, or just the key influencers? I think a little bit of both. We don't typically do this here, but one way to get around the incredible volume of information available is to take a sample of what's out there. It would have to be the right type of company, where there are many discussions and many references to their company or brand. For example, Starbucks customers discussing their experiences on personal "journal" type blogs is a good application of sampling. Let's say someone went to Starbucks and had to wait a really long time in line or had a similar problem. Maybe 25 people are going to see that personal blog entry; but if a similar sentiment appears on blog after blog after blog, that makes it more important and it creates an urgency for Starbucks to reconsider the way it is operating. Perhaps there are regional differences, and Starbucks needs to send in employees to evaluate what's taking so long. The blog research would be placed back into the development cycle to make a more pleasant experience for a customer. If it's appearing on all those micro-areas, in aggregation, it becomes a serious issue.

These are the real customers. If you're a prominent journalist-type blogger and you're talking about how there's a long wait at Starbucks, maybe more people will see that entry because more people come to your blog. But in terms of who you're measuring, as much as I want to know about the more high-profile references to certain issues, I also want to know about the individual customer experiences. We've found that some clients know about issues beforehand and want to quantify it, whereas others are completely unaware of what we will find. In both cases, clients typically want to watch the level of activity to see that it declines.

Q: Do most companies act on things quickly when they get information in real time?

A: It depends. There were times when we did daily reports. We've analyzed blogs or discussion forums for certain issues and for tone, and we've produced a report every day. That's not always the case. In fact, that's more for a crisis situation. In one instance, there was a rumor spreading about one of our clients, so they wanted daily information about where it appeared. For something like the long wait at Starbucks, it's definitely communication they'd want to keep on the radar—weekly or monthly anyway. As far as how frequently we provide reports, for traditional media reports we often provide quarterly reports. That obviously would be much too long a time to wait for customers who are monitoring blogs. We have self-service portals, as well, where clients can scan information themselves.

We have had clients who have acted online to clear up misinformation or point individuals to some background data. Offline changes, such as changing product features or company processes, often take longer. With the Starbucks example, the company can dispatch people to stores, to key locations, and monitor the wait times. They can also survey the public, or place comment cards in their stores, although those might take a little too long to yield answers. If they're wondering, "Is what I'm seeing in the blogs representative of what the public feels?" they can conduct a survey or other research methods. With awareness, there's an opportunity for a company to fix the problem or to change a product or service to make it better. Without it, you might be blindsided as criticism grows.

Big questions still loom. How is monitoring and measurement going to change? What are we going to see in the next ten years? How will a service provider meet the needs of the PR industry? It's definitely a growing industry. As companies become more involved in monitoring and measurement (we see this already with smaller companies outsourcing these tasks as a result of low cost, effective options), they will want more complex, technologically advanced products; products that can deliver the data instantaneously. In addition, the accountability model in PR has changed over the years. Having 25 clips in a clip book isn't good enough. Because money in a slow economy is tight and professionals are battling for budgets, you need to have monitoring and measurement tools that prove PR's worth to upper management. There's always this old argument that PR people don't get the recognition that marketing people or advertising people receive. Fortunately, over time this notion is changing and PR practitioners are now viewed as much more valuable assets within most organizations. You, as a PR professional, can contribute significantly not only to the branding or messaging/positioning of the company, but also directly or indirectly affect sales as well. With the greater accountability through new uses of Web 2.0 monitoring and measuring, there will be an increasing need for PR professional services.

Bear in mind the following key concepts to keep your PR 2.0 brands and their executives aware of today's fast-paced market communication:

- Take the time to find out how your brand communication is received in the market. It's imperative to monitor your communication, especially if your customers are a part of the Web 2.0 social networking community.

- Keep an eye on the influencers who help to drive your communication, whether it's positive, negative, or indifferent.

- Prepare your monitoring and measurement program to tackle the Web 2.0 complexities that might prevent you from tighter control of your communication on a daily basis.

- Realize that the Web universe is so sophisticated now it requires you to go beyond the pure number of mentions or gross impressions and measure new media with tools that enable you to evaluate whether the coverage promotes the right messages.

- Begin a monitoring and measurement program with the company's objective for the analysis. Ask the question, "Does the company want to monitor as much as possible to evaluate every comment on a blog?"

- Understand that less B2B service companies and more consumer-oriented companies are monitored on blogs and social forums. However, this soon will change as more B2B companies conduct business online.

- Use the information from social media monitoring to inject communication into the market. If you monitor a negative perception that does not subside after a period of time, damage control measures might be necessary.

- Keep positive social media chatter going by launching new campaigns or communications initiatives around what your customers like and find pleasing. They will continue to show loyal brand enthusiasm by sharing and spreading information on your brand.

- Change with the times. Put your old clip books away and let technology guide you into new monitoring and measurement forums. Your executives will truly appreciate analysis that provides more than just gross impressions.

A New Direction in PR

Chapter 6
Interactive Newsrooms: How to Attract the Media

In the PR person's perfect world, you want to have constant interaction with your media contacts. Stay connected to them at all times by telephone and e-mail, and for contacts you know intimately, use instant messaging (IM). When you do, journalists reach out to you constantly for information about your brand(s), industry research, expert quotes, executive interviews, and company statements. Yes, the media will always rely on you for human intelligence and one-on-one interaction. However, you can (and should) also provide an interactive newsroom that can prove to be a main source of credible information, especially when journalists research story ideas at all hours or use your media center to obtain breaking news. The newsroom is also a great way to maintain control of brand communication and is much better for the journalist to receive information straight from the brand, rather than another source (especially during times of crisis or uncertainty). You can't be there all the time. So, it's your responsibility to make sure your brand's newsroom is 24/7/365, updated daily and interactive with the tools for today's overworked and "always on deadline" journalist.

You've Got the Basics Covered

Hopefully, by now you have the basics of the Web newsroom down pat. Most journalists expect to see certain simple, required elements. You should have included in your newsroom the following key elements or features:

- **Contact information for your company's PR person/editorial contact**—Don't make a journalist search for this information. The PR contact information should be front and center on the first page of the newsroom, along with any specific directions on how the journalist should navigate this area of your site. Many newsrooms place the PR contact information as an option on the navigation bar. Other brands choose to have PR contact information appear on every page, in a prominent position. Additionally, journalists also see the contact information on each and every news release archived in the newsroom. It might seem redundant, but it's okay to be repetitive with the contact information. You don't want to take the chance that your busy journalist, in his or her mad rush for information, doesn't see the PR person's information upon first entering the newsroom.

- **Basic facts about the company**—Basic facts can be presented in the form of a company fact sheet or a company overview. The fact sheet is a snapshot of the company's executive team, its performance, products and services, and current situation. The fact sheet, of course, needs to be updated to reflect the company's most recent position in the marketplace. The company overview or "backgrounder" gives the journalist an idea of the history of the company and how it came together. This write-up usually includes the company's mission/vision and strategic direction. Editors look for the basic facts to get a feel for the company's background and then will search for more detailed information if there is an archived news release section in your newsroom.

- **A company's perspective on its industry or current events**—Discovering the company's spin is as easy as accessing company industry presentations or speeches by executives, or by reviewing past publicity that's prominently displayed in the newsroom. This proves especially helpful to the journalist to see what other publications are writing or have written in the past about the brand.

- **Access to financial information, if available**—Of course, if you're a private company, you won't post your financial performance. However, you might include in a fact sheet an approximate number representing your sales and revenues for a particular time period, or your aspirations for growth over the next several years. As a public company you are required to post your financials, which are open to journalists, analysts, and the public in the investor relations section of your site.

- **Easy downloadable images for stories**—Images and logos (if your company permits their usage; some don't) are great to offer to journalists who want to download them for their articles. Today, most newsrooms offer low resolution (72 dpi) for Web usage and high-resolution (300 dpi) digital files for quick download into print publications. Images enhance a story, but you need to have them clearly labeled with captions to describe the event or the individuals in the photo. The availability of logos is a sure way to get more brand exposure. If you take the time to organize your image library (whether it's by event or a time period), you will see the journalist's appreciation when your photos appear in an editorial. There will always be instances when a publication wants its own photographer to take photos. In these cases, the PR pro will be called upon to arrange the photo opportunity.

Newsrooms Serving a Wide Range of Needs

Today, the basic newsroom elements will only get you so far, especially when you need to communicate updated information in an instant. Newsrooms in a Web 2.0 world range from the basics to the more sophisticated media centers with searchable databases, video presentations, and podcasts. Then, there are the most advanced interactive Cyber newsrooms with blogs, Really Simple Syndication (RSS) feeds, and social media news releases. These more complex online newsrooms are also customizable and fully integrated to not only house your news and information, but also to distribute your news announcements (in the form of releases, media alerts, and newsletters) and monitor the progress of your communication.

With so much to offer in terms of advanced newsroom features, the question still remains—what do the journalists really want to find in a newsroom? It's safe to say that it depends on the journalist and his or her technology acceptance. In writing this book, some journalists declined the offer to be interviewed. When it comes to Web and PR 2.0, one journalist who writes for a publication in the high-tech broadcast industry shared her technological level of expertise: "…Truthfully, I don't use RSS technology. I do use the Web when I'm researching my articles for assignment, but it's mostly Google and other search engines." She passed on participating in an interview saying, "Maybe I'm not the best candidate for this interview." Is there anything wrong with the journalist moving at her own pace? No, absolutely not. It's only a problem when the brand moves at a slow technological pace and the journalists are ready for more interactive new media application. You need to be ready. There will always be journalists who are tech savvy and look for advanced newsroom features.

TEKgroup International, Inc. (www.tekgroup.com), developers of online newsroom software, conducts an annual survey to take the pulse of what journalists expect from an online newsroom. A comparison of the surveys conducted in 2005 and 2006 reveals that the online newsroom is a valuable tool for the journalist and the communicator. However, details of the 2006 survey disclose that editors are expecting different functions and features in newsrooms; some relied upon much more than others. Ibrey Woodall is the director of marketing at TEKgroup International. In an article she wrote for the Public Relations Society of America's (PRSA) *Tactics* magazine, she refers to the 2006 online newsroom survey and states:[1]

> "Primary features desired by journalists (85 percent) include the ability to request that only news related to their particular beat be delivered. The preferred method is via e-mail with a link back to the online newsroom (99 percent). The same method is preferred for pitched stories (97 percent). One journalist states, 'Targeted weekly e-mail newsletters are always the best way to catch my attention.' Other means of notification include wireless devices (13 percent) and Really Simple Syndication, or RSS (18 percent)."

Interview with an Expert

Ibrey Woodall is an expert in building online newsrooms. As Director of Marketing at TEKgroup International, she oversees the Advertising, Marketing, and Public Relations functions for the company. Woodall possesses almost 25 years of combined experience in the publishing, marketing/PR, and Internet arena, and provides her insight into today's newsroom requirement and also discusses the details of her company's annual survey.

Q: How have newsrooms changed over the past few years?

A: They've become a standard, as does most technology that actually serves a specific purpose and is beneficial to its users. Remember when cell phones were big and bulky and used only by a few? Initially, public relations professionals were intimidated by software. Their jobs were pretty hectic already; they didn't have time to learn how to code Web sites. With the advent of the online newsroom, a tool was provided to communicators that enabled them to do their jobs more productively.

It [online newsrooms] also enabled the journalists to do their jobs more productively. One of the many complaints we hear from journalists is that they can't get the information they need when they need it. Early on, there was hesitation from public relations professionals who believed that journalists would not use the online newsroom and definitely would not register to access some of the password-protected areas. TEKgroup's annual survey of journalists shows that 86 percent of those surveyed are willing to register. That's an increase of 3 percent from 2006. The key is to secure only specific sections that work for both your company and the journalists who cover your company's needs. We find that the industry password protects the access of high-resolution photographs and PR contacts, especially if cell phone numbers are posted.

Q: What does a journalist look for in today's newsroom?

A: First of all, they expect a company to have an online newsroom. All journalists who were surveyed felt, to some degree, the online newsroom was important. If your company doesn't have one, 94 percent of journalists surveyed expect you to have one in the future. Multiple elements exist that a journalist wants to access from a company's online newsroom. The top five would be PR contacts, news releases, searchable news release archives, product information, and photographs.

Q: How does TEKgroup international help its customers to build a newsroom that supports today's communications needs?

A: At TEKgroup International, Inc., we pride ourselves on being one of the first online newsroom software providers. Because of this, we've been very active in our research, as you see with the annual Online Newsroom Survey. We are also very active in educating the industry. We've partnered with the Public Relations Society of America, and we consistently provide updated material in the form of articles in industry trade publications and presentations at industry trade conferences.

There are two customers here that we have to support. One customer, the journalist, is after all, the end user. They have to get what they need quickly and easily. The online newsroom has to be designed and developed for that. Our research keeps tabs on what the journalists need. We relay that to the public relations professional.

The other customer, the public relations professional, needs to be able to focus on content, not code. The online newsroom software provides this capability. They are able to deliver the type of news and related assets that an individual journalist desires.

Q: What are some of the more interactive newsroom functions?

A: The entire newsroom is interactive because it's available 24 hours a day, fitting all deadlines. It's also interactive—the communicator is able to maintain it because it is a Web content management system, similar to any word processing editor. All posting, editing, and distributions are done by the PR professional. The PR pro no longer has to wait for the IT person to return from lunch to post a news release for them; they can get instant gratification. They post it and then view it. This immediacy is extremely important when dealing with crisis communications.

One of the more interactive and powerful functions within the newsroom is the capability to distribute your own e-mail alerts to registered journalists. This not only provides convenience and a return on investment, but it brings intelligence to the table. That intelligence is in the form of reports that identify which journalist actually returned to the newsroom via the e-mail alert and what other elements within the newsroom they accessed. This is a great report to submit to executives.

Q: Discuss one of your best case studies (newsroom makeovers).

A: Well, I'm partial to all our online newsrooms because we do establish relationships with our clients. The process of creating an online newsroom is very team oriented.

An interesting use of the online newsroom software came with the creation of the Carlson Hotels Worldwide newsroom located at http://www. carlsonmedia.tekgroup.com/. This is a good example of a common situation where too few communicators have to manage media relations for too many entities. The online newsroom software enabled them to manage the parent company site, as well as properties such as Radisson Hotels & Resorts, Park Plaza Hotels & Resorts, Country Inns & Suites, Regent International Hotels, and Park Inn—all from one single online administrative tool.

The online newsroom software is also a very efficient and financially responsible way to manage this particular situation. If each property decided to create its own individual newsroom, the cost would have affected the budget more, and there might not have been as consistent a message delivered throughout the properties.

Q: How do you think newsrooms will change in the next 5 to 10 years?

A: Online newsrooms will continue to evolve to meet the needs of both the journalist and the corporate communicator. Recent changes have included the integration of wire services, third-party media contacts, and media measurement. The key is to know and understand the particular purpose of your online newsroom and how it best fits your target audience. The newsroom is primarily the initial point of interaction between the communicator and the journalist, and that's why it is so useful in posting media elements. It's also extremely useful in the integration of media monitoring. From the newsroom, you send out an e-mail alert, you see which journalists accessed the subject matter, you monitor his or her publication for coverage, and you then analyze the type of coverage— whether it was negative, neutral, or positive.

You Can Manage the Newsroom Yourself

Taking into consideration Woodall's thoughts on building a Web interactive newsroom, you shouldn't be surprised at how much more hands-on you can be in a Web 2.0 world. Woodall mentioned the ability for the PR person to use a content management program to post updated information. Who would have thought 10 years ago that PR professionals would have their hands in Web programming? Learning to manage content makes you much more valuable to your brand. In my experience, whether a service provider customizes and installs your software or you purchase Web Edit Pro (developed by Interspire), content management tools are excellent and easy to use. Prices of "off the shelf" products range from high-end to lower cost tools. Then, there are also the open-source content management tools, such as Joomla! (www.joomla.com). These resources are free software options created by Web developers who continually build and make extensions and modifications to these tools for public use.

I recommend that you experiment and learn how to manage your own newsroom content. Now, there's always going to be resistance to new technology. As a matter of fact, I've met PR practitioners who are the most experienced (with respect to years in the business) but who accept technology at a slower pace. These pros were particularly reluctant to use the Web 2.0 content management tools. I remember one extremely talented colleague saying, "Take the money out of my paycheck, and get a programmer to manage the client's newsroom." This particular example is fairly drastic and even though my colleague was adamant about not trying new technological resources, he still received his paycheck in its entirety. Will proficiency with a content management tool be essential someday? It certainly wouldn't surprise me.

If your brand has the resources to use software that enables you to experiment with your newsroom content, what are you waiting for? Don't worry about your technological expertise. You don't have to be a 2.0 guru. The content management tool training process might seem a little intimidating at first, but you will improve with practice. There's always that initial fear of the unknown. Perhaps you think that you will erase a portion of your brand's newsroom, or that you might take down your brand's entire Web site. The occurrence of either situation is highly unlikely. The beauty of this type of tool is that you can work in a dormant area (one that is not live). You can always make a copy of a page to view, edit, and even look at source code (if you're that advanced). Then, once you are sure your new posts (this could include news releases, images, presentations, updated fact sheets, FAQ's, recent publicity, and the like) are linked correctly, or the information you upload is in the proper position, you can turn your page live in your newsroom. Being in control of one more part of the communications process is extremely gratifying. So, for those of you who want to have your hands in everything, the ability to manage your newsroom content is the best way to proceed forward in a Web 2.0 world.

The Leaders of Online Newsrooms

As Woodall indicated, newsrooms take all shapes and forms, but they all serve a definite purpose. Regardless of the size or interactivity, at all times the online newsroom is a primary point of interaction; providing essential information for today's busy journalist. So many exceptional newsrooms exist. A few of the interactive media centers and why they deserve recognition follow. Although all three examples cover different industries and have varying features and levels of functionality, they are representative of good, solid interactive newsrooms.

Online Newsroom Leader #1

Accenture (http://newsroom.accenture.com) is "a global management consulting, technology services outsourcing company."[2] As a global leader, the Accenture newsroom is set up to serve the needs of editors who have many different areas of interest. The site is complex yet amazingly organized with interactive tools for the media. This well-branded newsroom environment has a tremendous amount of features and functions.

Why is Accenture "Online Newsroom Leader #1? Of course, above and beyond the basic elements are the newsroom's best features, which include

- A tab on the newsroom's navigation bar to all media contacts globally. Contacts are arranged by capability/growth platform (such as, Business Consulting, Finance and Performance Management, Strategy, Human Performance, Outsourcing/BPO, and the like) and by industry (from airline and electronics to government and utilities).

- Archived news releases by date, with each news release providing the journalist with outside resources, such as links to related content including additional statements by executives, video testimonies, and editorial coverage and blogs on different topics.

- E-press kits are available to editors who need information on specific events or company initiatives. These e-press kits are "a press kit within a press kit" that include targeted news releases, images, statements, and related content.

- An advanced search tool enables the journalist to search by date and in his language of choice. A simple check box area provides journalists the opportunity to narrow their search to news releases, executive bios, press kits, photos, or events.

- The ability to sign up for media alerts and media requests enables the journalist special features within the newsroom, including the ability to select e-mail notifications to receive targeted news and use the Briefcase function, which is the journalist's own area for personal storage of information (called personal folders). The journalist must sign into this area by entering his/her media information and credentials (a great way for you to mine data about journalist contacts).

- Personal folders in the newsroom provide journalists with a password-protected area to store information they've researched and want to archive on Accenture's site for future use. As they find more information, they can add it to their personal folder or briefcase.

- Journalists can sign up to receive an RSS feed in the Accenture news-room. The feed contains updated content from financial reporting to new contracts. The information is easily downloaded automatically into the journalist's computer and viewed via Internet Explorer.

Online Newsroom Leader #2

Ford Motor Company (http://media.ford.com), "a global automotive industry leader based in Dearborn, Michigan, manufactures and distributes automobiles in 200 markets across six continents. With about 300,000 employees and 108 plants worldwide, the company's core and affiliated automotive brands include Ford, Jaguar, Land Rover, Lincoln, Mazda, Mercury, and Volvo. Its automotive-related services include Ford Motor Credit Company."[3] Ford has numerous car makes and models and as a result has set up a comprehensive newsroom that serves the needs of journalists who need to research and write about the many different automotive brands. This online newsroom leader clearly goes above and beyond the five basic elements with the following advanced features:

- The newsroom is broken into Corporate and Consumer sections. The Corporate section includes news and information on everything from Ford's affiliates and human resources to retailers and special events. The Consumer section includes news and information on customer satisfaction, e-commerce, marketing, safety, and service, just to name a few.

- Each Ford Motor Company brand (Ford, Lincoln Mercury, Mazda, Volvo, Jaguar, Land Rover, and Aston Martin) has its own online media center with the ability for the journalist to access on each car brand news, facilities, photos, videos, and PR contacts.

- The Executive Bio section goes beyond the normal company's presentation of the executive team. Ford Motor Company's People's section provides journalists with the means to find not only the executive's bio but also news releases, speeches, and remarks/statements made by the individual executive.

- An advanced search feature in the newsroom lets the journalist jump to a specific news section or to a particular media kit, car model, or country of interest.

- The Facilities section is a comprehensive area on the site that enables the journalist to access information on the Ford Motor Company assembly plants all around the world. The facilities are broken down according to brand and then region. Links lead the journalist to a review of plant information, employment, and production history.

- News releases all include special icons built into the release that enable the journalists with a simple click to add the announcement to their briefcase, view related articles, and send the content to a wireless device.

Online Newsroom Leader #3

America Online, better known as AOL (http://press.AOL.com), is considered the leading Internet Service Provider (ISP) in the United States. It also operates a Web network with 112 million monthly unique visitors.[4] The company's newsroom is clearly a leader in interactive features. Upon entering the newsroom, the journalist is able to view the company's latest news as well as the "most viewed" headlines in the month. The advanced features on this site include

- A Top News area has all AOL's recent news items, which can be accessed through the AOL News and Broadcast Center. From there, journalists enter into the password-protected Broadcast Room. AOL is partnered with The NewsMarket to provide the media with video delivered digitally (and in some cases on videotape).

- Other interactive and extremely informative areas in the Broadcast Room include multimedia press packs, a video and audio library, and a stills (still shots) and document library. Independent producers and journalists are allowed to order materials from this area of the AOL site.

- The Get Info area in the newsroom provides journalists with all their necessary media contacts. Also in this section, they can sign up for e-mail announcements and RSS feeds. The RSS feeds include a choice of Corporate Feeds, Consumer Technologies, Digital Entertainment, Digital Lifestyles, and Safety and Security.

- The What's Hot area has newsletter archives, a link to "Buzz on AOL," which provides links to recent editorial coverage, and Beta links in AOL Beta Central that gives journalists "a sneak peak of prereleases of AOL, AIM, and affiliate software and services."[5]

- Our Brands and Product Areas is the section comprised of hundreds of product blogs. Each blog, regardless of the topic (from AOL Journals to an AOL Picture blog) has tags (metadata or in simpler terms, keywords) that lead the journalist to additional blog entries on a particular topic of interest. The journalist can also take the time to blog about the entry or add it to del.icio.us (http://del.icio.us.com), a popular tagging tool that categorizes favorite blogs, articles, reviews, and the like.

Accenture, Ford Motor Company, and AOL are excellent examples of how you can enhance the journalist's newsroom experience. Although a journalist might not expect or require fancy features and functions, making additional interactive communications resources will provide them with the best and most comprehensive information for their stories. Of special note are the newsrooms that ask the journalist to add content to either a personal folder or briefcase. When the journalist opts to use this area of a brand's newsroom, it's a very easy way to track what content is being stored by your favorite journalists. You're able to tell the content that interests them and what you can possibly expect in terms of coverage.

Newsrooms are growing in interest, and more companies are realizing their value. Brands are no longer just building their newsrooms and leaving them stagnant. You can almost expect that the newsrooms of the future will surely move toward an interactive "standard," whether that means having executive blogs, social media news releases (with links to outside resources or interactive functions), podcasts, video, and so on, which is yet to be determined. Someday, you might find that incorporating an interactive standard has a direct correlation to more and better

coverage. As you build your interactive 2.0 newsrooms, keep the following key points in mind:

- Aside from your contact with the media, your brand's newsroom
  will be a main source of credible information as journalists research
  story ideas or use your media center for breaking news.

- Before you even think about enhancing your newsroom to include
  2.0 interactive features and functions, make sure you completely
  understand the basics. The newsroom basics include PR contact
  information, a company's basic facts or current snap shot, a perspective on industry events, updated financial information, and high-
  resolution images for downloads.

- Trends reveal that journalists definitely require the basic elements
  in a newsroom. However, an increasing number of brands are gear-
  ing up to include interactive functions for the more technologically
  savvy journalist.

- Whether you use a service provider to build your newsroom or you
  do-it-yourself with off-the-shelf software, remember that a content
  management tool will help you to keep newsroom information
  updated. Fresh content will have journalists returning to your
  newsroom, and including a briefcase function will enable them to
  store information in their personal folders.

- The online newsroom leaders are forging the way for smaller brands
  to see how the most advanced newsrooms operate. If your brand is
  smaller or even mid-sized, you might want to build your newsroom
  in phases. Cover the basics in Phase I and then add content features
  such as RSS, podcasts, and video to your media center in Phase II.
  In Phase III, similar to what AOL has done, you can use blogs with
  tags, del.icio.us, and technorati searches to check out all the chatter
  on a topic in the blogosphere.

- If you find over time there is a correlation between interactive
  information in your newsroom and the amount of coverage you
  receive by the news media and conversations among your customers, you will further enhance your newsroom's 2.0 offerings.

Endnotes

1. Woodall, Ibrey, "Journalists Relay What is Expected from an Online Newsroom—Meaningful Trends Revealed in 2006 Survey," *PRSA Tactics*, July 2006.

2. Accenture Corporate Web site, Company Overview, March 2007.

3. Ford Motor Company Web site, About Us, Company Overview, March 2007.

4. AOL Web site, Company Information, April 2007.

5. AOL Web site, AOL Beta Central, http://beta.aol.com, April 2007.

Chapter 7

The Social Media News Release: An Overdue Facelift

The news release isn't dead. On the contrary, it's evolving into a PR 2.0 communications tool. The traditional news release has transformed into a much more technologically savvy resource for journalists and the public, with the recent development of the Social Media Release (SMR) template. According to an article by Tom Foremski in the Silicon Valley Watcher titled, "Die! Press Release! Die! Die! Die!," Foremski makes a dramatic call to action. He demands changes to the traditional news release. For him, news releases of the past are a "nearly useless" resource. According to Foremski, news releases need to move away from "...committees, edited by lawyers, and then sent out at great expense...to reach the digital and physical trash bins of tens of thousands of journalists."[1] Foremski, a former *Financial Times* writer, feels the need to break down the news release to make a better communications tool. Each publisher should be able to gather relevant materials within the news release framework, create their own news story, and assemble the information more efficiently through the use of an SMR. As a result, the targeted information collected and used by the journalist is much more valuable in the writing and the news reporting process. Foremski's call to action prompted a revolutionary transformation. Are you ready for the SMR to change the nature of reporting news in the 21st Century?

A New Format to Spark Conversations

This is a question faced by every communication professional, as there are different schools of thought on the subject. You might agree with Tom Foremski that it's time to implement a drastic change to the widely recognized news release that's been a standard PR tool for years. At the same time, there's another school of thought. On the opposite end of the spectrum are the professionals who aren't quite ready to see the tried and true inverted pyramid style news release completely go away. For them, the traditional inverted pyramid format still carries value in reporting. The traditional Associated Press (AP) "newspaper" style news release served a valuable purpose for a very long time. It gave PR pros a communication tool that provided journalists with the "who, what, when, where, and why" of a story, all in the lead paragraph. Of course, there's a group between the two opposing ends who are looking to gradually make social media changes to the old-fashioned newspaper style release format, but not the drastic changes called for by Foremski. Although many journalists might concur that the news release needs an overdue makeover, not every one of them is ready to transition completely into the social media template. However, what most journalists and PR pros can agree on is a news release tool that's well written and extremely informative, with less of the corporate "speak" and more of the news that's accurate and timely.

What school of thought do you attend? You're certainly in good company if you feel that your brand's stakeholders, including the media community, need information in a format that can be easily gathered, organized, and shared. In a Web 2.0 world, the traditional AP style release isn't good enough to satisfy 21st Century reporting. However, the SMR is a communications tool that provides easy access to useful information, ensures accuracy of materials that have the "official seal" of a company, and offers the journalist content proactively before he or she finds it from a competitive source. In addition, if you are skeptical about social media, keep in mind that additional benefits include that it's user-driven with content which can be reworked and reshaped continuously. With the ability to use social media for collaboration and shared-interests, communities are created instantaneously, connecting online audiences globally. Best of all, social media is easy to grasp. You don't need years of technical training or an above-average aptitude to understand how to use this for effective communication.

Be Prepared for Social Media

Similar to the discussion about interactive newsrooms in Chapter 6, "Interactive Newsrooms: How to Attract the Media," you can ask yourself a related question: Will you interact with every journalist who requires a social media template, with the most advanced 2.0 features? Of course not; there are still many journalists who are not ready to use every 2.0 tool, and there are also those journalists who are just experimenting with this new format. However, all it takes is just one journalist who wants a sophisticated feature of an SMR to aid him in his reporting process. For that reason alone, you must be prepared. You need to understand what it takes to enhance your basic news release when you encounter a media professional who prefers sophisticated social media features, which might include

- Really Simple Syndication (RSS) feeds (direct news feeds on content related to the subject matter as well as links to content).

- Photo libraries with high resolution images. (These images are for download into a print publication.)

- MP3 files (a digital audio encoding method to reduce the size of an audio file for easy download) or a podcast.

- Video footage for Video-On-Demand (VOD).

- Links to previous coverage on a topic with the ability to use del.icio.us or Digg (www.digg.com) for social bookmarking. (Journalists can tag their favorite information by locating, classifying, and ranking noteworthy references and resources.)

- Technorati (www.technorati.com) is a leader in "what's happening on the World Live Web."[2] Because bloggers commonly link to other blogs, Technorati searches and organizes blogs, and tracks how blogs are linked together (recording the relevance of the links to your subject matter).

You've already learned that not all journalists share the same level of technological acceptance. Some are innovators on the cutting edge of what PR 2.0 has to offer, and then others might be Late Adopters of technology who wait for a technology to be widely tested and accepted by the general public. For you, as a communications professional, it is beneficial to be prepared with sophisticated tools in your news announcements, and there are several reasons why you would want to move toward a social media template. You should consider how it helps your media contacts, your brand's customers, and how it directly affects the conversations about your brand in the market.

- A social media template enables you to present different types of communication regarding your brand (from the core facts to exciting multimedia that can really tell a visual story).

- With a social media news release, you can direct the journalist to the information you want to present and have him or her cover it in a story, which is a better way to control the brand communication.

- Because of the increasing ease of use for journalists, you are providing a better means for them to develop their stories, which might translate into more accurate and a greater depth of coverage on your brand.

- You are helping media outlets with little resources to "do more with less."[3] Your social media template helps journalists develop their stories completely and accurately, with access to more information in a much quicker period of time.

- The SMR is also a consumer tool that makes it easier for the public to identify and share interesting content in their social networking communities. The social media template enables your brand to communicate directly to consumers so that they will continue to talk among themselves, to further promote your news and information in their forums.

Getting Started with Social Media

When you first decide to use a social media template, you might want to start simple. Starting slowly by adding in uncomplicated resources to your news announcement is easy. Then, you can always advance your way to a more highly developed SMR, such as Shift Communication's (www.shiftcomm.com) social media news release template. Shift Communications, inspired by Tom Foremski's thoughts on the traditional news release, was the first communications firm to launch a PR 2.0 news release tool. The Shift "In The News" section of Shift Communication's

Web site states how the company, "believes that journalists and bloggers are now fully adapted to using the World Wide Web for research purposes. The 'Social Media Press Release' merely facilitates their research by using the latest tools (social bookmarking, RSS, and the like) to provide background data, context, and ongoing updates to clients' news."[4] To review a great SMR, go to the Shift Communications Web site and download a PDF version of this template (the template is available free of charge, with no copyrights restricting its use). Clearly, you will see that the template is designed for the most advanced or tech-savvy journalist who has fully embraced all the incredible resources in a PR 2.0 world—he knows how to manage the social media interface and fully take advantage of the interactive portions of the SMR, all very quickly and with ease.

Remember, you don't have to be a guru to manage the new PR 2.0 technology. That's not to say that the true SMR abandons several of the original elements of the news release. Absolutely not! These new social media templates still contain a few memorable and meaningful components of the traditional release, including

- Client, spokesperson, and PR contact information
- A gripping news release headline and sub-head, if desired
- Main news release facts (however, core content is in a bulleted format)
- Approved quotes from brand executives, customers, partners, and industry analysts, if possible
- Company boilerplate information (standard approved verbiage that describes the main offerings of the company)

Let's begin with the social media basics and a few guidelines for your SMR. First, you want to include links to more information on the topic of your release (for instance, if your company has written any papers or conducted recent research). Also, it's important to provide the journalist with links to recent publicity on the subject. These links "click" to a media outlet's site where an article is posted or one of your executives was quoted. You can offer tags in your release, including del.icio.us and Digg, for journalists to bookmark their favorite blogs on related topics. Journalists are also looking for photos to enhance their stories, so you can use embedded photos in your news release, if possible, or you can have a link to a photo library that has several high-resolution images for download. (It's also a good idea to include a link to download your brand's logo.) Last, journalists can build their stories quickly and more accurately if you offer them key words to other associated and interesting information to search on the Web.

One very important question should come to your mind: "How do I begin to enhance my news release template, whether only slightly or to its fullest 2.0 potential?" If you are just beginning and want to proceed slowly and with care, you can use simple programming methods—simple techniques to start the SMR process. You can do it yourself or work closely with your in-house programmer to get the job done. Once more, as a PR professional you will better control your brand communication by including the features and functions that will help to get your brand increased coverage from the journalists and bloggers who received your social media release.

You Don't Have to Be a Web Developer to Create 2.0 Tools

The ability to add in your own 2.0 resources was a concept unheard of during the Web's infancy and even in the beginning of Web 1.0. Only Web developers were trained and relied upon for these tasks. Until now, there was always a clear divide between the communications professionals and Web developers. Times certainly have changed. Of course, there will always be those PR pros who don't want to roll up their sleeves to learn new PR 2.0 tactics. They're perfectly happy enabling the Web developers to do the programming. But, for those who do want to learn, your new-found 2.0 knowledge makes you that much more valuable to your brands!

Some easy tips for you beginner PR 2.0 programmers follow:

- Familiarize yourself with the information that is accessible to journalists on your Web site.

- Use resources already available to you, which reside on your brand's Web site (whether the information is in the public domain or is housed on the backend of your brand's Web site). Your in-house programmer or Web site development team will be able to assist you in finding the backend resources.

- Cut and paste links from your Web site directly into your social media template, including links to site pages with

  - Photos

  - Bios of management team

  - White papers or research studies

  - Video clips, if already posted on your Web site

- Find and use resources on the Web, including links to the following:

  - Past or recent publicity discussing the topic, your company, or quoting an executive

  - Groups or organizations that have a similar perspective on a topic or are partnered with your brand on an initiative

  - Influential bloggers who are writing about your topic, your product, or your service

  - Other Web sites for journalists and bloggers to gather more information, including Yahoo! News and Google News

  - Links directly to del.icio.us or Digg for journalists and bloggers to bookmark interesting information

If you currently use a content management tool in your newsroom, you are not limited to the information that is currently posted on your Web site. Rather, you can develop your own content, specific to your news release topic or communications initiative. For example, for a product launch, you can prepare approved quotes from C-Level executives on a page, or endorsements from customers who use your product, or industry analysts researching how your product affects the market. Using the content management tool, you can easily create pages with the new information and post these Web pages in your newsroom. When the pages are approved and are "live" for audiences to view, you can cut and paste the appropriate newsroom link right into your social media template. Journalists will click on the links embedded in your release and be able to access valuable information right from your Web site. Proficiency with the content management tool will enable you the flexibility you need to enhance your news release of yesteryear and make it more interactive and news-friendly for 21st Century news reporting.

When to Rely on the Experts

If you do not have the resources in-house to build your own SMR, once again there are Web 2.0 experts ready to assist you. There are a number of PR service providers, including PRX Builder (in conjunction with PR Newswire) and BusinessWire that are forging ahead with their social media templates. As a matter of fact, in PR Newswire's release of October 10, 2006, they use a social media news-release template to unveil the beta testing of PRX Builder's Social Media News Release Wizard. Using a social media template, the release offers a lead paragraph but then provides journalists the immediate ability to click on photo links and logos for download. The next section of the release is bulleted and provides the core content of the release. For example, the bullets discuss how the PRX Builder service "enables PR and marketing professionals to easily create Social Media news releases through a series of guided steps."[5] The PRX Builder Social Media Release costs only $6.00 per release. The releases are created in a simple XML document format. Communications professionals are able to easily develop and preview how the Social Media Release looks prior to distribution through PR Newswire. PRX Builder's Social Media News Release template also has approved quotes from the President of Whitley Media (the creators of PRX Builder) as well as approved quotes from Dave Armon, Chief Operating Officer at PR Newswire. Journalists (or anyone looking for quotes) do not have to wait for quote approvals as they have the approved quotes from executives right at their fingertips. For example, they are able to capture instantaneously what Mr. Whitley has to say about the PRX Builder service. One of the approved statements includes "The PRX Builder service is designed to make the creation of Social Media News Releases as easy as possible. We're excited about the prospects for expanding the use of social media services within the more traditional realm of press releases." Other great features in this news release include related links, photo notes, and a Technorati search of blogs discussing this news release. The PR Newswire release truly represents the tremendous possibilities of the PRX Builder service.

Interview with an Expert

Business Wire launched its Smart Release because "target audiences—reporters, editors, consumers, and investors—are looking for multimedia news 2.5 times more often than text only news.[6] The Smart News Release, just as it sounds, offers smart tools embedded in the news announcement. These resources range from text and photos to motion and sound. Business Wire developed the Smart News Release because the company thought it would be better for journalists who need quick access to multimedia. Journalists are looking for content that's ready to download, and the Smart News Release has one-stop access to Web and print-ready photos, logos, graphics, and audio and video. If you select Business Wire's Smart News Release, you will find the ability to track and measure the success of your announcement and a wider or "Smarter" reach.

Business Wire took the Smart News Release one step further with its EON service (Enhanced Online News Service). Business Wire and EON together offer PR pros the ability to use XHTML, Search Engine Optimization, social media, podcasting, RSS, and blogs in their news release formats. Laura Sturaitis, Senior Vice President, Media Services & Product Strategy for Business Wire, participated in a Q&A session on how EON truly enhances online news, reaching much larger audiences. Sturaitis heads up Business Wire's Media Relations, Content Licensing, Product Development, and ExpertSource teams in the U.S. She is responsible for the comprehensive and timely delivery of Business Wire clients' news release to print, broadcast, and online media organizations worldwide using Business Wire's multiplatform delivery methods; and for developing new media tools and services for the distribution, availability, and use of those news releases as part of Business Wire's file of breaking news content.

Q: Why did Business Wire enhance its news release template with social media?

A: Because of the proliferation of news online and all the places we deliver to; they are all multiplatform. We actually found very quickly that the visibility of those releases now better serve the audience that we reach. In addition, we're able to help clients enhance their releases and start thinking "bigger" about what the news release can do for them as they're writing it.

Q: Are news releases reaching more than just the media?

A: It's a new world. Today's news release goes well beyond just getting into the newspaper. We developed EON, which simply stands for our product called Enhanced Online News, a coproduction or a partnership we have with PR Web.

Q: Do you have to be a Web 2.0 guru to understand EON?

A: When we educate a client on EON, we start with the hardest and most advanced features first. In some cases many companies are already incorporating elements of EON, but might be missing subtle opportunities. For example, last year Business Wire began to deliver its files in XHTML. Many clients don't realize what XHTML is and how it serves an important function. Basically, clients already send us their releases in a Word format. Before they use a print version of that release, they often include different types of formatting, including bold, italics, symbols, sub-headlines, and the like. However, many times they forward to us a completely stripped-down version of the release because often they would see that once it was delivered on the wire, it was in plain text. Not because we delivered it that way; on the contrary, we delivered it very robust with lots of content. However, a lot of the media organizations, newsrooms, or the online sites are not set up to display the release with all the bells and whistles we were sending. Some of them, frankly, had a policy against including things like anchor text or hyperlinks because they didn't want visitors who surf off their site to go elsewhere.

Now, we're trying to tell our clients, "We're reinviting you to put all this stuff back in again because not only is it something that makes that news release easier to read, but it makes it more user friendly, more like a page of Web content as you're composing it. Actually, that's how it's being viewed when you can display it with its XHTML. You should be using links, putting in bold, and using subheads because these additional features equal importance and relevancy to the search engine.

Q: Does including XHTML give you better results with search engine optimization? Will your audience be able to find your releases easier?

A: A hundred things can be done to a page of content that can make it more important to the search engine, and XHTML is a part of this. Bold, italic, and certainly the anchor text (if you use anchor text, you're just using the plain words, then you hyperlink it underneath), and hyperlinks are key parts of that search engine optimization. These are things that writers of the release sometimes might not utilize. When you think about a headline or a subhead, that's what you see on the Google results, and its that headline or subhead that's going to convince you whether you want to click over to that full text or not. You need to remember this point when you're writing the release. We basically say to clients there might be 100 things you could put on a list of things that will help your search engine optimization. We also recommend the use of social media tags in news releases. Now this document is an interactive one because it's shown on Web sites that are not simply one-way street content but content audiences can interact with if they want. They can save it or even share it. Perhaps they might want to e-mail it to their friends, or they can Digg it—submit it to those social networks. It's no longer a straight communication from the communications department out to the media. A lot more back and forth happens because of the social media.

Q: What happened when Business Wire first introduced the Smart News Release in 1998?

A: When we launched the Smart News Release in 1998, it opened a whole new realm. When we incorporated the Smart News Release features (the video, audio, and graphics) a long time ago, it changed how that page was displayed and the click-through rate. When you have a multimedia, a graphic, or a logo running with the news release where it's showing alongside of the Google headline, people are going to click on it more. There's a much higher click-through rate for something that has a thumbnail next to it as opposed to a plain text headline.

Q: Would you say Business Wire is ahead of the curve because in 1998 not a lot of companies were jumping on board to see interactive video or audio?

A: We've always been very innovative. Actually, Business Wire was the first wire service to have a Web site. The very day we launched our site, we never launched for the story of Business Wire; rather every day from day one, the front page had news relevant to our customers.

Q: What do you think social media means for PR professionals?

A: It's very exciting, and it's very powerful. Right now, there's probably not a better time to be in PR. It's so funny when I hear people say it's the death now of the wire, or it's the death of public relations because now everybody has a voice and user-generated content. But, who's in a better position to capitalize on a world full of user-generated content than professional communicators and professional marketers, and those who have something to tell, a great story to tell, and the talent and skills to tell it.

Q: Are you finding that more Business-to-Consumer (B2C) companies are using EON or Business-to-Business (B2B)?

A: It's definitely started to be incorporated more quickly with the consumer companies. We have product announcements, rollouts, renovations, and updates. We have many different kinds of announcements, so it's "a no brainer" that brands will definitely use enhanced releases to tell the story; to show or use visuals rather than just tell a story with words. For B2B, it's being used in earning releases; you have links to the Webcasts and conference calls. That's been going on for a long time. Now, it's just become more formalized.

Q: Because journalists are such an important part of social media, does Business Wire talk to the media, do you research their needs, or do you just take it from the communications person's perspective?

A: Oh no, we feel like we serve two masters at Business Wire and always have—there's the client side, but the media is equally important because they're the ones we serve and inform of the clients' news. We have a staff of 15 media relations professionals worldwide that do nothing but make sure the journalists can get the client's news in any form they want. That's why it's called multiplatform. If they want a customized email, RSS, if they want a feed directly into their newsrooms, if they want to go on the Web, anyway they want to slice and dice it, we'll get it to them the way they want it. We're serving print journalists, broadcast journalists, bloggers, and citizen journalists.

Q: When you take the polls of these journalists, do you find more and more are asking for the sophisticated social media tools?

A: I think the main thing is that 98 percent of journalists are going online to search just like everybody else. They're going to Google to find story ideas. They're going to blogs. So, as much as you have to be present, that's very important. As far as social media tags and other features, I think that there's an increasing amount of people who are utilizing RSS and social network tags, including journalists as they are trying to find information that covers their beat. It goes back to Media Relations 101: When you write newsworthy content that can easily be found, contains the concepts and interests, and is targeted, it's all good no matter how it's delivered (even if that's delivered by carrier pigeon). With the social media news release, there's kind of a component that gives all the information to you in pieces, and then journalists reassemble those pieces on the other side and build their own story.

Q: Do you feel most editors are set up to see video and anything that is advanced on the media side?

A: Oh, certainly at this point. They're seeing the releases in various ways, and we'd say multiplatform because they're so redundant. They're not only getting the feed on their desks, but we think that journalists are pretty savvy to get what they need and see information in a variety of ways.

Q: How does the EON platform work?

A: Through PR Web, we have a search engine-optimized platform; a place for those releases to live so it's easier for those search engines to find them over a longer period of time. That's the trick because relevancy and "recency" are equally important. You could have really relevant content, but if it's older, it's not going to compete as well with something that's new. We did some really clever things to accomplish that: Everything from including the keyword in the URL so it's another instance of the keyword, to having a PDF. You know when you get search results on Google and it asks whether you would like to view as an HTML or as a PDF, having that available right under the headline makes it portable in effect.

Q: What about blogs? Are you able to see if someone is talking about your news release topic?

A: Because of the nature of blogs and of social media, it is first important to recognize that you must be part of the conversation. It is not advisable to push your news release to a blogger without permission and certainly not without being familiar with what they blog about. Communicators are sometimes hesitant to engage with bloggers, but treating bloggers using the best practices of media relations can be a very valuable audience to cultivate and target, if you are willing to engage. You can use RSS news readers and other technologies to monitor the blogosphere the same way you monitor for clips in MSM (mainstream media). But, the fact is the conversation is still going on—it's better to know it exists and have the ability to monitor it and become part of the conversation.

Q: Do most clients want to monitor a conversation to see if it's increasing or decreasing and then take the appropriate action?

A: Yes, you can't get all worked up about somebody on a blog saying something wrong. The beautiful part about the interactive nature of blogging and social media is if you're engaged in a part of the conversation in the blogosphere...if you are present and clearly identify yourself as an interested party or company spokesperson, if you don't like what they're saying, you go to their blog and comment. The happy surprise is often when anybody is being treated unfairly by a blogger, members of the community, fans of the company, happy customers, and others come to your public defense or correct incorrect information or impressions for you because they are also part of the conversation.

These new tools, technologies, and delivery and measurement options for news releases has really served to put the "Public" back in Public Relations.

Social Media Template: A PR Pro's Opinion

Many communications professionals are weighing in on the subject of the social media template. According to Phil Gomes, Vice President of Edelman, although the name Social Media News Release has all the right buzzwords, in his opinion, a news release is not an inherently social concept. He instead prefers the term "New Media Release" as a more apt descriptor.

Edelman decided to make its own Web-based proprietary software wizard, dubbed "StoryCrafter," for its clients. One of the first Edelman clients to take advantage of the enhanced news release format was Palm. "They were the first to use our software publicly for their Palm Treo Accessories announcement," explained Gomes. The announcement was released in April 2007, and since then the Edelman client has been eager to try new communications tools, including blogging.

Gomes discussed how philosophically, companies *want* to explore new technologies and tools that are available. However, if you walk up to a

Vice President of a company and say, "You must blog and you must podcast," you might be speaking in another tongue. When you discuss the news release and call it by name, everyone universally understands. Gomes stated, "There are wild eyed evangelists talking in *social media* terms instead of *communications* terms—regardless of the many voices, this isn't necessarily going to move the peanut forward."

Although there are success stories, Gomes feels that companies and communications professionals are still reluctant to embrace the social media release. After all, it was in October 2006 that BusinessWire celebrated the 100th anniversary of the news release. There has not been any attempt until now to give the traditional news release a facelift. He mentioned that although there have been significant improvements in distribution of the news release, there haven't been any substantial changes to its format. "Now is a great time to take a look at social media in the news release and explore how the Web affects communication." Gomes pointed out that the social media template makes multimedia a standard component and not an add-on. Additionally, communications professionals have complained for decades about the length and the language of releases; often news releases have become far too long and the language too technical to understand. When you use social media—for instance, hyperlinks in the body of the news release—you take the explanatory burden off the release as you can simply link your release to a data sheet with more technical product or industry information.

Palm's StoryCrafter-based releases are full of useful resources for journalists following Palm's news announcements. The template includes hyperlinks, multimedia, RSS, resources including del.icio.us and Digg, Technorati tags, track back, and comments on the release. Not all companies are ready to make the full conversion to social media, however many of the larger leading companies are paving the way.

Gomes believes that all industries will benefit from the social media template. The efforts seen in 2007 are mostly by the technology industry. However, just about any company can make a more useful news-release tool. "Eventually, professionals will begin to prepare their releases as they do B-Roll packages and will need to get used to telling their brand's news quickly and be able to share the information with audiences on-the-fly.

Someday, we all might want to walk around with our handheld video camcorders. In the new PR 2.0 toolkit, a camcorder is in your pocket." When asked if it will be more difficult and if it will take longer for larger companies to approve social media news releases with B-Roll video that's "rough cut and on-the-fly," Gomes commented that it depends on the organization's investor relations or legal department. Approval might have "extra check boxes." However, communications professionals will work with departments that touch regulatory issues and develop a series of rules for multimedia usage in releases. "Communications departments will quickly get hobbled if it's a constant, protracted exercise of Mother May I," mentioned Gomes. "The role of regulatory is critical, but at the same time, companies need to communicate quickly. A balance must be struck."

Gomes talked about his perspective regarding the relationship between traditional media relations professionals and journalists. He's spoken with several professionals who feel that new media is great; however, there's the underlying feeling that new media takes away a touch point between the PR person and the journalist. Gomes disagrees, "Who will win the hearts and minds of the journalist? It's the person who removes the barriers." That's exactly what social media does. Anything that makes a journalist's job easier is a win-win situation for everyone involved in the story. Of course, with or without social media, the release must deliver in a format that is easy to understand, simple to digest, and most of all is well written. Gomes further pointed out, "No format will ever solve the fact that many professionals have lost the craft of writing." For Gomes, the bottom line is that we improve the way we communicate. The social media template is a step in the right direction.

The news release's first facelift was a big change in the communications world. Keep in mind the following points as you consider the use of social media in your news releases:

- Use a social media news release template to enable your intended audiences to gather relevant materials within the news release framework, create their own news story, and assemble the information more efficiently.

- Not every journalist wants or needs the most sophisticated SMR. You can begin to add social media to your releases slowly based on the requirements of your audience and their technological acceptance level.

- Be prepared at any time to upgrade your news-release template with new media tools, including RSS, podcasts, multimedia, hyperlinks, Technorati tags, and the like.

- The true SMR does not abandon several of the original elements of the news release. These new social media templates still contain memorable and meaningful components of the traditional release.

- You can use simple programming methods or techniques to easily start the SMR process yourself or work closely with your in-house programmer to get the job done.

- If you do not have the resources in-house to build your own SMR, there are PR 2.0 experts ready to assist you. Many PR service providers are forging ahead with their social media templates to help brands move forward with a better tool for communications.

- With a social media news release, you are assisting journalists with little resources to "do more with less."[7] Your social media template helps them to develop their stories completely and accurately, with access to more information in a much quicker period of time.

- By incorporating social media into your communications tools, you help to change the way that news is reported in the 21st Century.

Endnotes

1. Tom Foremski is a former Financial Times reporter. *Die! Press Release! Die! Die! Die!* appeared in the Silicon Valley Watcher in February 2006.

2. www.technorati.com/about.

3. "Why Use Social Media with Your Press Release," October 2006. www.toprankblog.com

4. *Shift in the News*, "News Facts," April 2007. www.shiftcomm.com.

5. "Exclusive Distribution Through PR Newswire Ensures the Widest Reach of Social Media Enabled News Content. *PR Newswire.* October 10, 2006..

6. "The Smart News Release." *Business Wire.* http://home. businesswire.com.

7. "Why Use Social Media with Your Press Release. October 2006. www.toprankblog.com.

Chapter **8**

Social Networking: A Revolution Has Begun

Social Networking begins with blogging. What you refer to as the "the blogosphere" continues to grow daily. Suddenly, it's a crowded Web 2.0 world full of bloggers. Hundreds of thousands of bloggers—who refer to themselves as "citizen" journalists, each with the ability to opine—write and share information with other "tuned in" members of Web communities. No doubt you already know that 21st Century reporting and news distribution is no longer an exclusive function of the print, broadcast, or online media outlets.

The Start of the Revolution

With respect to these significantly different changes, PRWeb (www.prweb.com), founded in 1997 by David McInnis, answered a simple question that was on the minds of many companies: "Where did my press release go."[1] It's evident that social media has changed the nature of the news-release template and its functions. But, what happens when an announcement reaches different audiences in a Web 2.0 world? PRWeb answered this question for its subscribers by providing access to the most enhanced search engine-optimized distribution available for a news release. They offered distribution that gives brands the increased visibility they need. In essence, what PRWeb did was to begin its own quiet revolution to modify how PR professionals think about direct-to-consumer communication. The revolution has only just begun.

PRWeb realized early on that you're able to go further than the media in a Web 2.0 world. Of course, the company distributes its customers' news releases so that media professionals receive important brand messages and announcements. However, PRWeb does not rely solely on distribution to journalists. It has a direct-to-consumer newswire platform that focuses on "media bypass." PRWeb specializes in getting a brand's message directly to consumers, finding them where they "live" on the

Internet. You could say that direct-to-consumer distribution, as PRWeb calls it, "brings the 'public' back into public relations." Today, socially networked consumers decide what is newsworthy and relevant to them. They can decide what they want to talk about in their social communities. For companies to accommodate today's socially networked consumer, they need to change the way they market to them.

Reaching Audiences Through Social Networking

According to Mark Brooks, Founder of Online Personals Watch (www. onlinepersonalswatch.com) and a social networking consultant, brands must be able to better connect with consumers and push out to more people through those connections. When Brooks consults with his clients he tells them that Friendster, MySpace, and other social networking sites are giving 'people' visibility for the first time—more reach than ever before, and that reach extends to their friends' networks as well. "People are more conscious of the connections they make these days, and it's an entirely new psyche or discipline. It's quite exciting from both a social and marketing perspective," commented Brooks.

"Dr. Neil Clark Warren, of eHarmony.com, branded his company on himself, and people have connected with him and his persona, and brand, and that is the underlying principle of eHarmony's success. People are connecting with each other online at a faster rate. They're seeing each other's profiles more and more. Now, with blogs you can go one step beyond the profile. A blog is the best way to say, 'Here's who I am and here's what I have to say.'" Today, people want to connect—not just to the companies they purchase their products/services from, but also connect to the people behind those companies.

Brooks discussed how brands should speak out, and blogs are a great way to take a stance. "You ARE your company these days," he says. "A company's owners and spokespeople and 'brilliant people' need to be given the chance to connect with customers. You can't hide behind a brand anymore." Brooks consults with companies that still think they can stay quiet on issues. However, he disagrees. As a matter of fact, he advises his clients to take a stand or, as he puts it, "They don't stand for anything." Brooks thinks there is still some risk and most companies are taking the safe approach. However, the safe approach really isn't that "safe" for them to take anymore. If a brand doesn't connect with its audiences, if the executives behind the brand are not blogging, they're losing an opportunity, especially if they want people to talk. It stems back to the problem with advertising. Advertising is less and less efficient these days because people are tired of advertisements thrusted upon them and are better than ever at tuning them out. PR and word of mouth are becoming more and more important.

"So, how do you get people to talk? You don't do it by standing behind a company moniker. Social networks are a very important medium for getting people to talk about the people behind the companies," commented Brooks. If someone trusts the executives of a company, they're probably going to trust the brand. Brooks helps companies decide what they stand for, and then teaches them how to put up a blog. Their blogs should take a stance, which will impact the brand's PR and word of mouth marketing as social media enables audiences to share more information. The next step for Brooks' clients is video blogging. He realizes that blogging is still all text, and that people want to connect with you by more than just words. "Words are very safe and one-dimensional. Video is extremely important and I think we'll see more of it in the future. It ties in very well with social networking as it goes well beyond the profile and the blog to really let an audience know who you are in both words and in a visually dynamic medium." After all, two of the biggest questions a brand has to answer in a crowded marketplace are "What do you stand for?" and "Can I trust you?" Video blogging helps to answer these questions.

To Brooks, the social network comes down to the individual. That person has a social network and he/she wants to try to organize friends essentially because communication is so much easier and quicker these days. People have more and more contacts they associate with. Brooks thinks many socially networked individuals are spending less time with a core group of important people. Brooks believes there is a trend toward "collecting friends." He explains that it's a much younger generation that travels through this phase of social networking. They're just trying to collect a thousand friends. The integrity of the connections, in this case, does not mean much, and they're losing the meaning behind the social network. Jonathan Abrams of Friendster modeled the real world and encouraged people to connect with their real friends. He kicked "Fakesters," those with obviously bogus profiles, off the site wherever possible. Facebook followed suit by initially allowing only students who had valid university addresses onto the site. Then up popped Tom on MySpace. He changed everything. If you sign up for MySpace, Tom Anderson, the cofounder, automatically shows up as your first friend, even though he's a stranger to you. That sets the tone for MySpace. Any friend will do, even if you haven't met them. Online associations and loose connections are okay on MySpace. People use different social networks in different ways. WAYN (Where Are You Now) is for knowing where your friends are. LinkedIn is used for business connections. MySpace is popular for connecting with a favorite band, or brand. These days MySpace is trading its musical heritage for a more commercial agenda and enabling brands to establish themselves and have users connect with the brands, as people.

Brooks' clients are just beginning to embrace social media, and the main focus for him right now is to get them to put up their blogs and increase their presence online. He's encouraging people to start blogging, which is a core component of many social networks now. If they're not blogging, then they are losing a big opportunity. The key concept here is "people buy from people." Brooks recently picked up several Sony voice recorders and is sending them out to his clients so that they don't have to write their blogs. Instead, they can just talk during the day when they come across topics they find intriguing. Brooks' clients speak into the voice recorder and send the file to him for transcription and then posting on their individual blogs. The next step is to get them to connect with social networks, and it's important to point out that being connected starts with blogging. And, as the blogosphere continues to expand, blogging certainly is not restricted to consumers. Brooks' clients and many other professionals, from all different industries, are realizing that blogging is an excellent way to gain exposure for their brands.

The Leaders of Blogging

Tim Bray, Director of Web Technologies for Sun Microsystems (www.sun.com), joined his company in March 2004. At that time, there were already a few blogs, both on Sun's java.net property and also run individually by employees. At a meeting in April of 2004, Sun achieved an agreement that it would unleash all its employees to blog at will, and provide some infrastructure for them to use. Now, years later, several thousand of the organization's employees are involved in blogging. According to Bray, it was Sun and Microsoft that both cranked up the blogging culture at about the same time in 2004. The two companies were clearly the leaders in "blessing" their employees to blog under the corporate banner.

When asked to discuss the executives who have a blog at Sun, Bray stated, "It depends on how you define 'executive.' Visible executive bloggers include CEO Jonathan Schwartz, CTO Greg Papadopoulos, and General Counsel Mike Dillon. On the other hand, some individual engineers combining thought leadership with personality and good writing have as much reach as the executives." However, as blogs were unleashed at Sun, its Communications Department did not monitor these channels formally. The Communications Department at Sun was never reluctant to set up blogs, only the company's legal department. For the legal staff, the main source of worry was liability for what employee bloggers might choose to write. "Fortunately, to date none of the potential problems they foresaw have actually occurred. Marketing and Communications have not only been supportive, but also creative in figuring out a way to combine the efforts of Sun's bloggers and the more traditional marketing exercises to support product releases and other newsworthy events."

Bray sees blogs as an important communications tool and does not believe that blogs will ever replace forums or user groups. He feels the various social media tools serve entirely different purposes. For Bray, mailing lists, forums, wikis, and blogs all have a different role to play in business discourse, going forward. As for the future of blogs, Bray is unsure of this himself. He said, "Nobody knows. However, the large and growing numbers of people who not only have blogs, but also contribute to them on a regular basis suggests that the medium is here to stay. Some blogs will become increasingly multimedia-centric, with use of audio ("podcasts") and video; but there is no reason to think that old-fashioned writing, which is more searchable, linkable, and can be consumed faster, will go away any time soon."

How Does Social Networking Change Your Brand?

When asked, "How has social networking changed the way companies market to their customers," Stephen Johnston, Senior Manager in Nokia's Corporate Strategy Group answered, "To my mind, the Cluetrain Manifesto[2] was well ahead of its time. Its implications are only now being played out. In short, there is a shift of power from the companies to the individuals—people have always wanted, but can now get things on their terms." Johnston joined Nokia in 2003, and has since worked on Internet strategy, global macro and consumer trends, emerging business models, new collaboration tools, and corporate innovation. Since 2006, he has been leading a cross-company Internet innovation program that is aiming to facilitate Nokia's move into Internet consumer services.

Johnston discussed how social networking is very significant from a marketer's point because of the way in which it levels the playing field between brands and their customers by aggregating individuals and empowering them. He stressed how social networks connect with other people who share the same interests, however niche—so markets that were previously inaccessible can now make sense. Johnston used the example of groups on MySpace.com and how they can form around obscure subjects—for example, Canadian folk artists—or they can form around a brand—either coming together in support of it, or uniting in complaints. It's usually a bit of both. Johnston feels that social networks give individuals a voice—it empowers them to publish whatever they want to say, whether it's by posting their videos, pictures, or blog posts.

"These niches can be pretty vocal! The result of this is that individuals and brands are all just as important as each other. A 14-year old in Kansas can have more friends than a major multibillion dollar brand in any one social networking site," explained Johnston. For him, the implications are profound—companies can't possibly go around spotting "which are the latest up-and-coming social networking sites" and then waging a campaign to be the most popular. Instead, Johnston believes they need to focus on having the best products and, in particular, customer services so that their fans will be the ones creating the sites and evangelizing about their products. According to Johnston, taking the usual top-down campaign approach, to what is essentially a customer-owned phenomenon, will not work.

Identifying Trends in Social Networking

Johnston discussed the three biggest trends he sees: the shift in power from brands to individuals, the move from advertising to services, and the integration of the real and virtual worlds. As he outlined previously, brands lose their ability to control what is said about them within online communities. They need to focus more on delighting their existing customers to make sure they are evangelizing, not griping. As a result, there will be a new focus on helping companies engage in information-rich, two-way conversations with their customers, not glossy marketing messages pushed on increasingly savvy and aware individuals. Johnston pointed out that nowadays, few products are without services wrapped around them, and these are increasingly taking the form of social networking services. For instance, rowing machines now have the capability to interact with other rowing machines in the neighborhood, enabling the user to keep track of their scores and race other people who they've never even meet.

"These kinds of services add value to the product, and we at Nokia are introducing and enabling seamless integration of many services in multiple areas that add to the overall experience of our products, such as music and imaging services. The third trend—integrating real with virtual worlds—is one of my real passionate areas of interest," stated Johnston. He says Nokia is seeing the integration of real world data, such as location, direction, even traffic conditions, form an increasingly important part of the services' make up. Nokia's new N95 multimedia computer comes with built-in GPS and free navigation software that uses the Web to help customers improve their lives. "We'll be seeing many more examples of today's 'two dimensional' Internet services being supplemented by real world data to improve users' lives, which occur inevitably in 'three dimensions.'" Johnston knows that the net result will be less of a technology divide than we've seen today, in which people have to choose between playing on the computer or playing outside.

With respect to tracking and monitoring blogs, Johnston offers some advice. He recommends MyBloglog, which he explained is "a neat online service whereby you can see who's actually been reading your Web sites—it makes the Web seem a much more human and accessible place." He also mentioned in a similar vein, but even more relevant to this vision, a start-up company that demonstrates the real-world, virtual world overlap. It is a social network that you sign up for online, but also works with your Bluetooth-enabled mobile device. "You can be in a bar and your telephone will inform you there's someone there who recently visited your blog, or vice versa—you're browsing the Web, and the service lets you know if you come across a Web site of someone who you've recently been in close proximity to," explains Johnston. He's also looking forward to seeing a new breed of "mashups" that take the best of the Internet services and make them relevant for mobiles. "Things like being notified the minute the flat you're looking for is on the market, or you are walking past one of your friends' favorite shops and 'he wants you to visit it' will emerge. Time will tell which services are the ones people love and have viable business models."

Social Networks Go Far Beyond Friendships

Social networks are becoming increasingly popular by varied groups of Internet users. Many companies, groups, organizations, and consumers are just getting started with social networking. According to Wikipedia, the first social networking Web site, Classmates.com, launched in 1995. Classmates.com is best known for connecting people throughout the U.S. and Canada and has played a leading role in social networking.

The founder of Classmates.com, Randal Conrads, a Boeing engineer who was once a "military brat," created the company because like most, he had difficulty keeping in touch with friends.[3] As a result, Classmates.com began in his basement with an idea that served the purpose of helping people who move around, change jobs, get married, and change their names, stay connected. Today, if you just Google someone, it's impossible to search through thousands of entries to find that one person. Classmates.com satisfies an unmet need in society. Because high schools and colleges don't keep accurate records, technology certainly makes it easier to connect. For a free basic membership you can list your affiliations, post photos, and a biography. But, Classmates.com is for more than just finding people in high school, and if you're a member it goes well beyond friendships. The site is designed to make special connections between its users.

Classmates.com is different from other social networks. The Web site offers real names and not just screen names. These are real names and real people, with all the content being member generated. There's no need to purchase lists or obtain other types of data from services; the data comes right from the horse's mouth—the Classmates.com member. The common thread that makes Classmates.com so successful is there's power in the relationships. Although there's a lot of buzz going on with regard to social media, with Classmates.com you connect with people you've known well over time, or you've been acquainted with years ago. Connecting with people you recognize from your past is much easier than connecting with people you are not just meeting for the first time.

How to Measure Social Networks— An Expert's Point of View

Although it's reported that Classmates.com was the first social network site launched in 1995, concepts about social networks and how information flows through them have been around for many years. Perhaps the best example of this is social network analysis, a scientific field that has been evolving continually since the 1930s. Social network analysis is a quantitative science that, among other things, is used to measure properties in social networks, such as influence, trust, centrality, and network density. In the digital era, with billions of people communicating digitally, it's becoming increasingly useful as a way to understand how people are connected and influence one another.

FAS.research (www.fas-research.com), founded in 1997, is an independent consultancy that has been doing just that. They are pioneers in applying the sciences of social network analysis and complexity to the design of viral sales, marketing, and political campaigns. FAS' proprietary analytical techniques, social network visualization technologies, and data mining algorithms help clients see their markets as systems where people and institutions are connected and influence one another. This enables FAS to help clients harness the potential for change latent in the underlying social structure of markets, win new customers from existing ones, and systematically find a path to the tipping point for their ideas, products, or people.

Neal Gorenflo is Vice President of FAS.research and an expert on the use of social network analysis in business and the impact of technology on culture. Gorenflo's research on 3G, Internet, wireless consumers, and distance learning has been published in a variety of trade and academic journals. He discussed how FAS.research is pioneering the application of social network analysis in business and how the understanding and use of social networks, whether online or offline, is changing the way companies do business.

Q: How is social networking changing the way companies do business?

A: It's changing the way companies do business in a fundamental way, but we're still in the early stages of what I think will be a fairly comprehensive restructuring of our society brought on by social media and the culture of participation that it's fostering. So it's not just business that will be changed, it's everything. My perspective is that communications systems are foundational, that when a society shifts from one communication model to another, all institutions in society get reinvented according to the logic of the new medium.

This is happening as we shift from the broadcast paradigm epitomized by TV to a network model of communication epitomized by social networking. Identity, law, politics, culture, and business models are actively being reinvented as we speak. And while I believe we are early in this transformation, it's obvious that businesses take social networking seriously. We already see social networking and social media applications supporting businesses in a wide range of functional areas, including sales, public relations, customer service, product development, human resources, and knowledge management.

I think the key thing to focus on here is how social networking shifts power, and in the business context that means shifting power from producer to consumer. The flattening of organizations and the decentralization of power brought about by earlier forms of network communication technologies like e-mail is being radically extended by Web 2.0 technologies like social networking and blogs, to the point that the distinctions between producer and consumer are dissolving and consumer power is being radically enhanced. Technologies like LANs, e-mail, and intranets enabled companies to push power to the edges of the organization; but with the advent of Web 2.0, it is being pushed beyond the formal boundaries of the organization to consumers. The organizational pyramid is being turned upside down.

And this will be hugely beneficial for business. I think the power shift will result in better and, even more importantly, more relevant products. For instance, businesses are adopting the practice of engaging customers in deep and meaningful ways in every stage of the product lifecycle. This is borrowed from the software development community. And social media robustly enables the process.

The Firefox Web browser is a radical example of this model. It was an open-source software community that created Firefox, a volunteer effort with support from the Mozilla Foundation. Like all open-source projects, building Firefox relied on social media to coordinate volunteer efforts. Naturally, it was promoted in a way consistent with open-source production methods—the promotional work was distributed to volunteers using social media, and each doing their little bit added up to a whole lot of promotion. The Spread Firefox campaign was a hugely successful, volunteer-powered marketing campaign that helped catapult Firefox to roughly a 15 percent market share, second only to Microsoft's Explorer browser. This was like David taking on Goliath, except the battle is not finished. In any case, Firefox shows how using social media and engaging customers in a meaningful way in the whole product lifecycle can create serious competitive advantages in product quality, cost, and marketing efficiency.

In this environment, companies that employ authentic leaders— leaders who foster a culture of participation and earn their authority by their skill in facilitating many diverse stakeholders in creating value— will have a big advantage over companies that employ autocrats.

Q: How does FAS.research help its clients to understand social networks?

A: We help leaders understand social networking from a social science perspective using metrics and visualizations. I think leaders appreciate the value of social networks now more than ever, but they don't know how to quantify the value or how to best leverage them. From our perspective, social networking is all too often a curiosity rather than a real business tool. Our value to clients, on a high level, is two-fold. First, we give clients a way of seeing and quantifying the value of networks based on science, yet relevant to their business goals. Second, we give them tools and models that translate this unique insight into action plans that get results.

I can't emphasize enough the value of the mindset change we catalyze with leaders. Once a client begins to see his market as a system where people and institutions are connected and influence one another, it's like turning on the lights.

By making the system visible to leaders, we give them an increased measure of control. We put spotlights on the levers and gauges. And when they see how things actually work in their markets, they change what they do and how they structure their organization to take advantage of this more accurate view of reality.

Q: Are you able to graphically represent how groups are connected and how information flows?

A: Absolutely. There are two ways to look at what we do. Most of the time we help clients understand and leverage networks that already exist in their market. This includes graphically representing them. Visualization helps clients understand the structure of networks in their market, which means how individuals are connected within their communities and how communities are connected. By understanding the structure, we can design strategies to efficiently move messages, products, or ideas through the network. Visualizations help uncover the blockages and make visible the bridges from one community to another, and on a macro scale, the path from the periphery into the mainstream.

We also help clients design social networks. This is typical of the work we do in organizational development. Visualizing networks is also important here. The key idea in this context is that the ideal structure of a social network within an organization depends on the goal of and the type of work done by the organization. An ideal innovation network looks different from an ideal production network. We help organizations find their ideal form depending on what they do and what they want to accomplish.

The starting place is to first understand the existing network and how information and influence flow through it. Then you can design interventions that help you get closer to the ideal structure from the existing structure—and importantly, not lose the productive relationships in the redesign.

Q: When is the best time for a company to analyze its social network?

A: If we are talking about the social networks within a company, a good time is often before dramatic organizational change, such as a merger. Mergers are risky. It's well known that mergers frequently fail to deliver the expected benefits. One common mistake is that companies focus on the formal structure and ignore the informal social relations that are so important to innovation, problem solving, and just getting work done. These informal ties cross management levels and functional areas and are critical to an organization's health. Social network analysis can make these networks visible and quantify their value so that they can be considered in the new organizational design.

If we are talking about social networks in the customer base, there is a constant need because these networks are dynamic. New opportunities and threats emerge constantly. The sooner you get started, the sooner you can innovate a new sales and marketing model to obsolete your competitors' model. And if you read the advertising trades, the pain marketers feel in trying to extend direct marketing models is palpable. These magazines sometimes read like a long complaint about declining returns.

The source of the pain is no mystery. Direct channels are flooded and customers don't trust corporate messages. Time is ripe for change. Systematically scaling and measuring authentic word-of-mouth is part of the new paradigm. Unlike direct channels, the word-of-mouth channel is open, trusted, and more effective.

This channel is not without its challenges, however. For instance, the most popular word-of-mouth model does not scale. It's limited by the size of proprietary agent networks—groups of people recruited by service providers or companies to voluntarily buzz about products.

Our approach, on the other hand, does scale. Like direct marketing, the only limit is the size of your customer base or list. And despite what Malcolm Gladwell would have you believe, our research shows that everyone is a maven to some degree.[4] Our approach does not rely on recruiting uber-mavens; it's more granular than that. Everyone talks about products, but when and how much depends on the person and the product.

Using science, we help companies find where and when high concentrations of brand conversations are likely to happen and design marketing strategies to leverage this knowledge.

Q: How do you analyze social networks and how are you monitoring communication?

A: There are two ways to find the critical parts of a network: construct a mechanical model or use profiling.

To construct a mechanical model or network visualization, we need data that shows how people are connected. Online social networks, blogs, mobile phone call records, e-mail servers, patent databases, and co-publishing databases are typical data sources that have information about how people are connected. We take this data and apply proprietary algorithms to create social network maps and indices. Maps make visible the structure of the network. This helps with the macro-strategy—how to move messages from community to community. Indices quantify the value of each person's ability to spread messages and influence social connections. This helps with the micro-strategy—how to address each individual or discrete clusters in the network.

The profiling technique we use is similar to how the FBI finds serial killers. The FBI analyzes the commonalities of serial killers to construct a profile. This helps them know what to look for, not only in terms of the psychological profile but also where they are likely to live. We do a similar thing to identify people who play the key roles in spreading messages in a network—the hubs, connectors, and spreaders. We've found that each class is composed of people who share similar characteristics. Connectors, no matter where they come from, share some key values with other connectors. It's rarely a 100 percent match, but there are markers for each role that enable us to assign a probability that someone is a hub, connector, or spreader. This is incredibly valuable for direct marketing. It helps marketers design viral messages tailored to each role and target those that will most likely spread the message.

Q: Do you believe this approach is more effective?

A: Yes, and often dramatically more effective. Our approach is a true paradigm shift. Traditional direct marketing and communication strategy is based largely on segmentation. You break your target audience into groups comprised of individuals with common attributes, and you design specific messages for each segment.

While segmentation has been effective, this approach does not accurately reflect reality. It ignores the obvious fact that people are connected and influence each other. In our case, this fact is the core of our approach. We make visible and leverage the underlying social structure of a market. This is the difference between rowing a boat across the ocean and sailing using trade winds. Like sailors, we put nature to work for our clients. The end result is better returns.

Segmentation analyzes attributes of individuals while FAS' approach analyzes attributes of links and how people are connected is another way of understanding the difference. Instead of placing a statistical value on the sex, age, income, and behavior of an individual like segmentation does, FAS places a statistical value on the role an individual plays in spreading messages in their social network. Instead of looking for soccer moms, we look for connectors (the links between communities), hubs (the center of communities), and spreaders (individuals with enormous reach). Instead of paying attention to pockets of response, we pay attention to social patterns that have a high probability of being viral.

That being said, our approach doesn't replace segmentation or traditional market research, it overlays it. You still need to know the values held by individuals and groups in your target audience. Knowing how these individuals and groups are connected helps you move your message through the network systematically and tune it as it moves from community to community.

Q: Are many companies using social analytics?

A: It's definitely not mainstream, but it is a rapidly developing field. Up to just a few years ago, social network analysis was only feasible for large companies or governments. Cheap computing power and free, open source network analysis software has made the field more accessible. We've seen a number of competitors pop up in just the last two years.

The barrier now is in application. These days just about anybody can create a network visualization. The problem is that there are very few people who can tell you what the data means and what to do with it to create value. This is a challenge of interpretation, imagination, and experience, something that computers and software can't help with. This is where FAS is ahead. We've been solving business problems with social network analysis for nearly 10 years.

To give you an idea of what is possible now with enough computing power and experience, a European mobile phone carrier recently hired us to analyze three years of call data for more than three million subscribers (anonymized for privacy). For the macro strategy, we were able to break the subscribers up into distinct communities based on their calling patterns and identify the most viral communities, based on sociometrics which quantify mathematically certain properties of networks, including the strength and direction of influence. For the micro strategy, we created viral indices that were uploaded in the carrier's CRM. This enabled our client to make special offers to customers who have a high probability of influencing an acquisition or stabilizing other subscribers around them.

Q: Is the research you provide a lengthy process?

A: Most projects take four to eight weeks with just a couple workshop days with clients. It depends on the scope of the project, the availability of the data, and the amount of data to be analyzed. It also depends on whether our strategies are going to be applied incrementally or holistically.

Let's start with data. If data about how clients and prospects are connected is readily available, that speeds up the process, though the time also depends on the amount of data that needs to be analyzed. If we need to gather data for the analysis for instance, through surveying, co-occurrence search algorithms, or another method—that obviously adds to the time.

In terms of scope, this is an approach that screams out to be applied holistically. It benefits from integration between functional areas in a business, especially between sales and marketing because what we do can be thought of as a viral form of microtargeting. When you have an entirely new and more accurate way of seeing your customer base, it has significant implications for a client's organizational structure. When our clients see how their customers are connected, they immediately see the necessity to market and sell in an entirely new way and organize themselves in an entirely new way. When we have a client who can approach a challenge holistically, that can be a larger project because we could be involved in designing a new process or organization.

It helps to give an example. Let's go back to the cell phone carrier client I mentioned. This carrier is a new market entrant in Europe. It was successful in getting traction in immigrant communities early. The problem was how to bridge from the Early Adopter immigrant community and break into the mainstream. The carrier made subscriber call data available to us in anonymized form for privacy. This sped up the process, but it was a lot of data.

Despite the vast amount of data, we were able to literally map how all callers and communities were connected using the call data. This enabled us to identify the best opportunities to win new clients from existing clients based on which social patterns had the highest statistical probability to influence a conversion. We also identified the best bridges—actual social links shown in calling patterns—into new demographic communities. The whole project took six weeks. And the analysis and action plan we provided helped synchronize their sales, marketing, and customer service efforts focusing more resources on the hubs, connectors, and spreaders in their customer base.

Q: Where do you see your research efforts going in the next five or ten years? And what do you think is next in social networking?

A: In general, we want to deepen our understanding of how social networks operate and how to apply what we learn to important problems.

While we've focused mainly, but not exclusively, on solving business problems, we hope to find our moment to make a big positive difference to how people lead their day-to-day lives.

Not surprisingly then, we are doing more thinking about applying social network analysis to the design of social networking platforms. It's clear to us that the usefulness of seeing them from a technology or mass media perspective has almost run its course. As the technology becomes commoditized—and that is happening fast with the emergence of private label solutions—people are realizing it's the social architecture of these systems and how you manage the community that deliver the most value, not the technology.

And we are not interested in them as another diversion, as entertainment, as simply media. We are interested in designing social networking systems that help people create value in their day-to-day life online and off. We see social networking as a great coordinating technology that can help people organize themselves into geographically based mutual aid communities where all types of resources are shared, where the value and pleasure of social interactions is radically increased, where a culture of democracy and civic engagement can thrive, where people can better enjoy and enhance the natural and human splendor of their local communities, and where the social architecture of sustainability can show itself.

We think social networking has come at the right time. When combined with a shift in values that place a premium on authentic, self-organized experiences, social networking can facilitate the social changes necessary, at the scale and speed that is required, to promote true human fulfillment, resulting in social justice and environmental sustainability.

We are at a juncture where we, as a global society, have the power to either destroy ourselves or create an unprecedented global renaissance, an explosion of creativity in every field from every corner of the world the likes of which the world has never seen. The first chapters of both scenarios have already been written. We think social networking is one of the tools, if used wisely, that can help us ensure that our future is a bold tale about global renaissance, a continuing exploration of humanity's role in this universe.

Moving Forward with Social Networking

Social networking empowers the 21st Century consumer to choose what is newsworthy and relevant to them. Consumers are leading a 2.0 revolution in their social networking communities. They pass more and more information back and forth through connections, relying on an extended network of family, friends, business associates, and acquaintances. The movement toward social media enables easy information sharing. You should keep the following in mind as you advise your brand(s) about the importance of social networking:

- 21st Century reporting and the news distribution is no longer an exclusive function of the media outlets.

- There are direct-to-consumer newswire services, including PRWeb, that focus on "media bypass."

- Blogs go one step beyond the profile. A blog is the best way to say, "Here's who I am and here's what I have to say."

- Today, people want to connect, not just to the companies they purchase their products/services from, but also connect to the people behind those companies.

- If the executives behind a brand are not blogging, they're losing an opportunity, especially if they want people to talk.

- A social network connects with other people who share the same interests, however niche—so previously inaccessible markets now can make sense.

- Socially networked individuals are spending less time with a core group of important people. If they're just trying to collect friends, they are losing the whole point of the social network. It's that real world connection, which needs to be made for the networks to have high integrity.

- The concept of the social network and analysis of communication patterns has been around for many years. Social network analysis has been a scientific discipline since the 1930s.

- Social networks allow companies to cross boundaries and go outside the organization by involving customers in all sorts of brand communication. You will often see this placed back into the entire product development cycle.

- By using social network analysis, you can analyze the attributes of how people are linked. By data mining, not only can you find the connectors and the hubs, but also see specific communication patterns for better direct-to-consumer communication.

Endnotes

1. "About Us." *PR Web.com*. May 2007. www.prweb.com.

2. According to Wikipedia, the Cluetrain Manifesto is a set of 95 theses organized as a Manifesto, or call to action, that focused on the Internet as a connected marketplace where people would find new ways to share information.

3. Research obtained from John Uppendahl, VP of PR at Classmates.com.

4. Malcolm Gladwell discusses the role of mavens in his book, *The Tipping Point*. Mavens are information specialists who acquire knowledge and know how to then share that knowledge with other people.

Chapter **9**

RSS Technology: A Really Simple Tool to Broaden Your Reach

Really Simple Syndication (RSS) technology is as easy as it sounds. According to Wikipedia, RSS is "a family of Web feed formats used to publish frequently updated content such as blog entries, news headlines, or podcasts." RSS feeds enable online audiences to keep up-to-date with content from their favorite Web sites in an automated manner that removes the task of checking a Web site daily for new content.

As a result, more and more consumers are opting to receive their news and information through a news or media Web site or a portal (Yahoo!, AOL, MSN). RSS is a great way to receive an abundance of information, on a range of topics, which can be easily organized and reviewed. RSS is also the best way to stay current (in some cases up to the minute) because it gives consumers timely information and keeps them "in the know." When you decide to set up an RSS feed for your brand, you're choosing a direct-to-consumer approach—an effective and straightforward means to reach the public, different from older PR practices that typically go second-hand through the media (the influencer) to distribute news to customers.

The benefits of RSS feeds are unmatched. To put this into perspective, think about how much time each day you spend weeding through interesting and sometimes not so interesting content in your e-mail box. You probably have the same amount of time to visit all your favorite news and information portals to read about what's going on in your industry (or to stay abreast of the world around you). Very little time indeed. If you have an overwhelming sense of information overload, you are not alone and certainly can apply this same scenario to what your audience experiences.

You Can Cut Through the Clutter

RSS is an excellent way to reach your audience during the course of their busy and information-saturated lives. Without RSS, your brand's audience might be missing out on important information they are not able to access; whether it's from a lack of time or because your important announcements were intercepted by an overzealous spam filter and never made it to your customer's inbox. RSS feeds help to alleviate these concerns with a mode of communication that offers the ability to go beyond e-mail, e-newsletters, and HTML blasts. With RSS, you enable your audience to select and receive information about your company.

In this chapter, through perspectives offered by various professionals, you will come to understand that RSS is a powerful tool. As such, it should be included in your marketing arsenal. Keep in mind that RSS is:

- Spam free—your customers choose to receive it and you don't have to worry about spam filters that deter messages from reaching them.

- A communication tool that enables you to update, target, and control the frequency of your brand messaging.

- An excellent resource for companies that have readily available content and are willing to share a great deal of information with their audiences.

- Available to companies who have smaller budgets.

- A means to reach your customers directly and to drive traffic to content on your Web site.

- A tool that enables you to extend your branding—brand messages can be top of mind through an RSS feed.

- Measurable through the use of monitoring impressions, click-through rates (CTR), and Cost Per Measurement (CPM).

Increase Your Marketing Arsenal

If you are willing to spice up your marketing arsenal by including RSS feeds, you don't have to be a PR 2.0 guru to get the job done. The first step is making sure you have enough content on a regular basis. Next, you need to set up your content or RSS document in Extensive Markup Language (XML). To create an RSS feed by hand would be a tedious task and require some knowledge of XML and the RSS protocol. So, one option is to use an RSS feed creation program like ListGarden (www. softwaregarden.com), or FeedForAll (www.feedforall.com). With these programs you simply input the title of your announcement, the URL where it resides, and a short description that will be seen on the feed. Once you have put in this information, the software generates the RSS feed, which you then place on your Web site for users to subscribe to your program.

The best and most common method of implementing RSS is to use a Blogger or Content Management Software (CMS), one that uses RSS. These products do all the work for you. You create a post on the Web site and the software automatically updates your RSS feed. All the major blogging and CMS products support RSS; examples include TypePad (www.typepad.com), Wordpress (www.wordpress.com), Blogger (blogger. com), PostNuke (www.postnuke.com), and Drupal (www.drupal.org).

To view an RSS feed, you need software called a "feed reader" or "aggregator." You subscribe to a feed by entering the feed's link into the reader or by clicking an RSS icon on your browser, which initiates the subscription. The reader checks the feeds regularly for new contact and downloads any updates that it finds. Most major e-mail products now have feed readers, as well as most Internet portals.

Many companies have set up their own feeds, including IDC, Macromedia, and Deloitte & Touche, to name a few. But remember, as you familiarize yourself with RSS and learn more about the technology, you need to keep in mind that RSS is available only if there's a customer base that wants to receive the information. It makes sense that many of the larger companies were among the first to develop RSS feeds and to build to a customer base. A good example of a company that has instituted RSS distribution early on is Deloitte & Touche, which has an extensive RSS program.

Bill Barrett is the global and U.S. marketing director for Deloitte's Web site, www.Deloitte.com. He leads teams of marketing and communications professionals who develop and deliver various aspects of online marketing campaigns designed to drive market growth, build awareness, and strengthen strategic relationships with clients, prospects, and influencers. Since joining Deloitte in 1999, Barrett has focused on developing the Internet marketing channel, which serves as the hub for many of Deloitte's integrated marketing programs. Prior to joining Deloitte, Barrett held strategic marketing communications and information technology roles at companies such as Compaq Computer, JP Morgan, and Nestle Foods.

Barrett, who has been with Deloitte for approximately eight years, discussed the company's most popular RSS feeds which include (http://feeds.feedburner.com/DeloitteGlobal), Deloitte US (http://feeds. feedburner.com/DeloitteUS), and Deloitte Insights podcast (http://feeds. feedburner.com/DeloitteInsights). He attributes the RSS popularity to the real-time updates on latest information. These feeds are all syndicated via Feedburner, so that aggregators, blogs, and portals can pick them up.

According to Barrett, the benefits of using RSS feeds to an organization are the low-cost content distribution, and syndication of content to other sites, which leads to more exposure for a company. In addition, the end user isn't spammed as with e-mail. They can receive what they want and consume via their own browsers (no plug-ins or anything of that nature), IE7, Firefox, Safari, or leverage popular feed readers such as Google, Yahoo!, and the like. "RSS is a useful addition to a company's marketing arsenal as it extends your content beyond your own Web site. You receive more impressions and it's easy to manage and update, all at a minimal cost," Barrett explained. He added, "RSS feeds also help companies to build better awareness. If managed properly, just like your own site's content, the feed needs to provide content that appeals to the audience. With RSS, users control the information flow. Therefore, if your content provides them with little or no value, they'll turn you off."

With respect to increasing traffic to your Web site, Barrett believes that the nature of RSS certainly has that potential. Because your feed items link back to your site for full stories, video or audio content, and so on, appealing topics that are clicked-through can certainly increase site traffic. The syndication and viral nature of RSS feeds can open up content to new audiences that normally might not visit your site. For example, the Deloitte Insights podcasts have been picked up by many podcast aggregation sites, and they've also been picked up by university professors and used as course content for their programs. Professors finding this content off the Deloitte main Web site on their own is unlikely. Apple's iTunes store (to which Deloitte syndicates its podcast feeds) gave them that extension into the marketplace.

Deloitte measures the traffic from an RSS feed in several ways: Web site analytics (downloads and page visits) as well as Google's (newly acquired) Feedburner product that provides subscriber numbers, reach, and the like. Since the start of Deloitte's RSS program, the feedback from online visitors has been slow. Barrett feels that RSS is still a bit of an unknown to most of the firm's site visitors. The adoption of RSS has been slow, and in some cases users aren't even aware they are using RSS (iTunes, portals, and so on). Barrett expects that with IE7 and its built-in RSS reading capabilities, RSS will become more popular and they'll see a greater adoption rate. After all, he commented, "I don't see RSS as just a tech fad. I see it as the future for distributing content across sites (present in some cases). The biggest challenge, I think, is making it easier for users to leverage, as well as educating them as to what it is and its value to them."

What It Means to Be in Charge

If you are the communications professional in charge of brand communication, your responsibility extends far beyond understanding initial setup of an RSS feed program. RSS has a few different meanings for you. The technology might be the next logical step in the way a brand distributes its news announcements directly to its stakeholders. However, it's also a method, similar to the SMR, which is direct-to-consumer. Many PR service providers (Business Wire, MarketWire, PR Newswire, and PRWeb) caught on quickly by providing companies and marketing/PR agencies the ability to have RSS feeds through their sites in addition to the traditional PR newswire services. Suddenly, the ability to reach a targeted customer base without the need to go through the media was present and easily accessible. However, this new direct-to-consumer process is different for the communications professional. The change in distribution makes some PR professionals feel uncomfortable, once again, because you are bypassing the media or an important third-party endorser. Suddenly, you're no longer selling the credible third-party endorsement as a part of your PR tangibles.

With RSS, no journalist is writing about your brand, saying why it's so great or supporting your brand's cause with written or spoken word. Because consumers are continually seeking and demanding more information from their brands, you can't fight what your customer wants in an information-saturated world. If customers need to have as much information as possible, at all times, RSS (although you are bypassing the "typical" influencer) should be considered an important part of your communications planning. After all, your customer is still receiving newsworthy information that comes directly from your brand. The basics of public relations are credible and newsworthy information, which should make you feel more comfortable about a new social media tool that broadens your distribution.

The Pros Take a Stance

Hearing what other professionals are saying about their use of RSS technology is reassuring. Michael G. Schneider is Vice President of Public Relations for Success Communications Group (www.successcommgroup. com), a $60 million national public relations, recruitment marketing, traditional advertising, association management, and Web development/ interactive agency in New Jersey. Schneider had a great to deal to say about the value of RSS feeds for his communications clients.

Schneider recalls when RSS-enabled news kits started to become commonplace in 2004. He envisions this as the standard, not the exception, across the industry within the next five years. To Schneider, the ongoing challenge of making client messages more visible, digestible, and user-friendly, coupled with the simultaneous explosion of Web sites, e-newsletters, weblogs, and traditional news outlets putting more and more content online, made RSS a helpful tool in keeping pace with information in an automated manner. "The days of checking sites manually, scanning a few major daily newspapers, and chatting around the water cooler about last night's news as a way of staying informed has gone by the wayside," recalled Schneider.

Schneider discussed how RSS is not just useful in receiving information. Ever since his agency started producing more robust online news kits that enabled them to upload photographs, video, and content from both in the office and out in the field, they have constantly been looking for ways to make their clients message more "media friendly." Putting news kit information in RSS formats is just one of the tools that Success Communications Group has embraced to help accomplish this.

According to Schneider, RSS is relevant and can add real value across all industries and client types (nonprofit, corporate, governmental, associations, and the like). All subjects and interest areas can be broken into syndicated RSS-enabled information. After information is in RSS format, an RSS-aware program called news aggregators can pick up your information. Conversely, RSS enables any special interest group, advocacy organization, or company to "keep tabs" on a greater amount of information in a much more efficient manner.

Schneider discussed the other benefits of RSS feeds for his clients. "Speed and efficiency!" he stated emphatically, "Speed and efficiency!" When he began his career years ago, he worked in the corporate public relations department of a Fortune 500 company that would create a daily report of news coverage, what competitors were saying about issues and topics, and other news of corporate interest. This was pre-RSS. The process of generating these reports was time consuming and the information was old by lunch. "Today, RSS solves the problem for companies that regularly use the Web as a resource for information. They can easily stay informed by retrieving the latest news and information from sites and blogs that they are interested in. This is a big time saver," he explained. Scheider also mentioned another bonus of RSS: You can maintain your privacy by joining e-mail newsletters without providing your name and contact information. The number of sites offering RSS feeds is growing rapidly and includes big names like Yahoo! News, *The New York Times, USA Today*, and more.

Schneider believes that RSS feeds should be viewed as another tool that communicators can consider when disseminating information. If broad information dissemination to the media and direct to the public is your goal, creating an RSS-enabled news kit is something that might help get the word out. However, although Schneider places a great deal of value on RSS feeds, he stated, "I don't consider it the Holy Grail of awareness building and overall communication. Wire dissemination services are also useful. Today news releases are being keyword optimized to be more visible to Web search engines like Google and Yahoo! Many technological advances are taking place within the field of communication. RSS is but one arrow in the quiver of professional communicators."

For Schneider, technology is only part of this equation. He stressed how communications professionals need to remember that the content and quality of your message is really the key element. The old adage "You can lead a horse to water, but you can't make it drink" is something that he thinks about with regard to information technology. Companies, causes, and associations can do a lot to lead customers, supporters, and others to their Web site, but the relevance of their message, product, and information will ultimately keep them engaged, make a sale, or complete a call to action.

With respect to third-party influencers, Schneider realizes they can add a lot of credibility to your message. They can also disagree, not cover, or misinterpret your message. Moreover, it is becoming increasingly difficult today to determine who the third-party influencers are. "Citizen journalists, new media sites like Rocketboom.com, large national blogs, and e-newsletters can have larger audiences than many traditional news outlets. With this explosion of media, there's the ability to reach out directly to the public with your message. RSS-enabled news releases, news kits, and other media tools are one method of doing this," stressed Schneider.

According to Schneider, RSS is also not the only direct-to-the-public method that communication professionals are paying attention to. Social networking platforms such as YouTube, MySpace, and Facebook have created environments where messages can go direct to the public in mass capacity. Schneider explained, "Then once your message gets a foothold in these environments they can spread via viral marketing. RSS, social networking platforms, and other new communication methods make this a really exciting time in the communication field."

Last, Scheider discussed how many large, traditional media outlets have embraced RSS. *The New York Times, USA Today*, and others have RSS enabled Web sites. "With more and more information and news options offered today, RSS enables information to be tracked, shared, and collected in a method that is very efficient. Will RSS be replaced with something else? Perhaps, but the basic concept of what RSS offers is something that is here to stay," claimed Schneider.

Communications professionals who use RSS feeds daily see the value and endorse the social media tool. David Walton, Assistant VP of Marketing at JVC, is an Early Adopter of technology. He began experimenting with RSS and viewing feeds in 2004, then finally implemented them on his Web site in 2006. Walton uses RSS to keep track of everything from breaking news to the Netflix movies being sent to his home.

When asked how he felt about RSS as a useful addition to a company's marketing arsenal, Walton responded, "With major Internet portals integrating RSS viewing capability into their news pages, RSS can be a valuable tool to keep interested parties up-to-date about a firm's activities provided that it isn't turned into an advertising mechanism. News must be current and relevant. Headlines must be attention-getting, and most importantly must not have a commercial 'look.' If the RSS headline begins to look like an advertisement, it will likely be deleted—permanently."

With respect to Walton's company, JVC, they currently are providing RSS feeds for technical support information. Engineers and 'techies' have been the first to appreciate the RSS feeds. Walton explains, "I have the most recent questions posted to our FAQ site appearing at the top of my Yahoo! home page. Another division of our company has just started offering RSS feeds of news releases." Walton believes that although there is a tremendous interest in RSS, he doesn't think many magazine writers and editors will be interested in receiving the feeds on the JVC site.

However, their dealers and resellers might want to subscribe to the RSS feed for their own Web sites. Additionally, special-interest Web sites might use the feeds as an automated way to provide content. Walton stressed that if the material being fed is newsworthy and interesting, it will get republished.

Overall, Walton relies on RSS feeds to help him get the information he is most interested in receiving. "It is not a substitute for trade publications, newsletters, or Doppler radar. But, it can tell me what movies will be waiting in my mailbox when I get home," he explained. For Walton, RSS is not a tech fad. In his words, "No more so than the Internet, WWW, or e-mail, RSS is a simple, but effective tool that can put tremendous publishing power into anyone's hands. It's also a cool way to have a truly customized Web browser."

A Publisher's Point of View

Today, RSS is an integral part of our favorite media choices, from Yahoo! and MSN to online publications, including CNET, Broadcasting & Cable, and InformationWeek. You might remember that several years ago it was difficult to find the media outlets that enabled companies to sign up for RSS distribution. And once you did find the outlets that provided the feeds, it was almost impossible to find a live person to discuss how the feed worked for your client or what type of opportunities existed. Not anymore—RSS technology icons are popping up on both consumer and professional Web sites.

Reed Business Information (RBI) makes it easy for their Web site readers to find and take advantage of their RSS feeds. RBI provides business-to-business information in the form of printed magazines and online Web sites. The company has more than 75 brands across multiple industries, including entertainment, television, engineering, construction, manufacturing, publishing, printing, gifts and furnishings, and hospitality. Jennifer Wilhelmi is the Director of Online Marketing & Development at RBI. Her current role encompasses the online efforts around audience, business and fresh content development, as well as all marketing efforts, including

SEO, SEM, internal promotions, viral marketing, and branded/direct response marketing campaigns. Prior to her position at RBI, Wilhelmi developed expertise in the online advertising space, having managed Strategic Operations for DoubleClick's International Media division.

Wilhelmi discussed how RBI approaches RSS Technology and the importance of its use to their magazine brands and to their online audiences.

Q: Discuss how your brands are using RSS technology.

A: Broadcasting & Cable (B&C) is one of the brands within the RBI portfolio, based here in New York. I focus primarily on our 57 online Web sites and I work across our portfolio of brands to grow our online presence. We recently relaunched the Broadcasting & Cable Web site (www.broadcastingcable.com), which made RSS an even bigger part of our offering, but the features you see on the B&C Web site are consistent throughout our portfolio. We're going through the process of improving and relaunching many of our Web sites. I'd estimate that more than 60 percent of our Web sites are getting redesigned and have recently launched or are on the dock to launch sometime this year.

Q: Do most of them include the ability for the RSS feed?

A: Absolutely, that's a standard feature now for all our Web sites.

Q: Was that as a result of your customer base?

A: Well, it varied on a brand by brand basis, depending on the audience of our Web sites; some were actively looking for RSS feeds, others were a little slower to adopt RSS feeds depending on their comfort level and usage of the Internet. But, what we're seeing is that this trend of staying informed via the Web is definitely increasing. It gives us a lot of flexibility for getting our content out there for users to find or for users to leverage through their RSS readers. Beyond that, it is a great tool for driving users back to our sites.

Q: Are companies opting in to your RSS program?

A: They don't need to opt in. Basically, the way we set up our RSS feeds are around our discrete channels and blogs on the Web sites. So, if we're choosing to cover a company's news release, let's say something in consumer electronics, and it was on our *TWICE* Web site, then the *TWICE* editors choose to include it in their stream of articles for the day. Whichever category that article fell into, it would automatically be included in that RSS feed. The only content that wouldn't be in an RSS feed is something that's not ours or wasn't sent to us to be included in our news. If it were licensed content from a third party, we'd only include it in our RSS feed if we had permission to do so. It's pretty much our original news and the content, whether it is stories, product releases, or trade show information, depending on the type of Web site. Our sites house many different types of interactive content, but anything that's not in a PDF format that would lend itself to RSS feeds, we turn into RSS feeds.

Q: When did RBI begin offering RSS feeds?

A: We've had RSS for quite some time, but we've been expanding our RSS reach extensively this past year with the site redesigns and relaunches. B&C, for example, relaunched earlier this year and now they have RSS feeds around every single channel and every single blog. Blog feeds are new, but are now a standard element throughout the site.

Q: And you feel your subscribers have really grasped RSS quickly?

A: Some of them have, some of them haven't. It depends. We use it also for our partners. So, let's say a Web site approaches us and says, "B&C, we'd really love to have some of your news on our Web sites," and what we'd say is, "Why don't you grab our RSS feed and we'll send you our logo and you can include our news on your Web site because it's relevant for your audience." From our perspective, not only is it branding, but it drives the interested users who want to learn more about our Web site or news back to our Web site to see the full article. So, we find it a valuable tool not just for users who understand RSS, but also for our partners, as part of our bigger marketing effort.

Q: Is there a fee for associated partners receiving your RSS feed?

A: Typically, no. We get a lot of requests from people who want to have more news on their sites, but we wouldn't charge them for headlines and they wouldn't charge us to do that either. It's usually something that's free because we get benefits, we get branding and traffic back to our Web sites, and they get the benefit of offering more news or content that's relevant to their users on their Web site.

Q: Does it matter if the partner is large or small?

A: We look for partners who have a relevant audience to the types of people we're trying to attract. We probably wouldn't have an RSS feed for a construction company on an entertainment Web site because the audiences don't match. Providing must-have, relevant content to our users is a primary goal.

Q: Give me your own personal perspective on the benefits of using RSS feeds, and then also apply it to RBI.

A: Well, from a user perspective, I personally use RSS feeds to cut through all the information I'm bombarded with each day. I choose Web sites or feeds that are interesting both from a work side and a personal side. I customize them in a Yahoo! reader. Many sites out there offer readers that you can either download or customize on a Web site. It's interesting because a lot of people use those types of readers and don't even realize they're using RSS feeds. The terminology can sometimes be confusing to people because they actually do use them, but don't know what they're called.

From an RBI standpoint, that's even more important when we're dealing with the business community rather than consumers. Most of the people in our audience are business decision-makers. They're busy and they're inundated with information, and this is a way for them to get all their news and information in one place rather than necessarily having to visit ten different Web sites that are interesting to them. They can bring everything into their RSS reader and then follow up on the Web site if they need deeper information.

Q: Do you feel that using RSS is a useful addition to a company's marketing arsenal?

A: Absolutely—not only for the example I provided in terms of people putting it into their RSS readers, but for partnership opportunities and getting your content out there. You can be found in places the user would expect to find you. If, for example, you have relevant information about the broadcasting industry, then a user going to another Web site outside of B&C might still expect to find the most relevant news, which might be from B&C if they're the ones that broke the story.

Q: Do you feel that RSS is becoming part of your communications planning, not just an add-on?

A: We're realizing that more and more users are finding information from RSS feeds and search engines. We're more conscious of that when we write articles for the Web. We're really writing for that audience and for the mechanism in which they're going to find the article. We try to make sure that the headlines for these articles are straightforward and easily understood by the user because they're out of the context of our Web site. Where *Variety*, B&C, or *Publishers Weekly* might have inside industry jargon or terms, a user getting this into an RSS reader with a thousand other articles needs to know it's an entertainment article or a publishing article or a broadcast article. So, we try to put those types of keywords or triggers around it so that a user doesn't get confused. I can give you an example. I saw an article recently that said, "How to Run Your Business Like a Spartan," and it was off the *300* movie and was very eye-catching. But if that title was to be in an RSS feed, a user might not completely make the connection that it's an article for entrepreneurs about how to run your business. It's kind of vague. There might have been other key words they could have placed in the headline that would've still gotten the same message across but triggered "Oh, this is for small businesses" or "This is for entrepreneurs." We just want to make sure that when a headline is not within the context of our Web site, it's still relevant to users. That's how it plays into our editorial or content communications strategy. We try to think ahead about how the user's going to be receiving it.

Q: Do you think that RSS is helping companies or it's helping RBI to build better awareness and to drive traffic?

A: That is one element of it. We are doing many things to build awareness of our Web sites, and we make sure we are out there so interested users can find our info. Being a traditional print publisher and moving quickly into the online space, we realize that instead of having a controlled circulation, as we did in print, the users need to be able to find us online. And they need to find the answers to their questions really quickly. We're keeping all that in mind, and RSS is one element of that strategy.

Q: What kind of feedback have you received from your online visitors?

A: It's been positive, and like I said, it varies brand to brand depending on the sophistication of the industry, and whether they're using RSS feeds and readers. Some industries have been a little quicker to catch on than others.

Q: And will you continue to do formal research or just proceed based on feedback?

A: We'll absolutely continue to research and test and probably put more of our content into an RSS type format, and just XML in general, so that it can be used in different types of applications. That will really be based on what the users are looking for. And they will ultimately drive this. If it turns out they're not using RSS feeds and they're receiving information in another way, like through in-page widgets or through mobile, then we'll look to get them the information that way. But, our RSS feeds and XML effort in terms of making all our content into a format that can be read in multiple ways, that's kind of a combined effort for us. We want to make sure that if there are any applications outside an RSS reader we'd want to drop our content into, we have it in the most flexible form possible.

Q: Do you have an area set up for people with questions regarding RSS?

A: It seems as though most people have really responded to the little box symbol we're using around RSS. Online audiences seem to understand what that is at this point in time. We don't get a ton of questions, but what we do have on the Web site is a description of what RSS is and what they need to do to use it, as well as what it stands for, which is Really Simple Syndication.

We try to answer questions in our RSS feeds section where we explain RSS feeds and why you need them, but if a Web site or company wanted to partner with us, they would usually come to my team. That would be the marketing and development team. If they had a question about the actual content within the RSS feed, like, "Why did I receive this article, it doesn't seem like it's relevant to your Web site," they could go to our editorial team with their questions.

Q: Do you think Media Bypass is an issue with RSS feeds? Is this being blown out of proportion? What do you think about RSS as a direct to consumer tool?

A: I think it's fine. I think it helps us have that relationship with our end audience. What it makes us think about is the role of a brand online and how we translate that. For example, for B&C, our print audience knows us, loves us, and is a very dedicated audience. The ones who bookmark our Web site or come to us through an e-mail, we know they're very loyal to the brand. That's great because they have great brand recognition. However, users who find us either through a search engine, receive our RSS feed, or maybe encounter us on a partner Web site, might not have that connection with B&C that we'd like. They're consuming information on an as-needed basis. They're thinking "I need to see this news release" or "I heard about something that happened with the fight on HBO," and they type that into a search engine and somehow they get to our feed. In this case, they don't have that recognition around B&C. Without them going and clicking on the article and getting back to our site, we don't have a chance to really brand to them. Of course, we need to keep that in mind in terms of making our content relevant and useful and making it able to be found because our role might be different as the Internet evolves. Perhaps the fact that we are B&C down the road won't be as important, it's just that we have the most relevant news or we have the fastest breaking news or we have the best editorial spin when it comes to the Broadcasting and Cable industry. It's not a cause for concern; it's more of an evolution.

Q: Do you think RSS is more than just a tech fad?

A: I do. I think it's moving us forward toward something completely different from what we're used to today in terms of getting content into open standard formats like XML. Look how in-page widgets have taken off on sites like Facebook. I would put this in the same genre as RSS in terms of providing information to users when they are not necessarily on your Web site. RSS and other formats enable us more opportunities to get our content in front of interested users and it helps put the user in control of their customized content experience while saving them the time of having to go to multiple Web sites. I think some element of RSS or the underlying kind of open coding XML will still be prevalent in what we see going forward. It might evolve from the simple readers that we have today into more complex applications, but by building out our sites with XML feeds and essentially RSS feeds, we'll be ready for those types of transitions in the future. I don't think RSS is necessarily a fad; it will just facilitate more applications coming down the road.

Moving Ahead with RSS

As your customers require more information about your brand, you need to have the information readily available. Using an RSS feed is an excellent way to satisfy their hunger for information, in a manner they can review and organize easily. As you rely on RSS content feeds to distribute your important announcements direct to consumer, keep in mind the following:

- RSS is a straightforward means to reach your audience. Although it's a different approach for the PR pro, it is unmatched in terms of its effectiveness.

- With the ability to distribute targeted information and announcements, you reduce your audiences overwhelming sense of information overload when e-mail newsletters and HTML e-blasts pile up in their inboxes.

- RSS setup is simple by using software programs that guide you through an easy process without having to be a technology expert.

- Although RSS technology bypasses the "typical" influencer, it should still be considered an important part of your communications planning. After all, your customer is still receiving newsworthy information that comes directly from your brand.

- RSS will add real value across all industries and client types (non-profit, corporate, governmental, associations, and so on), and a variety of subjects and interest areas can be broken into syndicated RSS enabled information.

- RSS content feeds might get your information directly to your target audience, but the content and quality of your message is really the key element.

- Customers might find tremendous value in your RSS feeds; however, it's yet to be determined the number of journalists who sign up for feeds to find interesting information for story ideas.

- RSS keeps your brand top of mind. The more interesting, newsworthy information you make available, the more your audience will immerse themselves in your brand.

Chapter 10

Video and Audio for Enhanced Web Communications

Video applications appeared on the Web in the early 1990s. The ability to communicate through these applications has been available to you for many years. But, why is video on the Web such a focus now? Is it the fact that broadband is making audio and video more accessible to brands and their audiences? Or, did it take YouTube.com and Web 2.0 consumer video content sharing, video blogs (vlogs), and video podcasting to create an intensified interest? Is this awareness so great that it makes you want to pay attention to these PR 2.0 tools for your own brands? Let's explore the answers to these questions in the world of PR 2.0, where you need to embrace social media strategies and the 2.0 tools to capture your audience's attention.

More Than a Fad

Video is powerful and communications professionals have known this for years. There's strength in visual communications that tells an interesting story. Regardless of where you think the push for Web video emanated, you can clearly see that it's much more than a fad. Wikipedia says, "A fad refers to a fashion that becomes popular in a culture relatively quickly, but loses popularity dramatically."[1] Video will not lose its popularity. It dates back to earlier uses of Video News Releases (VNRs) in the 1980s and pre-Web streaming video, live or on demand. Pharmaceutical companies and other large corporations, including Microsoft and Phillip Morris, use VNRs in their communication efforts.[2] The popularity of using video in communications, especially on the Internet, is growing immensely among consumer and business audiences.

There's a reason they call YouTube.com "The Talk of Tinseltown."[3] The video-rich site has attracted a tremendous amount of attention from

Internet media companies, manufacturers, and Hollywood studios. Although early on many professionals were not sure how YouTube would make money, the Web site was noticed quickly by different audiences— more than just teenagers. YouTube continued to gain popularity when its numbers reached 4.2 million unique visitors approximately three months after launch. The interactivity on the site is fascinating for audiences. With the right mix of professional video clips and amateur content, the site attracts and retains audiences that can spend hours satisfying their "thirst for reality programming."

Web 2.0 Competition Is Heating Up

YouTube.com came on like a storm and made the "big guys"—Yahoo!, AOL, and Google—take notice. All felt compelled to get involved in the video mix and rightly so. Yahoo! launched its video site early in 2006 to get in on a video craze that was so easily achieved by YouTube. Video.yahoo.com launched with a Yahoo! Video page that included "a search box at the top and editorially chosen feature videos that are topical, interesting, or popular among viewers."[4] Yahoo! audiences drive the content by reviewing videos, reading the ratings, and then by forwarding links with video clips by using their Yahoo! Mail or Yahoo! Messenger.

Also in 2006, AOL made a big move toward video to gain the same type of attention as YouTube. AOL acquired a video search company, Truveo, in an effort to become a recognized player in the Video on Demand (VOD) market. Truveo's video search engine technology has a "Web crawler that can understand visual characteristics to help return more accurate search results."[5] AOL aimed to please its audiences with video searches that, until this point, were not as successful as text searches. With YouTube, Yahoo!, and AOL now actively engaged in video, Google had to make a quick move. Google launched its own video store where consumers could browse a main menu for video selections to purchase. It was also in 2006 that Google purchased YouTube for approximately $1.65 billion. Clearly, the thought leaders have set the stage for what could be the most important type of visual communication in the 21st Century. As a communications professional, you need to take the steps to use video at an enhanced level—moving from VNRs to Video on Demand (VOD) and real-time video on the Internet.

An Expert's Top 10 Reasons to Use Video

Jason Miletsky, CEO and Creative Director of PFS Marketwyse, remembers when he downloaded his very first video clip. It was in the early 1990s and he had just signed up for AOL (back when they still charged a per-minute fee). Miletsky wasn't looking for anything in particular, but somehow stumbled across a clip of John F. Kennedy's 1961 inaugural address. The physical size of the 20-second clip couldn't have been more than an inch square and took a full eight minutes to download. It was pixilated, garbled, and stuttered throughout. According to Miletsky, none of that mattered, "It was fascinating!" He said he watched it over and over again.

Miletsky admitted that the image quality of the Internet video clip was no match for its television rival. But the short, grainy, tiny video of Kennedy's speech was more than just a novelty of the Web—it represented *power* for the consumer. Of course, the TV entertained him on its own schedule, playing shows when the network decision-makers scheduled them. But, Internet video is entertainment and information when the viewer wants it. Miletsky feels that technology has been available almost as long as the Internet has been commercially popular, but it is now enjoying a bright spotlight over a decade later. Miletsky's top 10 reasons for the recent surge in video and podcasting on the Internet follow.

1. Improvements in Technology

As exciting as that very first video was, inevitably 8 minutes to download was simply too long for a 20-second clip. The concept of video on the Web simply couldn't fit into the reality of 12.8K modem speeds, monitors that displayed only a handful of colors, and computer speeds, power, and memory that are scant by today's standards. Today, the vast majority of companies (and a rapidly growing number of homes) access the Internet on DSL or better, from computers with considerably faster, more efficient processors, and monitors that not only display millions of colors, but do so in a variety of resolutions, providing an improved landscape for video to display.

2. More Accessible Production Capabilities
(smaller or built-in cameras, Final Cut, iMovie, and the like)

Apple's contributions to the acceleration of video's emergence and a popular Web medium can't be overstated. Even before the iPod paved the way for communication-on-the-go, Apple revolutionized video production by bringing it to the desktop with the introduction of Final Cut Pro. This off-the-shelf product, which was used to produce a studio motion picture in 2001 and began winning Emmy awards for engineering in 2002, enabled home users, hobbyists, and small companies to produce videos for a few hundred dollars as opposed to the tens of thousands required for AVID and other larger editing systems. The popularization and commercial acceptance of Final Cut, along with the improvement and subsequent price reduction of Web-ready cameras (including those built-in to many laptops), has brought video production capabilities to a far wider audience.

3. Improved Compression and Playback

Formatting issues have existed long before the VHS vs. Beta confrontation, and will continue to challenge developers as long as technology evolves. The Web, of course, has been no stranger to formatting issues that have plagued and hindered the expansion of video's usability on the Internet. Formats including WMV's, MPEG 4, and MOV have all struggled for dominance, each sporting their own benefits and drawbacks in regard to file size and image quality. Meanwhile, a confusing array of players, plug-ins, and browser capabilities have made convergence of media difficult for developers. Enter Adobe's Flash player, which has been nearly universally offered on most popular Web browsers to play FLV files, and the Flash CS 3 video encoder, a compression system that significantly reduces the size of videos without compromising their quality. Flash, which was once the culprit behind the alarming number of Web intro animations,[6] has matured to be the impetus to widespread video use on the Web.

4. The YouTube Factor

Once in blue moon, a Web site sees such unbelievable success that the public is forced to pay attention. Google showed up virtually unannounced to usurp Yahoo! as the king of all search engines; MySpace emerged as the most important socializing venue for young adults since the fraternity house; and YouTube, with its almost two-billion dollar sale to Google, focused the world's attention on a previously little known fact: Video on the Web is finally here.

5. The iPod Revolution

When the iPod hit the streets in 2001, it changed the music world forever. Music lovers were busy filling their device with 99 cent songs. At the same time, businesses realized that digital files could be downloaded to a portable audio device (a valuable tool to send messages to an audience). Seminars, white papers, news updates, and more began finding their way onto the iPods of business people everywhere looking to learn on the run. As newer versions of the iPod offered more memory and more features, including video playback, audio 'podcasts' evolved into video presentations, becoming so popular that even the term 'podcasting' has since become ubiquitous with on-demand video provided via the Web.

6. Increased Competition for the User

As the Web continues to expand, the competition to attract and retain audiences has become fiercer. This is true for sites looking to draw a general audience, as well as sites in a more limited vertical in a strictly B2B space. Brand managers and marketing directors, always on the lookout for new ways to attract eyeballs, are noticing that video on the Web and podcast capabilities are available tools that can provide a competitive advantage.

7. Less Time Allotted by Visitors to Understand Content

As wonderful a tool the Web is for providing information, the truth is that reading long bodies of copy from a Web page can be daunting, difficult, and tiring. The average user, with a limited attention span and a decreasing window of time to spend on any one page, is far more apt to

allocate energy listening to content rather than reading it. Tracking studies reveal the time spent on a page with only written content average less
than six seconds per visit (not nearly enough time to read the entire page),
but skyrocket to a minute or more when that same information is presented through a video.[7]

8. Higher Degree of Internet Marketing Sophistication and Integration

Web 1.0 brought with it a harsh realization: Traditional marketing
agencies weren't quite as hip as they claimed to be. Agencies viewed the
Web as a curious oddity they didn't understand, and wished they didn't
have to deal with. Web development became a function of "those guys,"
the "tech geeks" who understood the complexities of programming.
Today, though, the Web has been fully embraced by mainstream marketers as a necessary and welcomed addition to the service mix, and often
integrated into more widespread marketing campaigns. Video on the
Web has been a hidden jewel only recently discovered, as marketers are
beginning to replace static banner ads with converted TV commercials,
talking heads, and video-enhanced landing pages as the center point of
campaigns.

9. Expanded Use

Some uses for video on the Web are fairly obvious: Movie trailers are a
given, as are music videos and home movies (as capitalized upon by
YouTube). But, as amusing as watching a 14-year-old sing badly might
be, businesses have begun to turn their attention to more productive uses
of video on the Web. Sales and product training platforms have benefited
from it, as have online newsrooms and internal incentive campaigns.

10. Age-Ins Have Entered the Landscape

In the early 1990s, the Web was being commercialized by a generation
that had grown up on Pong, Pac Man, and 12–14 year olds busy helping
Mario rescue the princess. Those same kids have since graduated college
and, just as they demanded more from their gaming experience than even
Donkey Kong could deliver, they are also demanding more from their

Web experience than we could have imagined. As both our newest developers and our most sought after consumer market, the twenty-somethings are pushing the envelope of video, podcasting, and the Web further.

Lessons from a Thought Leader

The thought leaders are forging the way with video and podcasting. Cisco Systems is "the worldwide leader in networking for the Internet." Many people do not realize a network is critical to the success of a business of any size. Cisco's "hardware, software and service offerings are used to create the Internet solutions that make these networks possible—giving individuals, companies, and countries easy access to information anywhere, at any time. The Cisco name has become synonymous with the Internet, as well as with the productivity improvements that networked business solutions provide."[8] Cisco was among the Early Adopters of video. The company provided video conferencing tools to its customers in 2004. With the launch of Cisco's MeetingPlace, users were able to set up Web video conferencing all through a single Internet browser. Users had full control of voice and video, all in an effort "to shift its [Cisco's] enterprise customers to more Internet Protocol-based communications."[9]

Jeanette Gibson, Director of New Media for Cisco, understands the power of video and realizes how video has changed the way people communicate. Gibson has 14 years of experience in corporate communications and 9 years at Cisco, where she leads Cisco's New Media & Operations group. In this role, she is responsible for extending Cisco's leadership and innovation with new media and overseeing the vision and direction of Cisco's award-winning online newsroom, News@Cisco. Gibson is also responsible for developing and communicating the direction of Cisco's corporate blogging and podcasting initiatives and driving its Web strategy for communications Web sites, News@Cisco, and the Investor Relations and Analyst Relations Web sites.

Gibson referred to Cisco as an "Internet company," because they are committed to innovation and always looking at the Web for strategic communications. Cisco was one of the first companies back in the early 1990s to do a lot of e-commerce on its site. Most of Cisco's revenue comes through the Web site via its channel partners. "Being an Internet company, it's in our DNA to do anything that leverages the network and applications, like streaming video, that have been a part of our culture for a while. We do a majority of our communications via video, such as video on demand (VOD), so our executive team, at any event, can speak and the video is available via Cisco TV," explained Gibson. At Cisco, all employees can tune in and watch any program. Cisco TV is similar to a TV station where an employee can watch a sales manager talk about a new product, and watch the CEO, John Chambers, during the company meeting if the employee cannot be there in person. Cisco makes everything available via video. From a "culture perspective" video is the company's DNA—it's an integral part of the way employees work at Cisco.

According to Gibson, Cisco's CEO is very comfortable in the video environment. He likes video communications, so the company is equipped with in-house studios. "I can just pop in the studio and record a VOD (video on demand) for training purposes or education. I would say, probably in the 1990s, we started doing more of this as video streaming became more available. We did make a couple acquisitions that helped propel us into this space. They were video companies that enabled us to get what we now call Cisco TV on board, and that was probably the mid-to-late nineties." When employees log on to Cisco TV, they can see all the scheduled programs. If they need to know, for example, that a company manager meeting is scheduled, or if a broad company meeting is on the horizon, they can view it at their desk and watch the meeting live or watch a replay of the VOD. As a large company, Cisco communicates globally with its employee base using video.

Gibson shared how Cisco's audiences look externally to its online pressroom, which is called News@Cisco and is accessible by going directly to http://newsroom.cisco.com or off the main page www.cisco.com. If a visitor clicks on any news release, it takes her directly to the newsroom. It's here that Gibson considers Cisco's "main site" where they deploy much of its new media. This is the area of the Cisco Web site where users get all the updated news releases and anything going on that's considered "newswise" for Cisco. The site was reengineered around the year 2000 changing from a text-based site, which basically had a list of news releases, typical of the newsrooms in the nineties. Most were equipped with a simple list of URLs to access news announcements.

"We really looked at what our audience wanted. We knew we had to leverage what was coming out as far as video streaming technology and we deployed a video player on the site around the year 2000. Ever since then, we've been building that up more and we have more than 500 videos on our player now. They're searchable via advanced search. You could search for our CEO's name or a topic, whether its education or healthcare, and that video will come up in the player," stated Gibson. Cisco actually developed a player as a product to better showcase its video. It worked so well that the company ended up licensing the product and selling it to customers. Gibson said, "As an Internet company, we recognize the benefit of video. Studies show that you're five times more likely to retain information if you see it via video than just reading it. That's from an educational perspective with our e-learning group. They had been doing Web-based training for a while, and the benefit that we were seeing was that audiences such as journalists were coming to our site to watch our two-minute news clips."

Gibson believes that Cisco saw the evolution from the typical Video News Release that media relations professionals frequently used, into more of a one-stop video that tells a story and also could be produced in a viral way to expand your marketing practice as well. Cisco posted videos in its newsroom that were less than two minutes, were news style, and extremely focused on the customer. Cisco always focuses its video criteria on its target audience, the message the company wants to achieve, its cultural fit, and the use of powerful visuals. Because Cisco is so focused on the customer, its sales force is continually working to tell stories about how they're deploying technology for their customers. From a communications standpoint, the ability to have customers talk about Cisco's technology is an extremely beneficial type of marketing communication.

"We have a lot of customer videos and I think they've evolved from being the traditional prototype video to more this short, news-style video clips that we now can put on YouTube or put on our site for a journalist to watch or for a blogger to paste into their blog and make it more viral. We definitely think some of our most downloaded videos have been interesting customer stories; for instance, the one we did with the NBA talking about videos and wireless technology." Gibson believes that video gives you a chance to reach a broad audience. Other great examples of Cisco's videos include its philanthropy videos that have lasted over time to help talk about Cisco's strategy in education. Cisco's chairman completed a video about the importance of Internet and education. He discussed Cisco's programs at schools, which still get great hits. Cisco also created a video after its efforts post-Hurricane Katrina, in which they talked about some of the technology to help bring students' schools back up to speed. Cisco made donations to help repair some of the schools in Louisiana and Mississippi, and the video focused on how students have new classrooms where the traditional chalkboard is now a white screen. Kids can click on numbers and letters with a pointer and it's all computer-based. It's kind of like an electric or digital whiteboard. Another interesting video was Cisco's customer video around its implementation of wireless technology at the Indy500, where they put Cisco's wireless technology both in the car and in the pit. Cisco also did a video with Scott Adams, the creator of Dilbert, where it used video technology to illustrate how Adams was using the Internet to create his cartoon live over the net and taking feedback from people. This was a fun video showing Adams creating a cartoon in real time, which received a great deal of hits for Cisco. Gibson believes that anytime Cisco can put a human face on its technology and have the customers speak about the benefits, consumers can get a better sense of "who" Cisco is, they see the impact of what the company can do, and they can understand the relevance of the network as it applies to what people do every day.

Along these lines, Cisco launched a new advertising and marketing campaign in 2006, called the Human Network. The company is talking about the power of technology enabling you to do everyday things—it's a way of life. It's in the Human Network, which you might be looking at as your phone or PDA and downloading music, but the network is the underlying intelligence that enables you to do that. Cisco is running a campaign to try to educate consumers about the value of the network. It shows how the inherent intelligence of the network, which Cisco deploys, is helping you to get all the great content you are able to access via the Internet. Video is a great way to do that because people can see other people interact with the technology. They can hear firsthand accounts from a customer talking about the benefits of the technology and how Cisco is helping with the deployment. Cisco's campaign educates consumers on what Cisco does and discusses the significance of the network, which is a strategic message for the company. It also helps Cisco to promote video, which drives one of its key markets. "Obviously, [people] need routers and switches for power streaming video on the net, so the more videos people are downloading, the more bandwidth goes into it, the more equipment we can sell. So, video is a business driver for us, and it is helping us meet that need," Gibson said.

According to Gibson, one main reason for this type of marketing campaign is that a lot of consumers simply don't know Cisco. Gibson laughed as she remembered what most general consumers said when asked, "Do you know what type of company Cisco is?" Most say, "The food company?" They just don't know Cisco Systems, the network company. For Cisco, one of the challenges was just getting over the barrier of introducing the organization so that customers became more familiar with it, and that Cisco is the network company which has built the infrastructure most people know as the Internet. Consumers don't even realize they interact with Cisco's equipment every day by downloading music and working on their wireless networks. They aren't aware that Cisco helps to improve their lives.

Cisco is entrenched in social media. Cisco has made product introductions, including TelePresence, which is a new virtual meeting system. Cisco also purchased social networking companies—for instance, TribeNet, and Five Across—to get involved in producing social networking companies to help Cisco talk about how enterprise companies can benefit from networking. Internally, one of the Cisco employee projects is turning the traditional directory on its side and making it like a MySpace page where your directory is not just, "My name is Jeanette and here is my phone number." Instead, employees can watch a personal video, view a personal Web page, or blog. It really provides a better experience for employees. "We're using video in our daily lives as well as we're practicing what we preach. We're not just using video to post on YouTube; I have remote employees on my team who we talk with via videoconference using our IP phones. We have the video camera set up so that I can make a video for an IP phone call and then just see the employee's picture in front of me." Gibson's team does training videos for the company if they want to help people understand some of the tools Cisco offers. It's easy to go to the in-house studio and do a quick VOD, in just five minutes. As a result, you'll see their picture, hear them talking, and then you'll have their slides. There are a lot of different ways Cisco is using video for training and education internally. Cisco is starting to get employees to use more video. Employees have video cameras at their desks. They have a camera that floats around the communication team. At trade shows they take shots and do quick interviews of themselves, which tends to be more viral. "We're trying to become better at having a variety of ways that we showcase our content video. It doesn't have to be with a crew or professionally produced. It could also be something that any employee does. It works out that you get great content and the output that you're looking for," stated Gibson.

Cisco uses in-house video capabilities and there are times when they use outside resources. It's whatever is going to be more cost effective and wherever Gibson's team can get the best expertise. If Cisco is doing an internal video, they tend to use their own resources. However, if they're going to do anything externally, they check with the internal team first, who might recommend a video crew. With News@Cisco, the online newsroom, Cisco started with external vendors because it needed to move quickly. If Gibson's team does a shoot in Boston, they have a crew there ready to go. If a shoot takes place in Jordan, where they take the CEO for the organization's Jordan Education Fund, then they hire a crew. It's on a case-by-case basis in terms of what makes sense, but Cisco definitely has the resources internally.

Cisco is creating a rich package of information that helps the user consume the information in a compelling and interesting way. "We look to create a story with an audio podcast or have a speech that's related to that, maybe in the healthcare arena. We can take a clip of the demo that maybe an executive did on stage during his/her speech and link to that demo. We may even put that demo up on YouTube. Right now our videos on YouTube are not exactly 'the fun, comedic type of videos," admits Gibson. The videos are from a culture perspective. For Cisco, it's about product and technology demonstrations and training videos. If you go on YouTube and search for training on routers, you can see what the Cisco marketing teams and communications teams have posted. Cisco's CEO typically does a demonstration of new technology when he's giving a keynote speech. A five-minute clip of this demo will be posted on YouTube.

Cisco is evaluating different formats, looking at how it can be more viral and how to blog more, which is the next big focus. Cisco uses blogging in its day-to-day communication plans. Anytime Cisco has an announcement, it evaluates "what is that personal, authentic statement" it can put on its blog. Recently, Cisco has found success with video blogging at a partner summit. This is an annual summit Cisco holds with its channel partners. There are about five thousand channel partners there, as well as Cisco's internal crew. The event is Webcast and recorded. As a result, Cisco ended up with a number of video blog posts on the partners, about 30 posts in one week that were just quick, 30-second to 2-minute videos. "People really enjoyed the videos because you got that behind-the-scenes of the event, and customers are saying, 'Here I am, here's what I'm talking about,' so it wasn't just us talking and thinking of how we can give people a sense of our culture and our personality as well as our strategy and vision by being more creative with video," said Gibson.

Gibson feels that streaming video and VOD is providing Cisco with a Return on Investment (ROI). The company has been able to leverage its video over and over for the different communications vehicles that's absolutely made it worth the time and effort. They are no longer spending $20K to $30K on videos. That day has come and gone. Now, Cisco focuses on how to be more efficient and productive. It uses new tools and leverages technologies in a cost-effective and more efficient way. "There was an education video that our marketing team did on the ABC's of voice over IP. The emergence of voice on the Internet is a popular topic, and that was a 45-minute training video that one of our VP's did mostly for customers, and they put it up to help educate channel partners. We took 10 minutes of that training video and put it on iTunes. It still remains one of our most popular downloads and it's an audio podcast. We didn't even put it up as video, but we're looking at doing more videos on the how-to of networking," Gibson said.

Moving forward, Cisco is redesigning its site to better accommodate video. "It's funny because we've had so many requests and interest in better ways to highlight video that we actually turn to outlets like CNN and CBS on how we should redesign our site." Gibson's overall message on video was that there are many ways to get in because video is not very expensive. Cisco is experimenting by taking one project at a time and evaluating the success of each. If a video strategy works, it is rolled out broader. That's where they are with video blogging. Gibson feels that with such great response from the customers, employees, and executives, Cisco will not only continue to use streaming video for the executive team, but also more frequently for the company overall.

An Agency's Perspective

Not every company is a Cisco Systems. There are many organizations that are only just beginning with video. You might be working with B2B and B2C companies and realize there are different rates at which companies are ready to employ streaming video. The executives of Peppercom have been discussing and recommending to their clients the use of streaming video as a social media tool. Peppercom focuses on providing award-winning, innovative public relations campaigns that help drive a company's business and affect its bottom line.[10] Both Ted Birkhahn, partner and managing director of Peppercom, and Andrew Foote, account supervisor and manager of Pepper Digital, discuss how they encourage B2C and B2B clients to use Web video to reach audiences online. Peppercom wants its clients to consider streaming video as a tool to use for whatever it is they want to communicate to their key audience.

Q: When did you start recommending streaming video to your clients?

Ted: I think a lot of it has really been an outgrowth of the traditional video highlight packages and the video news releases that have been around forever that we've always been recommending to our clients. With the rise of broadband, there's been a tremendous opportunity to get out there in a new way, and really leverage Web sites for companies and have different types of videos, whether it's a product announcement or a tutorial, or anything of that nature. It's been happening this way for the past couple years. We've really been pushing it and saying, 'Look, you should really be doing this…here are the things you can do…here are the possibilities,' and just moving forward from there.

Q: Are there certain types of clients who are gravitating more toward video as a social media tool?

Ted: Obviously, the larger clients with bigger budgets and large Web infrastructure/architecture are the ones who employ video strategies. We tend to make the recommendation from a strategic standpoint; what is going to make the most sense for your brand, and then a lot of times clients actually work on getting things set up and uploaded to their Web sites. However, when you're working with a smaller client, they just don't have the budget or the resources to actually make it happen. Certainly, we're willing to work with them in many cases to get the video posted to the site and do different things; but, yes, typically it is the larger clients.

Q: Who were among your first clients to start Web streaming?

Ted: Whirlpool, Panasonic, and Valspar are examples of clients that are using online video effectively.

Andrew: It's important to consider how B2B and B2C clients use Web video. When most people think of digital marketing, they tend to assume that it's a B2C play. The fact is, there is a tremendous opportunity for B2B marketers to utilize video and audio streaming to reach key stakeholders. Several of our B2B clients, like TPI and Marsh, are exploring the possibilities of online video as a communications tool. Our goal is to help them determine how to strategically utilize online video as a component to a larger communications initiative. It can't just be video for video's sake.

Q: What are the benefits of streaming video for your clients?

Ted: There are a lot of benefits. You're able to eliminate the cost of the old-school hard copy distribution, such as videotapes and DVDs. The time delivery is pretty fast and there's no duplication process. You can typically view video or download it and, in many instances, people can take video with them. It's mobile. They can put it on their video iPod. It's just a great resource when people are out there trying to research a company, trying to learn more; they can go to a Web site and the visual aspect, of course, is the most powerful thing. Just standard podcasts are great. Text is important as well, but video really brings things to life, and that's one of the reasons that Peppercom has been recommending video to its clients.

Andrew: Video is a great way to connect on an emotional level with your customer. For a long time, text was the primary format for Web-based communication. Obviously, you can still make powerful connections through written words, but you can really enhance that message through video. Also, the rise of video sharing sites like YouTube and distribution channels like Brightcove are enabling companies to connect with new audiences. The ability to tag content improves "find-ability"—people who are searching for industry-specific content can discover videos produced by companies.

Ted: Even though we've mentioned that this plays into the big companies, it also levels the playing field for the smaller guys. It enables them; those who don't have the dollars to do the big ad spend can potentially reach a very broad or target audience, if that's what they want to achieve by using video. That's a game changer for a lot of companies. You look at the BlendTec. About one year ago they started posting videos on YouTube, showcasing the power of their consumer blender. They were doing all this kind of wacky stuff; they would throw golf balls into the blender, and the title of this series was "Will It Blend?" It was all about showing the YouTube audience and the online video space, "What can we blend up in this blender?" Of course, the golf ball was chewed up to bits. They also took a broom and placed the handle upside down and literally chopped the broom handle up with this blender. Not only is video incredibly powerful, but it also showcases, without a doubt, the performance and strength. They've done about 15–50 different videos on YouTube, and all have received a million plus hits. To turn around and equate that to an ad spend, it's invaluable.

Andrew: And they likely spent next to nothing in terms of production.

Ted: BlendTec's campaign was highly visual. They obviously struck a chord with the audience because it's cool. Who doesn't love to see something get destroyed or chewed up. It just worked and they definitely leveraged an opportunity with their audience.

Q: How does streaming video help you to target your audience?

Ted: A lot depends on the particular client and the target audience they're trying to reach. However, not all streaming video is made for the World Wide Web. A lot of it can be developed for a company's intranet, the way they communicate with employees, face-to-face, who are spread all over the world. It is especially useful in crisis situations where you want that reassurance of the chief executive that "things are okay and here's how we're handling the crisis situation." You can do only so much in a letter or in an email. You stream a video of the CEO talking to the employees; it can be a lot more reassuring and makes a powerful statement.

Andrew: Streaming video can also be used to communicate with the public during crisis situations. Take the JetBlue crisis, for instance. Several days after the surge of negative press, the company posted a statement from its CEO on YouTube. It was a great two to three minute apology and action message that was completely genuine. It wasn't overly scripted or crafted. It resonated with the audience and, as a result, received very positive feedback and support from the community.

Streaming video can also be used as a customer support tool. Product tutorials and step-by-step instructions are enhanced with visual support. Web video is also effective for internal communications. Example uses include e-learning, meeting recaps, software demos, and HR policies.

Q: Overall, has your video communication with your clients been successful?

Ted: Yes, we believe so, although it varies from client to client. Generally, most people have positive experiences with it. I think many apply some hardcore metrics to it. That's really working as a means to figure out how to better measure the impact of the video.

Q: What software or vendor services do you provide to your clients to get the Web streaming done?

Andrew: Typically we work with a variety of vendors, and we don't have an in-house production team that's producing video. We leave that up to a variety of skilled producers. It really depends on what type of video you're doing. If you're doing some type of news announcement, obviously you want to work with a production team that has those types of skills. If you're doing something a bit edgier and more creative, you want to work with a producer who can pull that type of thing off. First and foremost, it's accessing our database of those types of people and making sure it's the right group for the job. When it comes down to post production, editing, and actually getting things uploaded, we'll work with a variety of vendors.

MultiVu and PR Newswire are good examples. The multimedia news release is huge right now. And as with Whirlpool, for example, whenever we're issuing something in a news release format, we're always providing links to videos of the product, or of the actual event or static images, just to give reporters and bloggers as many options as possible to tell the story a bit more visually and colorfully.

Q: With respect to distribution techniques, are you using anything to maximize the client's reach?

Andrew: PR Newswire is just one example. Other options are distribution companies like News Broadcast Network (NBN). NBN has a new service called Viral Infusion. Beyond producing Web video, NBN uploads it to every conceivable video sharing site that makes sense—Google Video, VideoJug, Revver, and Myspace are just a few examples. Another consideration is "find-ability." The Web is massive and it's cobbled together. How do you actually find and access this content? Paid video Search is an important tactic. Working with companies like Google, you can purchase keywords that are relevant to specific videos. This ensures that your videos rise to the top of natural search rankings. Also, if you're producing video podcasts, directories like iTunes are effective platforms.

Q: Are you doing more podcasts or more Web video applications?

Ted: One of the greater benefits of podcasts is the instant syndication. Why not podcast it? It's essentially an MPEG (a digital audio/video media format), a QuickTime file, or an MP3. You can certainly just stream it, but why not slap a feed to it so that if you're going to be doing something in more of an episodic fashion, you can blast it out.

Q: With podcasts, are companies jumping on the bandwagon?

Ted: Not all, but we are. We did a podcast last year. I guess it really was an extension of our blogs. We just thought it was natural. I think like everything else, it's a little bit of wait and see. You get a few to try it and once they try it, they like it. I think people are more likely to start a blog before they get into a podcast because they just feel more comfortable, well, probably for a variety of reasons. They feel more comfortable writing out their thoughts than speaking and recording them. But, certainly, we're hoping there's going to be more and more interest down the road.

The right way to approach it; certainly walk before you run. A lot of people out there are reading the marketing books. They're hearing about the latest viral marketing and video and they immediately think, "How can I get one of those." But, at the same time, you should start small and see what the possibilities are; for instance, just doing tutorials or announcements through video or a multimedia news release. Get comfortable with that and then work into bigger applications, including video podcasts or a series of them. There are some companies that are dipping their toes in the space. One example is Whole Foods. They started, about a year ago, with just a standard blog and now they've really upped it to podcasts. They have a new video podcast called Secret Ingredient. You can check it out if you go to the Whole Foods Web site—at the bottom of the page, there's a link to Secret Ingredient. It's a video blog all about cooking. There's a chef-type guy on there. He's in the grocery store. He's interviewing shoppers, and there's humor involved. He's mostly asking the shoppers questions about different types of food and giving tips on how to cook.

Q: What is a best- or worst-case scenario with either Web streaming or podcasting?

Ted: From a PR perspective, digitally it's always been that you should communicate your information through a third party to your key stakeholders. That third party is typically the mainstream media. Now, that's still very much a part of any good PR program. Whether it's streaming video, blogs, or podcasts, it really enables you to communicate directly with your key stakeholders. It's a very powerful thing. It also can be a very dangerous proposition if you don't do it right. One of the biggest obstacles I think for companies to get involved in this is overcoming the risk factor, or the fear factor because you lose a certain element of control out there once you start playing in the space. Our message to clients is: If you do it the right way, content is relevant, and you have the right safeguards in place, anything you do has risks attached; but we think the risk is certainly worth the potential rewards.

Andrew: I agree with Ted—"Content is King." Audiences are smart. They can spot a sham from a mile away. You have to be totally genuine and relevant. Don't just post something on YouTube. Make sure that it actually fits.

A big takeaway for a lot of marketers is to always remain authentic. Buick is a good example. They had this clip on YouTube a while back that was basically meant to look like the "average Joe" captured it. The footage was of Tiger Woods golfing. It was intended to look like someone was secretly recording one of Tiger's TV commercial shoots. So, you see Tiger getting ready to deliver his line, and a loud airplane keeps flying overhead so he has to stop. He keeps stopping and starting and laughing, and it looks like someone is taping all this. Then, suddenly, you see these security guys come over to this videographer (who is secretly taping) and they make him turn off the camera. Well, it turns out it was a professionally produced piece created by an ad agency. They tried to make it look like it was an underground video that popped up on the Web when, as a matter of fact, it was just completely manufactured. Just looking at it, you can really tell because they did a very careful job of making sure that the Buick emblem fit into the video. It basically got "called out" instantly by viewers. A lot of people responded on YouTube with comments like: "This is lame." So it's all about just being totally real and not fooling yourself.

Q: Are you finding that it's easier to measure the results of really great Web streaming?

Ted: It's fairly easy. There are a couple ways. There's the quantitative way, which is online and it's very "trackable." Most companies out there are looking at standard history at the landing page of the video. They're also looking at the number of streams, how many people are actually clicking on this, and then they're reviewing the number of subscriptions. If it's podcast feed, they're just checking out the number of feed subscribers. So, those are basic quantitative measures that people are evaluating. Then, the real interesting measurement is the qualitative methods. That's when you have a feedback mechanism; it's not just, "Oh, here's a video, stream it." If there's actually a way to bring the community into the conversation and have a comments feature, they'll let you know very quickly whether it's a success.

A good example of that is the Whole Foods video blog we mentioned earlier. They have been receiving a lot of praise from their audience saying, "Hey, great job, keep it up. This is awesome." I think there were a few sprinkled in saying "Oh, this particular one is kind of lame. Try this or try that," and it's a great way for them to kind of modify their content and let the audience guide them through development. That is invaluable feedback and granted, you can't necessarily attach numbers to it, but companies can establish some internal guidelines for what success means. If it means 50 positive comments over the course of a month, we're doing awesome. That's great guidance. Another one of the qualitative type things is if something is posted to YouTube, obviously it's the same format. The audience is going to let you know whether they like it. You can take a look at just plain views or how many people have viewed the video on YouTube. Everyone can see that. It is very clear under the video—they show the number. There's also a star feature. You can rate something from zero to four or five stars, and that's a great indication. They have their feedback right there. You can also look at how many people have marked something as a favorite, which means "I'm giving this the seal of approval and I'm recognizing it." You can also look at how many people have links to it. There are a lot of tagging tools that are out there to tag something. All those social bookmarking features are a great tool. You can search and if your video pulls up and there are 30 to 50 people who have linked to it, they're basically saying "Hey, this is cool." And, right there, it's a good indication of success. Unfortunately, with the metrics there's no one system to fit one number. So, you have to pick and pull from a lot of those different resources to establish your own guidelines and go from there.

Q: Does Web streaming video or podcasting provide some kind of return on investment?

Andrew: The ROI is a company's ability to create content designed to reach audiences in niche communities. While it's not mass syndication, the intimacy of online video leads to customer interaction and brand loyalty—something that is difficult to achieve through TV. And, certainly the metrics help: video streams, plays, downloads, and subscriptions are all very trackable and reportable.

Using Video/Audio for PR 2.0 Communication Success

Streaming video, VOD, video blogs, podcasts, and video podcasts are all amazing social media tools to use in your communications planning for both B2B and B2C companies. There were several key take-aways that the experts in this chapter emphasized:

- Streaming video and VOD tell an interesting visual story. These applications are changing the way companies communicate to audiences (mainly direct to consumer).

- Video and podcasting can be used internally on a company's intranet for training, demos, for highlights of meetings, and clips from executive presentations. Externally, applications can be used for customer testimonials, product demos, and support tools, and can also be included in company news announcements posted in a newsroom area on your Web site.

- The use of video has evolved from being the traditional prototype video to more of a short, news-style clip that can be posted on YouTube or put on your site for a journalist to watch or for a blogger to paste into their blog and make it more viral.

■ Both B2B and B2C companies are posting their video clips on YouTube and other video content sharing sites with the understanding that they need to keep the content appropriate for audiences.

■ Video and audio applications on the Web eliminate the cost of the old-school hard copy distribution, such as videotapes and DVDs. The delivery time is fast and there's no duplication process. You can view video or listen to podcasts, download them, and in many instances, take them with you. These applications are mobile.

■ There are expert resources that enable you to increase your brand's reach and go beyond just producing and posting video content on your Web site. Your video can be posted on every conceivable video sharing space from Google Video to YouTube to MySpace.

■ The best approach is to walk before you run. You should start small and see what the possibilities are—for instance, begin by just doing tutorials or announcements through video or a multimedia news release. Get comfortable with that first and then work into bigger applications, including video blogging, video podcasts, or a series of them.

■ Your audience will let you know if they like your video content. Measurement includes plain views or how many people have viewed the video, star feature ratings, comments with feedback, and marking your video as a favorite. In addition, if you can search and if your video pulls up, and there are 30 to 50 people that have linked to it, that's a good indication of success.

■ If you do streaming video the right way, that means your content is relevant and you have the right safeguards in place. Although anything you do has a risk attached. However, that risk is certainly worth the potential rewards.

■ A big take-away for your brand is to always remain authentic and relevant to your audience. Don't try to fool people with scripted or overproduced video content that has no real value.

Endnotes

1. "Definition of a Fad," *Wikipedia.com*. June 2007. www.wikipedia.com.

2. "Definition of a VNR," *Wikipedia.com*. June 2007. www.wikipedia.com.

3. Sandoval, Greg. "YouTube: The Talk of Tinseltown,"*CNET News.com*,'sMarch 30, 2006.

4. Mills, Elinor. "Yahoo Launches New Video Cite," *CNET News.com*. May 31, 2006.

5. Sandoval, Greg. "AOL Acquires Video Search Engine," *ZDNet News, Truveo*.. January 10, 2006.

6. Flash introductions are typically 10–60 second animations that appear on the home page of many Web sites before any actual content is displayed. Thankfully, nearly all these animations included "Skip" buttons, enabling impatient audiences to bypass these superfluous introductions.

7. Miletsky reviews and evaluates PFS Marketwyse Web site tracking studies weekly.

8. "About Us," *Cisco.com*. July 2007. www.cisco.com.

9. ZDNet News, Marguerite Reardon, "Cisco adds video to conferencing suite," December 2004.

10. "About Us, Welcome," *Peppercom.com*. July 2007. www.peppercom.com.

SECTION **III**

Embracing PR 2.0

Chapter **11**

Social Media: Immerse Yourself and Your Brand

W eb 2.0 and social media (such as message boards, forums, podcasts, bookmarks, communities, wikis, and Weblogs) are not just heating up for consumers—they're hot! Remember that you're a consumer too, and you can't truly understand what audiences want and why they demand social media unless you're heavily engaged in it yourself. Unfortunately, time is limited, and the demands of your day pull you in many directions. What happens? Consumer audiences can become much more skilled in social media than the communication professionals who deliver their brand messages. Don't let your audience outpace your brand. If you feel you and your brand fall into this category, I recommend you quickly step up your game and practice what you preach. The more you personally get involved in social media, the more apt you are to deliver P.R. 2.0 strategies that enable audiences to drive their communication. You will be satisfying their daily craving for social media. PR 2.0 is definitely not a "fad." If you don't embrace PR 2.0 or you don't act with urgency, your lack of engagement is a disservice to your brand. The public wants social media. They won't accept anything less. Your job is to know and deliver the needed communication.

Be a Social Media Consumer

Based on the experts I've interviewed for this book and their many experiences with social media, both B2B and B2C brands will benefit from social media. What does this mean for you? The time has come to take your 2.0 knowledge and skills to the next level. Don't wait another second to begin your own blog if you haven't already. Sign up for Facebook.com, MyRagan.com, LinkedIn.com, Classmates.com, or MySpace.com and don't just check back occasionally—become actively involved. Roll up your sleeves and use those interactive 2.0 tools in your PR planning, including RSS feeds, podcasting, and streaming video for your brands. The more comfortable and proficient you are with social media, the more you will be able to apply meaningful and effective PR 2.0 strategies (strategies weaved into customized social media communications programs to reach groups online) when the opportunity arises.

Being aware of the level of your audiences' social media sophistication and interactivity is an important point that I can't stress enough as you move forward. You should study your audience's behavior. Try employing some of the newer research techniques to aid you in better understanding your consumer or business professional's level of 2.0 adoption. You need to assess their interest and use of social media. This holds true for all your influencers, too—those VIPs you need to communicate to in a bigger effort to reach your customers. But remember when using social media that you are using a direct to consumer approach, reaching outside your usual universe of influencers or company partners/channels.

A 2007 study conducted by eMarketer.com revealed a significant percent of time consumers spent online at user-generated sites versus company-generated sites (by age group). Of course the numbers presented in the study will change in time. Of particular interest was the group called the Millennials or Gen Y (ages 13–24), who were on user-generated sites 51 percent of the time as compared to Gen X (ages 25–41), who spent about 35 percent of their time on these sites; and Baby Boomers (ages 42–60) even less time, at 27 percent. When these groups are not on social networking sites, yet still on the Internet, the remaining percentage of time is spent on company-generated sites. This is a tremendous consideration and opportunity for brands to use social media tools incorporated into their PR strategy and planning and overall Web communications.

Rethinking Communication Based on Consumer Behavior

Obviously, this isn't your "Father's" Internet anymore. Your brand needs to change and be flexible with the times. What was popular in Web 1.0 has changed or is no longer being used. For instance, at one time you might have raced to your e-mail inboxes to retrieve e-mail messages. The days of being thrilled over e-mails in your e-mail box are over. Consumers are long past those days. I'm not surprised that today many forward-thinking companies are rethinking e-mail communication. As a matter of fact, *Fast Company* published an article titled, "E-mail is Dead." There's still a great deal to be done to make e-mail communication better.[1] According to Doug Belzer, the author of the article, "The average e-mail account receives 18 MB of mail and attachments each business day." This is a stifling amount of communication and information, comparable to what the author describes as a "crushing tsunami."

Three companies—Capital One, Union Bank, and Reuters—are building new e-mail models to accommodate today's Internet users. Capital One is teaching its employees how to manage and control e-mail by crafting better messages, shortening subject lines, and by creating succinct body text that uses bullets, bold text, and underlines. Clear and concise e-mails save time. Union Bank came up with an RSS solution. Rather than broadcasting e-mails to all Union Bank's 10,000 employees, the new model has targeted RSS feeds that enable employees to receive information through a feed based upon their job description and location. Reuters also has chosen Instant Messaging (IM) as an alternative to e-mail. Certain instances occur when meetings need to be arranged and conference rooms secured, and according to Reuters executive VP David Gurle, "If you use e-mail to conduct business transactions in a conversational way, you'll end up with a full inbox." However, Gurle's opinion is that e-mail will never be replaced by IM, and I agree with him.

The excitement of e-mail and even IM has waned because there are so many more interesting and better functioning types of Web communications. Today, online audiences are racing to the Internet to socialize. According to a weekly survey of online activities of Internet users by age, among the participants surveyed in the Millennial group, 78 percent of them are downloading and listening to music, and 55 percent of them are reading blogs. And, even though the Millennials clearly take the lead in Web 2.0 and the use of social media, Gen X is not far behind. As a group, 57 percent are searching, downloading, and listening to music and 42 percent are reading blogs.[2] Knowing that the Baby Boomers have their favorite Web 2.0 activities is even more amazing. Among this group,

40 percent are watching and reading personal content created by others and 38 percent are maintaining and sharing photos. Also according to this weekly survey, even mature audiences (ages 61+) are spending time utilizing social media. Approximately 36 percent of this group is watching and reading other's content and 43 percent are maintaining and sharing photos (even more than the Boomers).

If you did your own informal research and were to ask 10, 20, 100, or perhaps 500 consumers what they want from Web 2.0 and their brands, you might find consensus on similar preferences and behaviors. From my experience, and based on what I've heard from the many experts who shared their experiences, consumers want to

- Receive direct communication from their brands
- Have easy access to brand(s) and any information regarding products and/or services
- Be able to ask questions about products and services
- Get a quick response when they have an inquiry
- Hear a voice from a company and know a company's position on certain issues that might affect their industry
- Believe they can trust the people behind the brand
- Drive and control their communication
- See how other people feel about a company, its products, and/or services.
- Interact with people who have similar viewpoints
- Share information with others, including photos, video, podcasts, and blogs
- Discuss favorite books, movies, leading ladies or men, teen heart throbs, artwork, and anything else they can share their thoughts about openly in a community of members with like interests
- Contribute information and create content in an open-source forum

Giving Power to the People

The consumer preference "to contribute information and create content in an open-source forum" is one of the greatest accomplishments of the Web 2.0 platform. To enable consumers to participate in a content building forum is the penultimate of social media, where the users build, test, and add to the contents in the forum. The finest example that comes to my mind is Wikipedia, which truly exemplifies Web 2.0 and how people engage and interact in a community. So much is available to discuss when it comes to Wikipedia and the notion of wikis. The best person to provide insight and expert perspective on the wiki is Jimmy Wales, founder of Wikipedia. Jimmy started Wikipedia and literally gave "Power to the People." For consumers, Wikipedia means community control over communications and endless opportunity. Although Wales did not invent the concept of the wiki—the term was coined by Ward Cunningham, meaning a Web site you can edit—Wales realized that if people have the tools they need to collaborate, then they can do more than just "code." They can build whatever they want. For his first concept, Wales focused on the encyclopedia. To him, it was a way for people to come together. Wales had the idea in 1999, and he was "just obsessed with it and very excited." He was actually in a big hurry because he thought it was so obvious, that someone else would do it before he did. But it turned out that for two years or so, as he and his team struggled with a first version of Wikipedia, nobody else was doing what he was doing, not even close.[3]

Get Your Audience in Your Backyard

Where do you rate yourself on the social media scale? Are you savvy with social media or are you just getting started? Ragan Communications (www.Ragan.com) is an excellent resource that has been helping communications professionals to learn and engage in social media whether they're beginners or advanced in Web 2.0. In an interview with Mark Ragan, CEO and publisher, he discussed how communications professionals are getting involved in social networking on his Web site. His first point focused on social networking and what it offers B2B companies— the powerful ability to build their brands in unprecedented ways.

By sponsoring a social networking site, or building your own social networking site and branding it after your company, you are engaging and allowing other people to partake in a very intimate conversation between your company and them, and then solely between your customers. "There's a user-generated aspect that's significant. As long as my audience is in my front yard having a barbeque and drinking beer, all assembled in my space instead of the guy's yard down the street, I can come out the door and sell them some hot dogs. The whole notion behind gathering your audience in your yard is that you would rather have them there than in someone else's yard," explained Ragan.

A second point of interest is that you're going to see an inevitability to move toward social media. He feels it's somewhat present now, but somewhat invisible unless you're really engaged in this topic. And, inevitability that is going to mean that if you don't do it, your competitor will be doing it. So you better get out there now and get everybody in your yard "eating your hotdogs and drinking your beer because otherwise they will go to somebody else's yard," as Ragan puts it. He stressed that you need to feel a sense of urgency to engage in social media. "I think there is urgency. Although my colleagues in my profession, which is niche publishing, look at me like I'm crazy. They keep saying, 'where's the economic model? We don't see it.' I just ignore them. They continue to print publications and basically serve their audience the way they've always served them. Instead, I've chosen this other route that is not much of a risk because the costs are very, very small."

As of today, there are almost 8,000 people on the social networking site www.myRagan.com on any given day. Approximately 700 of the online users are completely engaged, either writing blogs or responding to forums. Ragan openly admits that he likes to watch the whole thing happen. He can practically eavesdrop on his customers. He sees what they're interested in. He can see what's keeping them up at night. He can also see what's driving them to drink. Then, he is able to respond to their needs by sponsoring the appropriate conferences and seminars that answer their questions and solve their problems. It's a smart plan. This type of interaction gives an instantaneous way to look at what hot issues are affecting customers. "We're doing a social media conference—as a matter of fact, our third conference on social media. It's no surprise to me that we're already three times ahead of where we would usually be for a conference a couple months away. I think it's because of the social media site that we have. There was such a buzz among the rank and file in the industry that it's rubbing off on our other products already."

To some extent, MyRagan steers customers in a favorable direction. It builds the brand even deeper into their lives because the cutting-edge customers are out there on the Internet in communities everyday, and for Ragan, it's better when they're out there on a social networking site called MyRagan. This is a distinct advantage. With respect to disadvantages, he has colleagues in the industry who would say the pitfalls come from the fact that Ragan might be undermining his paid content by allowing a lot of user-generated content to be posted online. However, the problem with that argument is that paid content has been undermined for the past 10 years. He believes that if you sit there and simply gripe or cry about it and throw up walls around it, that's not the solution. No matter what, it's happening anyway and there's nothing you can do to stop it. You should take the position, "If you can't beat them, join them." If you look at the tremendous growth of the site, Ragan's approach has worked.

Ragan remembers first focusing on social media when he was "tired of driving the car into that brick wall each and every day." The brick wall Ragan speaks of is that same brick wall that has affected all niche publishers, which is free content on the Internet. Some publishers feel free content on the Internet has pretty much destroyed the economic model of all niche publishers. Ragan was grasping for ideas on how he could continue to make money as a provider of training in his market, which is internal communications and PR, keeping in mind that audiences are less and less willing to pay for content. He had a gut feeling that whatever he chose in the end was going to have to be an Internet-based solution. He started looking around at the popularity of MySpace and Facebook and realized that there was this tremendous power in bonding your customers to you through a community type of medium. Of course, he realized early on that a question comes up: How are you going to monetize this type of solution? You can monetize it the way you monetize any kind of system that is enabling you to build a crowd of customers around a brand. Simply, it's to sell them other "stuff."

"I may not be able to maintain my subscriptions, but I'm selling them an enormous quantity of books and manuals and seminars, conferences, Webinars, audio conferences, special reports, and research reports. What social media enables me to do is gather thousands of people in my front yard who I might not have interacted with otherwise. And, then I can go out there and start selling them what they need," commented Ragan. Even better, his social networking solution is growing quickly, relevant to the size of the overall market he's looking to attract. It certainly is not going to be a Facebook or MySpace because it's a niche market. However, it's experienced unprecedented growth. The site launched on May 3, 2007, and in just over three months it attracted about 8,000 members to the site without doing any real marketing. Without any promotion, the site grew by 200 users per week

When asked about his audiences' behaviors on blogs, Ragan mentioned that they are discussing the concerns in their industry, such as "How do I measure the effectiveness of my communication?" or "How do I beat the approval process, which has become a nightmare at my organization?" He knows that these are the hot buttons or sensitive issues. The difference now, as a result of social media, is you are surrounded by user-generated copy that generates great stories. What you get now is the kind of information that you used to have to conduct with a focus group to receive. Ragan has people blogging on subjects, telling real-life stories, and first person narratives. For instance, what it's like to have your boss take your communication and rewrite it even though the boss has no expertise in the field. It's so important to hear the "first person Readers-Digest-type stories that are just filled with color, drama, and narrative," which you can then turn around and use in your promotions and direct mail copy.

It goes one step further. You can monitor the stories and actually approach a member of the community who wrote a particular blog entry and then ask that individual to speak on the topic at an upcoming conference. "There's so much power behind that. We have people, for example, the Director of Internal Communications for NASDAQ, on our site. I can see what's on his mind and I can one day go to him and say, 'Hey, did you see that we're doing an event with Southwest Airlines' hoping to have a conference at some point at NASDAQ'…or maybe it's a Google or eBay executive who's on our site," explained Ragan. He found that this model for a conference works particularly well. For three years, his organization was searching for a partner, and then Southwest Airlines said they'd be willing to do it. This was a tremendous breakthrough for the company.

The feedback from communications professionals on MyRagan is positive. Not one person has offered a negative comment. No one has said, "I don't like the site, or this site isn't worth my time." Of course, Ragan realizes that there are many people who sign up for the site and aren't active. These are the people who come back every two weeks or so. However, about 10 percent of his audience is really engaged. "The same rule applies for most social networking sites, including Facebook and MySpace. What's that statistic I always hear—it's that 10 percent of the population online produces 100 percent of the content," he said. Ragan's 10 percent is busy on MyRagan responding to forum threads and checking in everyday to see if they have mail. They're the real active people. They're hardcore and Ragan believes that these numbers are going to grow.

MyRagan is considered "the first ship in the fleet of three." He was proud to discuss his "Mother Ship," a huge daily newspaper modeled after *The New York Times* for corporate communications and PR people. "It's this massive Web site that has the bells and whistles," he stated enthusiastically. The last ship is MyRaganTV with free video content for professionals to access. Approximately 150 videos have been produced that his team will be uploading to the site. He's positioning MyRaganTV as the YouTube of the PR and corporate communications industry. The channel will enable you to go out there and view hundreds of videos that Ragan has produced. More important than that, just like YouTube, it will enable you to go and post your own video. He discussed how if you have a little marketing company in San Diego, and it's a one-person shop and you want to promote it, you would do a video of yourself talking about your expertise and go to MyRagan TV and be able to upload that. Of course, he'll have an approval process on his end, mostly to prevent inappropriate content.

The news division part will be the videos produced by Ragan Communications, and then there's a community blog. If a user doesn't want to go to all the trouble of getting his/her own blog software, he or she can use the platform that's available to upload and run personal video blogs. There's also the YouTube-like embedded code function so that if you like a video posted by Ragan Communications, you can just grab that video and put it on your own site. "We have one thing that I'm not sure if YouTube has. We're also going to have an editing function that enables you to see a five-minute video, and if you like everything but the last three minutes, you'll be able to edit the video on the site and then embed your edited version," he said, excited about the possibilities. In addition, you can rate the videos, comment on them, and you can embed them on your own site. There will be 15 different categories, including PR Showcase, Internal Communications Showcase, Community Blog, Most Recently Viewed, Most Popular, and so on. If you are familiar with YouTube, it's basically a clone of YouTube, but for the communications industry.

Ragan offered advice for the communications pro. He recommends that you spend a lot less time studying the issue and "just jump in." Realizing that social media is cheap, and doesn't cost that much to start, is important. He did mention that it was much more labor intensive than it is dollar intensive. A perfect example he says, "I'm standing in my neighborhood right now, in old town Chicago, which is a very cohesive community. The other day I was walking through the neighborhood with my daughter and thought I should start a social networking site for the area. It would cost $100 for the software. Then I'd stick leaflets in everyone's door. Before you know it, you'd have several hundred people on the site within a matter of 2–3 days. You'd have a business running. And, once you reach critical mass of several thousand people, you start going to the merchants. Anybody can do it. A woman living at home with her kids can launch a social networking site for a couple hundred bucks a month and start building a business around her particular niche. The only way to do this is to take this advice and just jump in. The whole notion of Web 2.0 is the creation of platforms that enable the everyday person to create and drive communication."

An Expert's Perspective on Social Media Tools

Marketwire (www.marketwire.com), headquartered in Toronto, Canada, has also been focusing on ways to help clients engage and join in the online community. The company is another expert resource that you can turn to with solutions on how to make news releases blog friendly, and how to deliver your news to community-driven online content forums and social media sites such as Digg, Del.icio.us, and Technorati, and virtual worlds such as Second Life. Thom Brodeur is Senior Vice President, Global Strategy and Development, at Marketwire. He's been with the organization for approximately four years and just six months in his current position. Brodeur is responsible for new product development, strategic planning, mergers, and acquisitions worldwide. He shared with me his thoughts on how communications professionals need to feel comfortable with social media before incorporating these tools into their PR strategy and planning.

Q: How much research did Marketwire conduct prior to offering clients social media tools?

A: We didn't do formal research studies. Informally and on a fairly regular basis, we are in touch with our clients of all types and sizes: public companies, private companies, nonprofits, IR and PR agencies, and so on. Much of what we do through our sales force is a kind of 'on the ground' discussion about what clients look for and what kinds of problems they are trying to solve if they do not easily see services or solutions available, whether it's from us or other providers they work with. We started to see a lot of this sort of questioning or commentary coming from our clients late in 2004. In early 2005, we released our SEO Basic and SEO Enhanced products, which are our products for search engine optimizing news releases. I think for a long time folks just thought SEO was only useful for their Web sites and not for any other form of communication.

Following that, in early 2006, we began social media tagging news releases for clients as well. The whole idea of social bookmarking, community outreach, and the ways you could reach those communities came quite a bit later than just basic search engine optimization of news.

Q: What would you say are the most popular social media tools that brands are using through Marketwire?

A: This is a two-pronged answer. The most popular social media tools are both what they are using now and what they should be using. They are absolutely using hyperlinks, various landing pages on their Web sites, newsrooms, and the like. They are also experimenting in many places with writing corporate blogs, as you know. I would also say they're involved with MySpace and other social communities. What they should be doing, in our opinion, the thing we work very hard to encourage our clients to do, is building topic-specific Del.icio.us pages, for example, networking with influential bloggers, and basically just getting involved. Like with anything, it's hard to understand something unless you try it. Overall, we're finding that agency communications professionals, corporate communications groups, PR professionals, and even investor relations professionals, are paying attention to social media a little bit more than in the past.

We encourage clients to build their own social media mash-ups[4] and social media newsrooms, or at least to work with service providers whether it's their newswire like Marketwire, or their agency, or others who are capable of helping them design and develop these kinds of resources. We also think companies should be distributing social media releases, both to traditional media and of course to the blogosphere and online social communities. They should be using strategic hyperlinks in their social media releases to give their audience a complete look at the story. Gone are the days of "tell it all" in your 400-word news release. Use strategic linking to your advantage. You can send somebody to another destination right from that traditional news release that really enables the story to expand and gives a fuller or bigger picture. These are things people should be doing more of. We're starting to see that there are always Early Adopters. You have the Early Adopters and then you have the folks who are the Laggards—or the critics—forever procrastinating on what's new and what's next.

Q: Would you say that B2C are Early Adopters of social media and B2B brands are a little slower?

A: From our perspective, there's obvious utility to both markets, but what you've seen is that consumer brands really leveraged social media earlier. This largely occurred because, if you think about it, even in the traditional sense, consumer brands are typically more interested in pushing their messages to the public because of the benefits of word-of-mouth and viral marketing. What we suggest is that this is every bit as important for B2B brands, and there are a couple ways that we look at this. Obviously both B2B and B2C can benefit from social media, but, from our perspectives, in different ways. B2C brands should be using all the elements of social media to distribute their content whether that's photos and images, videos, podcasts, audio files, news, and other information in as many forms as possible so that they can generate word-of-mouth buzz. B2B brands, we believe, should use social media for two purposes. First, as a means of presenting themselves differently—not always relying on the tested, tried, and true 'traditional media' standard via a traditional press release and traditional distribution of that release. And, second, as a way of making their message a bit more user friendly in a world that is adopting social media elements in the mainstream—effectively 'consumerizing' complex B2B brands through new media approaches.

When you think about communication to consumers, the idea here is that you're communicating at the most basic level. Anyone can understand your message because you make your message digestible. And sadly, in many cases, a lot of B2B brands haven't learned that the way to drive pull-through and demand is for their brands and/or products to use a consumer communication approach. The idea of helping the end user understand how your B2B product or service can help them creates the dialogue between the consumer and your channel (whether online, retail, or otherwise) to ensure that the products the channel is embedding into their end-user products have been requested, talked about, blogged about, and so forth by the consumers who will use those products. They can equally make their story easier to digest and recognize that they're no longer just telling their story to channel partners, or technology and/or system aggregators, or other types of companies who can do their translating for them. So, from our perspective, what this means is B2B brands ought to be using RSS, wiki technology, blogs and social media press releases, networks, and online communities to do a lot of their 'storytelling' for them.

A good example might be a company that frequently changes prices and wants to allow its distributors to subscribe, maybe via RSS, to receive automatic notification of price changes. B2B brands could also use wiki as an alternative to e-mail. Instead of having multiple strands of e-mails around a specific project, set up a wiki. Everybody goes there, contributes their content, their ideas, their thoughts, argues with one another, has an open, spirited discussion about the content and subject matter, and goes on from there. This is where a lot of process improvement can happen, and external audiences can be exposed to the extent you want them to and also give them the opportunity to participate. Then, of course, use a blog for an internal communications newsletter. Save yourself some paper, save yourself some HTML e-mail traffic, and send people to a destination where you are not only delivering news one direction, but also people are commenting and providing real-time feedback. IBM obviously is a clear market leader in allowing their employee base around the world to leverage blogs as a means of communicating with one another and discussing important company information.

Q: How reluctant are communications professionals to use the new social media tools that you have to offer?

A: In general, I think this goes beyond what we have to offer. We have this basic tenet that's tried and true to just about every facet of our lives, and that is how much you use something personally. Whether it's an automobile, a certain kind of food, whatever your personal experience is with a product, a service, a thing...whatever that brand means to you...whatever that category means to you on a personal level will, in many cases, drive whether you adapt to it or adopt it. A Pew study recently indicated that professionals who have experimented with blogs (roughly 39 or 40 percent of Americans) are likelier to use these tools in their work because they've used them in their personal lives. When you think about it, the biggest issue is that individuals who avoid these kinds of things are either afraid social media isn't appropriate for their audience or doesn't reach their audience, or because they haven't tried to engage in using a social media tool and are afraid they either don't or won't know how; although we could argue that the population is shrinking pretty fast. A recent Inc. 500 survey said 66 percent of the respondents indicated that social media is important to their business. That's a pretty remarkable statistic.

Other interesting stats that we share with our clients appeared in *Time* magazine. Approximately 9 of the top 20 Web sites in the United States alone are social media sites. And, 68 percent of American Internet users trust a person like themselves opposed to 17 percent who say they trust a PR person, or 28 percent who say they actually trust the company's CEO. The whole idea of why this is so proliferate in our marketplace is because people trust each other more than they trust messengers. This speaks to the broader topic of how does the use of social media among online audiences change the way communications professionals work? From our perspective, you look at fast-growing companies and the communications professionals who support those companies, whether they are agency or in-house practitioners. It is those Early Adopters and forbearers of this kind of technology who are driving the dialogue. What we've learned is that with the exception of technology companies, larger blue chip organizations, in many cases, are a little bit slower to adopt a little warier because they have so much more information to protect and steward; they can be a little slower to adopt because of the fear of the unknown.

Q: Do you feel that social media tools are easy to grasp?

A: Yes. To reinforce the point from earlier, it's all about use. The more you work with these kinds of resources, which is no different from working with your personal computer, laptop, VCR, or DVD player, the better you will get at it. With practice, you will be more comfortable.

Q: With a higher comfort level, are communications professionals incorporating new social media tools into strategy and planning?

A: I would say that there's an underlying element of peer pressure in our lives. Nobody wants to be the last kid in the neighborhood to get the new Xbox and to know how to use it and game on it effectively. Among PR pros, there's a pervasive approach around reaching audiences; that's what we're taught as communications professionals when we get out of school. You need to reach your audience. That would largely indicate that we're still one-way communicators. Social media has sort of flipped that model on its head because the communication comes from the other direction. What we're finding is that more and more communications professionals are being forced to plan social media into their tactical media relations and communications plans because they have to *engage* their audiences now. Communications professionals are doing a lot less 'telling' today than they are encouraging dialogue and discourse among the influencers (in most cases, consumers and other advocates) that are important to them. It's a very different ballgame today.

Q: Now that consumers are driving the communication, and social media is direct to consumer, does this make PR professionals nervous?

A: I think it makes us nervous, not because it's a new thing, only because it's different from how we're conditioned. When you're conditioned to wash your clothes a certain way because that's how your mother taught you and that's how you've been doing it since you were 12, and someone else comes into your life, your husband or significant other, and says, 'Hey, I wash my clothes like this,' or 'I like my clothes to be washed this way,' your conditioning is challenged. You either bristle or you're nervous or you send the wash out to be laundered for a while until you feel you can comfortably wash your clothes this *new* way. It's about personal experience. The more you wash clothes a different way because now you have a different perspective, the more comfortable you become with it.

What we're finding is that, when you look at the workflow of a communications professional, typically the way it has always worked, the news release or news alert or communications tool that's used to communicate happens at the end of the cycle. You can measure it, monitor it, and you can hope that the media and influencing community you sent that communication to is actually going to do something with it, publish it, reprint it, write a story about it. With social media, what happens now is that news release, that news alert, that tool comes first. Then, the conversation starts and the real dialogue begins as you're engaging people or communities, at the beginning versus at the end of the life cycle of that particular communication. Workflow is changing a bit and any time you change a person's process—their procedure or their workflow—you're absolutely going to get people who are immediately engaged by that and they're riveted. Why? They engage because it's something new and it's something different that they want to embrace. Then, there are the rest of us who say, 'Wait a minute, that's not the way I've done this all these years; it's going to take me a little while. Let me settle it with myself and think about how I can adapt, if at all.'

Q: What advice do you offer to communications professionals about social media tools?

A: Do it! Start experimenting with these tools in your personal life. Go to Wikipedia. Use a wiki. Create your own blog using a free online blog tool or participate in your corporate blog, if there is one you can participate in. Go to YouTube and watch or upload a video. Take a look at Flicker, download a podcast, create a podcast, use an RSS reader, sign up to receive something from an RSS feed, so you know what the distribution mechanisms look and feel like. Use these tools so you're clear about what you can and cannot use them for, and recognize that these forums aren't going away. The more familiar you are with them, the better prepared you'll be to engage them. Think about it from this perspective: If you're a traditional communications professional, a PR professional, even an investor relations professional, if you never read a newspaper or have never seen a broadcast, would you be good at what you do? Probably not. If you don't do any of these things social media-wise, you probably won't catch up either. Among my younger communications contemporaries I might well be considered a dinosaur when it comes to using these kinds of technologies and tools, and I'm only in my late 30s. I find them less intimidating when I understand what's under the hood though. The only way to get under the hood is to open up the hood and start looking and tinkering. And, you can always ask others who are good mechanics about their experiences as well.

Moving Forward Through Understanding and Experience

The way your brand communicates is morphing into a new experience for both the consumer and the PR professional. As you move forward with social media for your programs, you should keep in mind:

- You're a consumer too. Get involved and engage in social media so you understand the nature of the resources. With comfort and understanding, you'll be better prepared to deliver PR 2.0 strategies.

- Every audience has a certain level of social media sophistication. Be aware of this level and degree of usage and introduce the tools that groups will react and respond to with enthusiasm.

- When consumers are social networking in your backyard, it's an opportunity for you to hear their intimate conversations and understand their needs. You can listen and develop information (products/services) to solve their problems and satisfy their needs.

- Social networking and social media are relatively inexpensive. For a small investment you can get closer to your audience, and it's much more labor intensive than dollar intensive.

- You should establish relationships in the social networking community similar to the manner in which you strive to develop relationships with traditional influencers. The blogging community is growing and targeting influential bloggers who can be an active part of your communications strategy.

- Realize that you might be conditioned to operate in a specific manner and your workflow process hasn't changed in years. Social media will shift your workflow because it alters the timing of the communication tool. News releases, for instance, are no longer at the end of the cycle when the consumer or B2B audience receives information via a third party. Instead, with social media, the communication is at the beginning of the cycle.

- Take the time to develop your social media skills so that you don't get left behind. As a communicator, you need to be tapped into what's in the news, and social media is making the news. It's also the way audiences are receiving their daily news and information. Grow with it!

Endnotes

1. Belzer, Doug. *Fast Company; Next Tech.* "Email is Dead. July/August 2007.

2. Deloitte & Touche USA LLP, "The Future of Media: Profiting from Generational Differences." Provided to emarketer on April 16, 2007.

3. You can review the full Q&A interview with Jimmy Wales, Founder of Wikipedia, at the close of Chapter 12, "The Pro's Use of PR 2.0."

4. According to Wikipedia, a mash-up is "a Web site or application that combines content from more than one source into an integrated experience," July 2007.

Chapter **12**

The Pro's Use of PR 2.0

When it comes to PR 2.0, levels of acceptance and adoption vary between you and your professional peers. One of the best ways to gauge where you fall on the PR 2.0 spectrum (from the Innovator and Early Adopter to the Late Majority and the Laggard) is to talk to as many professionals as you can and to be socially involved in online communities. You need to hear how your fellow professionals are involved with Web 2.0 resources and PR 2.0 strategies, how they are moving forward using consumer driven new media tools (either strategies for their brands or how they personally are involved in 2.0), and their overall challenges and successes. Everyone has a story to tell, whether it's an experience with blogging, social networking, podcasting, streaming video, or Really Simple Syndication (RSS). Each experience is different, valuable, and will provide you with ideas and new techniques to add to your arsenal of communications strategies.

From the small online start-up, such as Art eXposed (www.getartexposed.com), a small NJ-based company that supports and promotes an online community of artists, and the large public company, such as BMC Software (www.bmc.com), to the practices of the social media gurus, professionals with different skill sets are taking steps to engage their brands in social media. In this chapter, you learn from the personal stories of an Innovator, Jimmy Wales, and from Early Adopters, including long-time consultant and tech guru Steve Lubetkin and Jane Quigley, a technology expert at DigitalGrit, who have been practicing PR 2.0 for years. These professionals are from extremely diverse companies and wide-ranging backgrounds, yet believe and share a common view—you need to understand and engage in social media to reach powerful communities.

Social Media for the Start-Up

Mark Skrobola, artist and founder of Art eXposed, spends at least 50 percent of his day social networking and using social media tools to drive consumers and artists to his online art gallery. When Skrobola first started out, he knew that Art eXposed needed to be a part of MySpace. Registering under his business name, he quickly set up a MySpace page to drive the artist community to his Art eXposed Web site. He started by looking for artists and having them join as his friends. If he liked their artwork, he would not only make them his friends, but also make their friends his friends. The more friends he acquired, the more his extended network grew. How did this affect his business? Skrobola went from signing up three artists on his site in January 2007 to more than 22 artists exhibiting their work (and paying for his online services) in a matter of 4 months. Skrobola finds the MySpace classified ads and blog to be an effective way to communicate to artists and art enthusiasts. MySpace has a great events area and through MySpace, he was able to inform his entire MySpace network about the Art eXposed kick-off event in June 2007.

On the Art eXposed Web site, Skrobola is actively blogging, which helps to increase his page rating in the search engines. He uses Technorati (www.technorati.com) and Feed Burner (www.feedburner.com) to get his site noticed, ultimately leading to more traffic to his blog. Skrobola is working with his artist community to get video demonstrations and interviews uploaded on YouTube.com (to further increase the number of patrons frequenting his site). These videos will also be posted on his blog. "Today everything is visual. Consumers want to feel comfortable about buying high-quality artwork. There's no better way than a good visual image to judge the value of the artist and his work. Video enables you to get very personal with the artist, more so than a traditional portfolio picture or written words on a page."

Engaging the Large Corporation

Whether you are an entrepreneur using social media for your start-up company or you work for a large corporation, today's Web 2.0 audiences are dictating the social media strategies. For example, Ynema Mangum, executive producer of TalkBMC at BMC Software Inc., became actively involved in Web 2.0 when her company launched its public blogging and podcasting channel called TalkBMC (http://talk.bmc.com) in June of 2005. According to Mangum, corporate bloggers were recruited for a variety of reasons: as a result of their activity and quality of content on their internal blogs; because they voiced a demand to blog or be heard; and/or because the producers felt they always had something interesting or unique to say.

Mangum feels that BMC was early on the blogging scene. "There were very few blogging platforms to choose from. We chose Plone (www.plone.org), an open-source content management system that supports blogging. Being a large and proprietary software company, we felt that our choice would give us some early and positive press around embracing open source and also enable us to go outside of our IT organization and be more experimental. No one knew at the time if corporate blogging would 'take' or if it would fail," she explained.

BMC at one time or another had about 20 bloggers. Their roles ranged from individual contributor, to middle manager, to the executive level. The highest blogger titles included BMC's CTO, Chief Architect and Corporate Strategist. Mangum admitted that the list of company bloggers did not include all that many marketing and salespeople but let more technically literate individuals speak. They also made it a point to ask individual contributors to join so people outside BMC would get a feel for the internal culture and the quieter contributions made by the "very brainy people" at BMC.

Similar to the discussion with Tim Bray of Sun Microsystems in Chapter 8, "Social Networking: A Revolution Has Begun," Mangum said that the company's communications department does not typically monitor BMC's blogs. The blogs are reviewed and moderated for comments with profanity and for potential competitor hacking. However, BMC doesn't tell their bloggers what to write about or how to write it. The company does sometimes suggest topics if bloggers appear to be having a block. It is never a requirement; nor do they ever pay anyone to blog or to be interviewed for a podcast.

Mangum feels that blogs have a place in a social media community that is made up of a number of things: wikis, knowledge bases, forums, user groups, blogs, podcasts, videos, discussion threads, and so on. Blogging is one part of a potentially powerful community and it's important to think carefully before launching a new way to communicate with potential prospects, customers, analysts, investors, and generally interested parties. "Fortunately, the communications department at BMC was extremely flexible and open-minded about blogging. In fact, they suggested (and continue to suggest) the first bloggers. They are very involved in our content and I believe they will be deeply involved in the future of social media at BMC," she said.

Blogs have a bright future, she believes. Blogging and social media are changing the way her business communicates with the market. "The future of blogging and how companies use it (versus strictly personal social sites) is going to be different for every organization. The following entry from Mangum's blog lets you experience her frame of reference as she focuses on social media with respect to BMC's audiences.

From the Entry: *Marketing IS Conversation*

"Markets are conversations" was a concept first published in the *Cluetrain Manifesto*. It's 2007 and social media is hot. That concept needs an update. *Marketing is conversation.*

I drew a bubble cloud on my white board at BMC to illustrate this point. In the middle of the cloud were "conversations @ BMC." Outside of the cloud lived all the areas we want to influence. Conversations=relationships= revenue. It's that simple. And, if you are in business, you want to scale your conversations so you can influence your market, show your thought leadership and drive brand awareness, and build collaborative relationships with your audience to build your content and messaging. As marketers, you no longer have to do this alone. Now, you do it fully aligned with and collaboratively with your community.

And, oh boy, the technology is here for scaling these conversations.

Many companies that are full force into Web 2.0 built a "roll your own" internal solution for managing these conversations. Now, we're all ready for an update. At BMC, we've looked at multiple vendors who have content management systems developed specifically for social media. Some are not quite there yet with features and functionality; others are just repurposed content management systems looking to be the next Vignette.

I've seen one that is vastly different than the others, yet right on, in that the technology is built with social media in mind. It's almost like the developers actually understand *Cluetrain* and the importance of these conversations because virtually everything done in this system is a conversation—whether it's a poll, survey, blog, or whatever. And, you can render different views of the conversation on the fly. So, if I decide I think my audience would respond to a listed view better than a detailed view, I can change it right away. And, I can configure "listeners" to get feeds about what others are saying about me. It's kind of sneaky and cool, like putting your ear up to a door and listening to the conversation on the other side, then opening the door and responding immediately when you hear something said about you....

The battle rages on in marketing organizations everywhere between the Web 1.0 traditionalists and the Web 2.0 savvy professionals. Both views are sometimes needed while we're in this transition. But, content is, more than ever, king. Build that content with your community. Because...well, you know. *Marketing is conversation.*

The Consultant/Guru's Point of View

Mangum is in good company when it comes to passion and involvement in Web 2.0 and social media. Steve L. Lubetkin, APR, Fellow, PRSA, is the managing partner of Lubetkin & Co. LLC, a diversified public relations, Internet broadcasting, and communications consulting practice. The company's Professional Podcasts LLC subsidiary is a leading producer of audio and video podcasts (digital multimedia programs distributed via the Internet) for corporate clients and other organizations. Lubetkin formed the firms in 2004, after successfully managing communications during the completion of the $47 billion Bank of America-Fleet

Bank merger. Throughout his career he has held senior executive positions in corporate communications at Bank of America, FleetBoston Financial, and Summit Bank.

Lubetkin is an Early Adopter of social media. He said he got involved in social media after Steve Rubel gave a presentation on blogging to the PRSA National Board of Directors. In January 2005, he started blogging and podcasting the following month. When he realized he had some skills specific to podcasting (having prior experience on the radio as an engineer and news anchor from 1975 to 1979 at stations in Central New Jersey), he focused on selling podcasting services to clients. He's been extremely active in the space since that time.

Lubetkin started using a blogging tool that was offered by his former Internet Service Provider (ISP). Eventually, he realized he needed a more robust tool and switched over to blogger.com. His blog is referred to as "Lubetkin's Other Blog" to distinguish it from his first blog. "I need to be completely up-to-date so that I can advise my clients on the most effective approaches [in social media]," explains Lubetkin. He creates podcasts for his clients as well as for his own account with his work featured in the April 2006 issue of the *Philadelphia Business Journal* (www.philadelphia. bizjournals.com). In the past couple years he's produced podcasts for NAPL, a trade association for the excellence in graphic communications management (www.napl.org), The American Institute for CPCU (www. aicpcu.org) and PRSA, the Public Relations Society of America, (www.prsa.org), and other organizations including Sun National Bank's Sun Home Loans mortgage subsidiary (www.sunnb.com) and Rutgers University School of Business Administration (http://camden-sbc.rutgers. edu/BusinessCommunity/outlook.htm).

When asked what he thought about the driving force behind social media and PR 2.0, Lubetkin said he believes it's a combination of a consumer driven initiative and better technology. He explained that it wouldn't be feasible, for example, for consumers to produce and upload rich media content like video and audio without enhanced bandwidth, storage, and production technologies (affordable cameras and recorders, affordable software tools). However, Lubetkin feels that there are PR people who are enthusiastic about technology for its own sake. They want to demonstrate that they are on the leading edge. It is in their business interest to push clients into technologies that might or might not be appropriate for that client's business objectives. Lubetkin warns that if the technology doesn't help the client meet their business objectives, maybe it shouldn't be pitched to them.

Of all the social media tools, Lubetkin feels that podcasting is more effective than blogging because blogs suffer from writer fatigue and often an inauthentic voice. "A Chairman may get tired of doing a blog and delegate it to his PR people," states Lubetkin. "Not to mention that you have to leave the negative comments on the blog. That can be difficult." Lubetkin, who is clearly in favor of podcasting, recommends it to his clients because this social media tool enables you to reach a highly mobile audience of people, who will seek out valuable content for listening or watching on their own terms and at the time most convenient to them. Lubetkin also believes that his clients' podcasts get downloaded at a significant enough volume level that makes them happy and meets their expectations. "One client views downloads as the ability to reach a global audience without having their business development experts having to give those many face-to-face presentations," he stated.

Lubetkin believes social media will continue to evolve. The next step is for social sites like MySpace and Facebook to become less of the "walled garden" kind of either-or choice and become a central place for people to link with other people. "Look at Pulse, the new beta site from www.plaxo. com. They are offering to link up all different sites in a single interface. That is probably more efficient than having to log in to multiple sites."

Lubetkin also sees the value of RSS for his clients. He described RSS as a crucial technology because it enables you to collect all the data sources you want to monitor in a single environment where they can be tracked at the keyword level.

Best Practices from the Technology Evangelist

Jane Quigley, Senior Director for DigitalGrit, the full service interactive marketing firm, began exploring and experimenting with social media more than five years ago. "Once RSS feeds really became standardized, I found it was a great way to get news. Now, I have about 183 feeds that I read, some daily, some weekly. Then about three years ago, I started a blog at LiveJournal as an experiment and I was hooked." Today she has three to five blogs that she's working on at any one time, and she also helps other people set up their own blogs. Quigley tried to stay away from any real forays into social networking at first—she started a MySpace, but never used it. She set up a profile on LinkedIn and forgot about it for a long time.

It was late in 2006 when Quigley started getting more involved with social networking services. It started with Twitter (www.twitter.com) first, and then she expanded to other micro-blogs, including Jaiku (www.jaiku.com) and Pownce (www.pownce.com). She started a Tumblr (www.tumblr.com) and began with Facebook right before the platform opened. "That was a revelation for me—the viral nature of the Facebook platform. Now, I'm on 23 social networking platforms. But, I use and heavily contribute to Twitter, Facebook, Pownce, and my blogs daily. I also use wikis professionally and personally as communication and organizational tools," she stated. In addition, Quigley beta-tests software and services (Mac-centric and social networking-focused) and finds that she gets a lot of invites from her social network "friends."

Quigley remembers the first types of resources she started to use to communicate personally and professionally. For her, RSS feeds were first, and then LiveJournal, Blogger, and LinkedIn came next. Getting more involved with social media, she started experimenting with del.icio.us and began commenting on other people's blogs. By 2005, Quigley was really hooked on RSS feeds (especially after Apple incorporated an RSS reader into Safari). "Not only was I exploring my own voice, but I also began talking to my clients about corporate blogging in late 2004—with no takers," she recalled.

Quigley's position at DigitalGrit and her Web 2.0 experience has enabled her to carve out an "Industry Expert" niche. "I'm also an Emerging Technology/Services evangelist—I like to try to adapt new technologies and services to our clients needs before they are in their sightline. Our clients always want to know what's going on with new technology. What is the value proposition for them? And, more importantly, *when* they really need to start thinking about it." Every time she speaks to her clients, she talks about the new things she's looking at, how she thinks they might be appropriate for their space, and gives them an estimated timeline as to when she thinks it'll become important.

For those looking to get involved in social networking, Quigley recommends the following resources to develop and maintain contacts: LinkedIn, Facebook, blogs, IM, Twitter, and Pownce. Her company uses Twitter, IM, and Facebook for status updates, and some project management.

Quigley has a select group of blogs:

- **Jane's Tumblr**—A collection of links, pictures, and feeds she wants to keep around. For Quigley, it's "a brain-dump kind of thing."

- **www.socialdays.com**—A blog she started that discusses social networks/media.

- **www.settingcontexts.com**—A blog focusing on David Allan's GTD productivity system, as well as software services/apps. This blog is Mac-centric.

- **www.secondlife.com**—With a partner, Quigley has a conference center in Second Life that they rent out to companies looking to explore metaverses without a major initial investment.

- **DigitalGrit's corporate blog**—With podcasts and an internal wiki.

Quigley believes companies need to realize they do not own their brand anymore. People are using a company's assets and developing their own brand experience, such as making YouTube videos (commercials—positive or negative), developing blogs that hold companies responsible for the customer experience, and creating Facebook groups that try to change new corporate policy. She believes we're all consumers and our experiences are shared, easily and virally, with our networks at large. The example she provided was "Like that '70s hair commercial, 'You tell two friends, and they tell two friend, and so on...' Now, it's just done, uploaded and shared in minutes." Technology and increased bandwidth all have played a part in the drive toward social media. Five years ago it would have been tough—because of bandwidth issues—for YouTube to succeed. Also cameras were more expensive. No camera phones. Now everything and everyone is accessible 24/7.

Quigley cites as a favorite example iLike (www.ilike.com), a Web site that enables users to download and share music. It debuted in October 2006 and had built a community of three million users in seven months. "They were one of the first apps on the Facebook platform and literally had to run around Seattle pulling servers from friends and friends of friends to handle the traffic Facebook generated. After (almost) three months, they were at eight million users and at one point were signing up more than 300,000 users per day. Before Facebook opened up its platform it would have taken much more than a year to get that kind of user base and traffic that took less than three months to build."

Quigley feels that one of the most effective social media tools for both B2B and B2C companies are widgets, which are becoming a major tool in distributing content (and advertising) in a strong, viral manner. New companies are building widgets that can be used to purchase content—from newspapers—even video. People will pay to get exclusive content, or to preview content (TV Shows, and so on) before anyone else. She believes that metaverses (like Second Life) will play a role once they can scale in a larger way (capacity in one place is limited right now). But there's been some great examples of companies using Second Life to gain great success, such as IBM, which uses its space there to hold meetings, corporate events, and so on.

Quigley thinks that what happened in the first 45 days of the Facebook platform has been the turning point. Instead of the "walled garden" approach of Facebook, people are going to be able to share applications, advertising, widgets, and all social networking tools across all platforms and incorporated into the operating system (OS) of choice (or direct from desktops). "People are already aggregating their content so that people who 'follow' across platforms are only getting the same posts once instead of 4 or 5 times. I think the race to monetize Facebook and social networking, in general, will bring new tools, services, and applications that will force transparency and openness of the platform," Quigley explained.

Q&A with a Social Media Innovator

Each professional gets involved in social media in a different way. For Mangum, it was blogging. Lubetkin found the value of podcasting early on, and for Quigley it was her great interest in RSS feeds that started her passion and further experimenting with all types of social media both personally and professionally. One of the most well-known Web 2.0 gurus also had a great deal to say about his start with social media and his innovation that truly changed the way consumers access information on the Internet. In a Q&A with Jimmy Wales, the founder of Wikipedia, he shared his unique perspective and insight into the world of social media.

Q: Have you always been ahead of the curve with technology in the past?

A: Yes, to some extent. I was a very Early Adapter of computers. My mother was a gadget person. We were the first people I knew who had a Betamax, VCR, with the Beta tapes, and we had eight tracks too. My mom, like me, was an Early Adapter of technology and because my uncle owned a computer store, we had computers in the house when I was very young. I was always experimenting with technology.

Q: When and how did you come up with the idea of Wikipedia?

A: I had been watching the growth of the presoftware movement—or open source software as most people know it—for several years when I had first heard of this idea of software that's released under free-license that enables anyone to copy it, redistribute it, modify it. At first, I was skeptical. I thought, that was kind of fun, it's a little hobby for some people. But, it just kept growing and growing, and then I realized that's the main software that really runs the Internet and it's all free software. Volunteers write it and they are the people who had a need to share the software.

Now, we're starting to see some business models merge around this. I thought that this kind of collaborative, public effort of writing software would emerge first because if programmers needed tools to share code with each other, they could write their own tools. They have, for example, a program called CVS, which means Concurrent Versioning System. CVS is where programmers can check out and check in code changes and share codes, so if you and I were working on some software together, I can check out part of it and make some changes and check it back in. You can be working on some different part of it, and then it merges our changes in a useful way. Programmers invented things like that to enable them to pool resources. However, I realized for the rest of us, if you and I wanted to collaborate on a document, our best choice might be just e-mailing back and forth a Word document. That really breaks all facts if you have ever tried to collaborate with eight or ten people by e-mailing around Word documents. It just doesn't work.

My idea is to give people the tools they need to collaborate so that they can do more than just "code." They can build whatever they want. The first concept here was the encyclopedia. It was to allow people to come together. As soon as I had the idea in 1999, I was more than excited. I was obsessed. I found myself in a big hurry because I thought that it was extremely obvious that someone else would implement my idea. It turns out that for two years or so that we struggled with a first version, which was not a success, there wasn't anybody else even close to what we were doing. Then, it was in late 2000 that I stumbled across the wiki editing concept, which I didn't invent. It had been around since 1995, when Ward Cunningham invented the wiki, meaning the Web site that anyone can edit. Ward had invented this small underground phenomenon on the Net, which no one really harnessed for a large-scale project. I launched Wikipedia as a part of a socializing cultural tradition of free software, open source, and the wiki combined.

Q: Did consumers understand the concept of Wikipedia right away, or did it take some time?

A: It did take some time and it didn't all at the same time. From the very early days, the participation and the page views and all those measures doubled almost every three to four months. But, remember, in the beginning the first doubling means that the participation went from 10 people to 20 people and then from 20 to 40 people and so on, but it's hard to say if that's fast or slow. It sounds pretty fast, doubling every three to four months, however, there was a ramp-up period before Wikipedia became "public."

Q: Did you ever think that Wikipedia was going to be as big as it is today?

A: When I was looking at the rankings for referenced Web sites, I thought that Wikipedia could make it into the top 100 or maybe even the top 50 sites. But, now it's in the top 10. I never really thought it would be that big. In a way, it makes a lot of sense because the reason that referenced Web sites are only in the top 50 or couple hundred is because they aren't that good. The idea of having this massive resource available for free makes it no surprise that it's so popular. After all, so many sites have only a small amount of information for free, like Britannica, and most make you pay to get full access to information.

Q: Who inspired you to do what you do today?

A: I would have to say my mom and my grandmother, who owned a private school that I attended when I was young. There were four kids in my grade growing up. It was very informal learning. We had some structured classes, but we also had a lot of free time to explore whatever we wanted. This had a big impact on me, not to mention that in my family there was this huge dedication to the idea of knowledge, education, and learning. My mom and grandmother made knowledge, education, and learning core values for us growing up.

Q: What would you like business professionals and consumers to know about Wikipedia?

A: I guess the main concept of Wikipedia normally is communicated pretty well, although sometimes you'll see major mistakes. But, the Wikipedia community is very passionate about quality, and that's why the Web site is as good as it is. At the same time, it's an open-ended project. Wikipedia is always a work in progress, so there are errors and there are problems. The community tends to sort out the errors and the problems fairly quickly, but obviously, things happen and incorrect entries don't get sorted out as quickly as we would like.

I always suggest that people think of Wikipedia primarily as a starting point. Depending on your purpose, it might be the only source that you need. So, if you just read some news story about an event that happened in Albania and you don't really know where Albania is, or what's going on there, you could access Wikipedia and find out information on the region. This would be a basic summary of the facts. However, for other more in-depth research, you would need to rely on other sources after your initial search for information on Wikipedia. You might read the Wikipedia article, but then follow and read all the sources, and even get a couple books on the topic. Then, you can always take some of the knowledge that you get from all the other sources and go back to check Wikipedia. You can add to it and even fix it, if necessary.

I think when you use Wikipedia you should always take it with a grain of salt. As good as it is, there's always human error. Encyclopedia Britannica is riddled with errors, and even with a very high-quality product, the best work is still the nature of human knowledge. You should never take something as given, but really check up on it.

Q: Do you think that college students are embracing Wikipedia as a resource site?

A: Yes, massively. A college newspaper recently interviewed me. When they first reached out to me they told me about a survey conducted on campus regarding the Web sites students are using, and 90 percent of them are using Wikipedia. They said, 'Does that surprise you?' And I said, 'Yes, I'm surprised the number is so low.' I think it should be 100 percent! Who in college doesn't use Wikipedia? I think that, in general, it's become really huge with most college students. However, with the popularity, there are a few concerns. For example, if students don't do what I recommended earlier because they, too, need to take Wikipedia with a grain of salt, always follow up and check the references. When I was in college, if I had turned in a paper citing *Britannica*, that would have been very bad. Even in an encyclopedia, you're supposed to be doing your own research. You should go to Britannica to get some background, but then you have to do some real homework. The same goes for Wikipedia. It can be a problem if students think they can cite Wikipedia. They really shouldn't.

On the other hand, I can't think of a better Web site or better tool for college students. I always like to give the example, if you're reading a novel for class and the novel is set in World War II. The novel briefly mentions the battle of Iwo Jima. So, you think, 'Ahhh, I don't quite know what that is. I know the battle was in the South Pacific and it was something important, but I don't quite know the strategic implications or what happened there.' You can go to Wikipedia and read an article on Iwo Jima and then you go back to your novel, which you're reading for literature class, but with a richer understanding and you have a greater knowledge of the background material. It makes you realize the motivation behind the battle so you know why it occurred. That's the perfect use of Wikipedia as opposed to if you were trying to do your thesis on Iwo Jima, I wouldn't recommend starting with a Wikipedia article. In this case you should be doing some original research.

Q: What function does your organization, Wikimedia, serve?

A: The Wikimedia Foundation is a nonprofit, charity, 501C3 organization that owns Wikipedia, Wictionary, Wiki News, and all our other projects. The Foundation survives on donations from the general public. The vast majority of the money we've received has been small donations— $50.00 to $100.00 and €50 to €100. We've seen a significant amount from Japan and from other countries around the world. Last year we had donations from 50 different countries. Wikimedia is very much a grassroots organization, very volunteer driven, and is politically neutral. We try to think of ourselves as something like the Red Cross for information and, we're here to help everybody get the information they need.

Q: What is Wikia?

A: I have a completely separate company, Wikia, which was launched in 2004 to provide community-based wikis inspired by the model of Wikipedia.org—the free, open-source encyclopedia. With respect to the Wikimedia Foundation, it is a nonprofit educational resource with projects that include dictionary, encyclopedias, textbooks, and things like that. However, my company Wikia is all the rest of the library. It could be political advocacy. It could be just fun stuff, such as what we call an uncyclopedia, which is a parody of Wikipedia. The uncyclopedia is very funny. Wikia is also really big in gaming. We have the World of Warcraft Wiki. Players of this huge online game document things in the game and offer each other help along the way, and there are approximately 3,000 different communities. This started toward the end of 2004 and it's been growing faster than Wikipedia did at the same stage of growth. It's really exciting and getting big fast.

Q: What advice would you give communications professionals about negative publicity and social media?

A: I can talk for a long time on this topic because I think it's really, really important. One of the things we see today with Wikipedia is that whatever you type into Google or Yahoo!—you know, any company name and various keywords—the Wikipedia article is probably the second or third link. Sometimes even the first link and sometimes it's even ahead of the official Web site of the company. It's tremendously important to a lot of communications professionals that the Wikipedia article is accurate. But, I think communications professionals have to be very realistic and understand that it has to be neutral and accurate. You can get into a lot of trouble and, in particular, you don't want to have something on behalf of your client that's going to cause any kind of embarrassment. However, if the company in question has some controversies, you have to understand that Wikipedia has to cover those controversies. You can't go to Wikipedia and start blanking out the controversial sections. You're just going to get reverted—it just doesn't work that way.

What I recommend is that all PR professionals do not edit Wikipedia articles directly. Instead what they should do is go to the discussion page. Transparency is something that's really valued by our community. If you show up on the discussion page and identify yourself as a member of an agency and that you have concerns about an article, you're then able to provide the correct information and even links and resources that clear up the miscommunication (if this is the case). If you provide the information, you will have to trust the Wikipedia community to deal with it in the proper fashion. It might take a little bit of time and can be a little frustrating, but in general this method works very well. If it doesn't work, you can always escalate the process by e-mailing Wikipedia directly, where there's a whole team of editors who monitor the incoming e-mail queue and sort out issues and concerns.

I'm personally involved at that level of monitoring. I feel this is a very effective method for correcting errors or for getting some balance in an article. That doesn't mean you're going to ultimately be happy, certainly not if you're looking for a "puff piece." Wikipedia takes an impartial view. So, when you write something and you hype it up a little bit, or you make it seem very favorable, you might use certain words of language that are not appropriate for an encyclopedia. For instance, with the phrase, "XYZ Corporation introduced a new product," you might write, "XYZ Corporation introduced an innovative ground-breaking product." In another forum this might be fine, but it isn't right for Wikipedia; it's not our house style. What's going to happen if you put something like that in Wikipedia? Our people are just going to fix it up.

Q: Does Wikipedia have concerns about companies/PR professionals and self-promotion?

A: Generally, I think communications professionals get it. We do have problems with people doing self-promotions, but this tends to be small businesses—in fact, very small. We also have this problem with bloggers at times, and lot of high school rock and roll bands trying to get in a Wikipedia article. They should go to MySpace where it's acceptable to brag about their music. Or, maybe they should go to YouTube, but certainly this type of article does not belong in Wikipedia because there are no sources and no references. The Wikipedia community will most likely delete an entry if they cannot find multiple, independent reliable sources.

Q: Any final thoughts on social media?

A: There's one phrase that I've heard that I like a lot, which is 'conversational marketing.' The idea is that the Web is a giant conversation; it's just one giant, nonstop conversation, going on in all these different communities. If you understand and respect that, then you should join in the conversations. But, you have to understand that it's very different from a broadcast-oriented world where you control the message and you put your message up. That will still exist and it's still an important tool in marketing. But, conversational marketing is very different. The conversation about your product is no longer just between you and your customers. Now, you actually get to listen to your customers talk to each other. The difficult part—you can't control the conversation; you can participate in it, but you can't control it!

Go Ahead, Get Passionate over Social Media

From the blogging beginnings to first experiences with podcasts and RSS, every professional engages in social media at a different pace. A common notion: You can see how professionals from small companies and large companies to the industry technology experts see the need to use social media and be passionate and "obsess" over it. It might start with a personal test of tools, but certainly translates well into client efforts and unique PR 2.0 strategies for your brands. The convergence of public relations and social media is a powerful proposition and one you need to take seriously. As you venture into social media or become more proficient, you should remember the advice from the experts.

- Blogging is a great start. However, you shouldn't tell your company's bloggers what to write about or how to write it. You can, however, suggest topics if bloggers appear to be having a writer's block.

- Social media, especially blogging, is changing the way businesses communicate with the market. The future of blogging and how companies use it is different for every organization.

- With podcasting you don't have to worry about negative comments. The recommended tool enables you to reach a highly mobile audience, who will seek out valuable content for listening or watching on their own terms and at the most convenient time.

- You can be enthusiastic about technology, but you shouldn't push clients into technologies that might not be appropriate for their business objectives.

- Social media is advancing quickly with a predicted next step for MySpace and Facebook to become less of the "walled garden" kind of either-or choice, and become a central place for people to link with other people. A next generation of social networking sites will offer to link up different sites in a single interface, without having to log in to multiple sites.

- You can listen to your customers talk to one another. The Web is one great big conversation that's nonstop and goes on in all these different communities.

- The social media community is transparent. You must respect the neutral and accurate views of a community and realize that controversy is the nature of the Web and PR 2.0. You can't change the controversy. You, can, however, identify yourself and inject facts and information appropriately.

Chapter 13

The Mindset of the PR 2.0 Journalist

What do you need to keep in mind in your PR 2.0 interactions with journalists? First and foremost, even if your journalists are engaged in 2.0 and social media (personally or professionally), that doesn't necessarily mean 2.0 takes precedence over all the tried and true PR rules of communication. Why? Because journalists, regardless of a level of technological acceptance or a desire to engage in social media, still expect and require a few very important characteristics from their trusted PR sources. Exhibiting the desired characteristics, on a regular basis, is the difference between the average to good PR resource and the great PR source. Social media applications (wikis, blogging, social networking, streaming video, RSS, podcasts, and so on) are for the most part used as communication resources that serve to enhance the communication or interaction with your contacts.

How to Reach PR Greatness

You learn from the journalists in this chapter, through their candid commentary and advice, that they have a clear expectation of their PR professionals, and these expectations relate directly to the field of Public Relations and the "traditional" PR communication practices, It's your ability to deliver excellent information that's timely, credible, accurate, and above and beyond what journalists can ultimately uncover on their own. For the journalist, this defines the PR person's value. Some journalists go as far as saying they would forego the fancy social media interactions just to obtain the best, relevant information and a deeper level of understanding on a particular topic of interest.

Journalists want and appreciate interactions with PR pros who are (1) tapped into their needs, (2) understand their publication's audiences and industry trends, and (3) offer precise information that is targeted and suitable for their stories/interests. That's so much more valuable than your ability to deliver a "cool" social media interaction. If you don't understand the journalist's intended audience and interests, you clearly are not following the natural and "traditional" rules of PR in your communication with influencers.

You're still building relationships and these rules, for decades, have built the strongest relationships. The intimate relationship that you develop provides the best transfer of information, in the timeliest fashion. (Of course, I still believe the most intimate communication is face-to-face, but you can't always achieve this easily.)

Social media or not...today's journalists and the journalists of the future will always be focused on your knowledge, ability to deliver credible information, and overall responsiveness (which could be at a moment's notice).

Although you should familiarize yourself and be ready for social media interactions (perhaps that includes providing journalists with a social media release or an interactive newsroom), beware of communication with them exclusively through a social networking site—*Time* magazine reporter Jeremy Caplan addresses this in an interview at the end of this chapter. A journalist always lets you know the best way to reach, interest, and keep your brand top of mind.

Advice from the Influencers

Similar to the shared stories of the PR 2.0 pros and gurus, every media person has a story to share and advice to give a communications professional on the best way to reach a media outlet and what will pique interest. Feedback about new media strategies and how they want to be engaged from several members of the media follows.

Anne Holland–Publisher of MarketingSherpa.com

Anne Holland is the President and Publisher of MarketingSherpa, Inc., a research firm that publishes Benchmark Guides, Buyer's Guides, and "How To" Reports for advertising, marketing, and public relations professionals. Holland is a 20-year veteran in the publishing industry and a well-respected figure in the digital marketing arena. She has been quoted by *The New York Times*, *Business 2.0*, *CBS MarketWatch*, and *Fast Company* on numerous occasions and offers you some good advice and a better understanding of how the media thinks and builds winning stories from her point-of-view.

When it comes to the best Web 2.0 and social media, Holland says that journalists tend to trust third-party sources, beyond the company-voice tools, which make the best resources for stories. This includes finding external bloggers and podcasters who mention your brand and/or interview your executives. "For certain beats, such as technology reporting, journalists are more likely to read blogs other than just a company's," explained Holland.

Holland knows that journalists look to the newswires that feed into Google News, Yahoo! News, and the like, which is more of a tool to reach your end audience as opposed to the journalist world. "Journalists are not eager to troll news releases anymore because they know that these are being disseminated directly to consumers now," she said. Holland pointed out that as a result, journalists look in obscure places, including blogs, message boards, e-mail discussion groups, and podcasts. She feels that they are poking into the corners of the Web that their readers haven't discovered yet, and this is the same place your messages need to be. "If a possible source posts news releases much more frequently than other individuals—there's one company I know who has posted a release every day for the past 60 days—then it does raise your profile in my mind because every single morning when I check my e-mail feed from the wires, your name is always there!"

Holland spends a great deal of time on the Internet. She naturally checks out her MarketingSherpa blog and the bloggers who mention or hotlink to the site. However, she doesn't spend a lot of time in forums. She's a member of several intimate (300 members or less) industry e-mail discussion groups for key beats her publication covers. She often scans the e-mails she gets looking for story ideas. "If a topic comes up there, I might assign a reporter to it. It's more of a topic idea generator, not a lets-write-about-this-company thing. If I ever thought someone was trying to fake me out by posting queries to catch journalists' attention, I'd probably 'out' that person to the forum administration and get them kicked off. It's very bad form if it's not a genuine post."

Holland rarely reads a company blog from a vendor in the field. She's more likely to sign up for e-mail from a brand (no reporters she knows sign up for the blog RSS feed). Holland said that it's not useful because you can't forward anything to colleagues. If you have a really great blog and you offer an e-mail feed, she might sign up for it and read it, and maybe consider you as a potential good story source. In all cases, it has to be genuine—something you'd write even if you didn't know she was reading it. "It's got to have behind-the-scenes insight or unknown factoids I won't find someplace else. If it's how-great-we-are crud, I will stop reading it," she mentioned.

In Holland's opinion, PR pitching strategies have changed over the years. For her, it's still about personal relationships. If you get back to her with useful "stuff," if you answer the phone when she's on deadline, if you're intelligent and conspicuously make her job easier, then Holland will, in turn, help you out too. If you send her ill-fitting pitches on a regular basis, she'll eventually start ignoring all your e-mails. In fact, Holland said that if you offer it, you must be willing to respond to it. If this is the case, you can even reach out through IM. However, **never, ever, ever** IM a journalist out of the blue. If they IM you, of course, respond; but Holland suggests that you shouldn't use this as an invitation to start hitting journalists with IM pitches. "That can be more annoying than the phone. Especially, reporters on tight deadlines will want to hunt you down and kill you if you interrupt their train of thought with an unrelated pitch," she warned.

Holland believes that the PR person is a valuable resource to the journalist. In fact, if she needs a source and reaches out to a PR pro for an interview and that person gets back to her in a super-timely fashion, then that's valuable. When the PR person is there and ready to react when Holland "cries" for help (although she said she doesn't do that often), that too is extremely valuable. Holland realizes that technology certainly helps the relationship along. "Now, I can sign up to be e-mailed news from you. I can surf the Web and see what your customers say about you. I can surf the 'way back' machine and pick up past stories and quotes your CEO would prefer stay hidden," she said.

Holland, like many journalists, realizes the value of the PR professionals is their quick, responsive nature, knowledge of their brands, and valuable/credible information to complete their stories. Regardless of social media or 'plain old traditional PR,' this is the natural expectation of the journalist in any good relationship.

Jeffrey Chu–Business Senior Editor, Fast Company

Jeffrey Chu, senior editor at *Fast Company*, is no different from the many editors out there who long to interact with great PR people. Chu has been writing for many years and now, as a business senior editor for *Fast Company*, he shared his checklist of do's and don'ts for the PR 2.0 communicator. In his opinion, despite social media the pitches are still mediocre.

At the time of the interview, Chu was fairly new to *Fast Company*. He believes that the use of social media tools is a preference and it really depends on what you're looking for when you're developing a story. Social networking Web sites are useful for finding sources, and he mentioned that blogs, in some cases, are useful for story subjects. But, the rest of the "newfangled technologies," as he called them, often contribute more to the clutter than anything else. Chu is not a blogger and he rarely spends time in forums unless he is searching for information on a particular subject. He does, however, use Facebook as his primary social networking site and he also has a Friendster (www.friendster.com) page.

Chu said that he really hasn't seen any novel PR pitches through social media tools. E-mail is the main source of the pitches he receives. On the whole, he feels that PR pitching is "garbled and/or littered with errors and/or just not that professional." I agree with Chu's frustration. Communications professionals should not allow themselves to get lost in the "looseness" of the Internet. Good communication skills shouldn't stop in 2.0. They should get only better.

The interactions with journalists that I first experienced and learned from my own mentor were never left to just "spell check" on a computer. These communications were well-thought out and reviewed even when there was a crisis or the severest time crunch. In fact, there was no spell check when I was starting out. At the time, the only tools we had were our own "eagle eyes," as the Vice President of Padilla, Spear, Burdick & Beardsley, Andrew Edson, used to say. We would read something once, maybe even twice for flow and grammar, and then read it backward to make sure that all the words were spelled correctly. Do you know anyone who does this today? Not many communicators take the time, especially online. It's very important that your communication, no matter how creative you are or want to be, doesn't lose momentum (or credibility) if the Internet makes you fall into a lazy frame of mind.

Chu had some strong opinions about blogging and the PR pitch. For him, blogs are not the right forum for the PR professional to use to pitch to a journalist. "It seems a poor use for a blog. I wouldn't take such a pitch too seriously. If the PR person wants to pitch me, the best thing he or she can do is to find out more about me and my publication and my interests, and target the pitch in a very obviously informed way. That's the problem with so many pitches: we're obviously just names in a database," explained Chu.

Chu thinks that the most valuable PR person is the professional who has a real understanding of his publication's focus, as well as a willingness to discuss ideas at length. Unfortunately, he can count on his two hands the number of PR people he's come in contact with who he feels are good and meet these expectations.

Chu doesn't really concern himself with how much knowledge the PR person has if he's receiving a social media release. That's not what brings him the best story. Chu feels that PR professionals should spend their time understanding journalists and the field of journalism first. "The social media elements are just bells and whistles, but until you understand how to deliver a compelling message, regardless of media, that's irrelevant," he said.

Chu says, "I think technology has made PR people complacent. I get a ton of lame e-mailed pitches, often addressed to the wrong person or the wrong company. There's much less of a face-to-face relationship." Chu values most of those PR people who contact him first to have coffee and to understand what he's trying to do with his content. Once the conversation is started, it can flow from there. The key to great PR 2.0 is always to establish a relationship. Nothing has changed. In this day and age of advanced technology and increased bandwidth and applications, PR pros should not forget to pick up the phone.

Yes, social media can be very personal and it's all about conversation. Perhaps there's a line that needs to be drawn between your interaction with journalists through social media tools (such as social networking and blogging) and your professional services. In an interview with Jeremy Caplan, Business, Technology and Social Issues Reporter *TIME* magazine, he offered PR professionals a best practices approach to the journalist and social media.

Q&A with a Top-Tier Journalist

Q: What do you think are the best social media tools for journalists, whether it's RSS, blogs, podcasting, or social networking, which help you to develop your stories?

A: I basically use a tool in each different area, and I find that it's helpful to rely on as few tools as possible. Getting overwhelmed with all the available resources online is very easy. The best approach for me is trying out several and then figuring out the single most efficient/effective tool and just learning to master that particular tool.

For instance, there are numerous RSS readers. I've tried a few and found that Google reader is the most efficient. It enables you to access RSS feeds or blogs from wherever you happen to be as long as you have Internet access. For instance, if I'm on the road or if I stop at an airport, I can read whatever blogs I'm interested in reading at that particular time. Basically, Google provides an easy way to keep track of however many blogs you follow, whether it's ten blogs or a hundred or as many as several hundred. In addition to reading a blog, it enables you to categorize it and save or file it for future reference, or forward a blog entry to someone else. Google reader is searchable so that you can always access that content later, and it's a terrific tool for managing the huge amount of information that most journalists and PR professionals digest everyday.

Another tool that I find particularly useful for digesting podcasts is iTunes (www.apple.com/itunes), which is free software from Apple. You can use iTunes on either a PC or Mac and, basically, it enables you to subscribe to podcasts on just about any subject under the sun. A few that I particularly enjoy listening to and find useful are: *Meet the Press*, *On the Media*, *This American Life*, and a variety of shows from National Public Radio (NPR), one of which is *Story of the Day*. These are examples of podcasts that come out regularly—in most cases, once a week—but in some cases daily. You can listen to them wherever you are and they're all free! It's a great way to keep abreast of the news when you're not in a place where you can read.

In terms of social networking sites, I find LinkedIn to be fairly useful. I use it to connect with other journalists. I also use it to refer people to others who might be in need of help with something, perhaps with a project. I also use it to refer colleagues, or maybe for people who are looking for a job. I've also used LinkedIn to find sources for stories. In some cases journalists prefer to go around PR people. They can go directly to the people who work at a particular company or who have worked there in the past. I'll use my LinkedIn network to find sources who have experience in a particular industry, or who might have worked at a particular company that I'm writing about at some point in their career. I would easily be able to find this type of information noted in their LinkedIn profile.

Only in rare instances would I refer a journalist colleague to a PR professional who was profiled on LinkedIn. If I knew someone was writing about a particular subject and there was a PR person who I trusted and whom I thought would be helpful for the journalist and vice versa, I might make that referral. I have to say though, in general, I am wary of connecting with PR people in unfamiliar networks for a number of reasons. First of all, as a journalist you want to remain impartial. You don't necessarily want to connect in what could be perceived as a social way with a PR person; you want to keep some distance.

Second, you might not want to create the expectation that you're going to be available for a PR person's regular contact. Because, depending on the person, they might abuse that opportunity to be in touch too regularly. Third, I try to limit the number of people in my network to just those individuals that I'm in contact with regularly. There just aren't too many PR people who I'm in regular contact with. On the other hand, a PR person who makes effective use of LinkedIn, by connecting to people in a variety of industries, might be able to offer a resource that's of value to journalists. They can act as connectors that serve a useful purpose—but only if the journalist asks for that connection.

With respect to user-generated video, I cannot say that it's terribly useful in terms of regular research and reporting. On occasion it is, and I'll use a tool like Digg Video (a community-based popularity Web site with an emphasis on technology). But, that tends not to be something that's really a part of the reporting process. I just haven't found video of that sort to be useful in the past. There have been a couple occasions where video has been of interest to me—for instance, illustrating product usage. I've seen a couple videos where a PR person demonstrated how a consumer could use a technology service or product. Seeing the product in action and a quick demonstration of a real-life scenario was an interesting way to learn about a product that was efficient, in comparison to reading a couple pages of dense text. Seeing a short video of the product in use—a real-life scenario—helped bring it to life. That's a case where it was useful. But, in general, I don't find that there's a lot of value added to see a video produced about something that can be explained briefly in text. Unless it's something that you really need to see to understand, I think those cases are probably not as common as some might think.

Another consideration with video, it takes time. That's really one of the biggest issues for me. If you have ten minutes between meetings to find something that you're thinking about and want to dig into further, you probably don't want to spend eight of those ten minutes trying to load up a video. You have to see if you have the right software, see if it's relevant, and then it takes two minutes to load and then, in turn, the video isn't really that relevant or useful. For me, it would be most efficient, in many cases, to read a quick paragraph summarizing things.

Q: Do you feel that readers on Time.com are engaging in social media on your site (RSS, blogging, podcasts)?

A: It's a work in progress for us. The Time.com editors are continually looking for more ways to engage readers. Invite them into the conversation. Readers can comment on the Time.com blogs and there are many

Time.com blogs on various subjects from technology to politics. Readers can participate in dialogue on the site. We're looking forward to finding more ways to get them engaged and involved. We're constantly working on the best way to do that.

Q: About how much time do you spend on the Internet blogging or checking out forums and gathering information?

A: As a journalist, I spend a tremendous amount of time online gathering information and reporting. I don't spend too much time blogging, but that might change in the future because I find it's a nice format for journalism in the sense that it's flexible in terms of length. In a story in a magazine you often have to fit into a particular predetermined length, which might be a page, two pages, or five pages. It has to fit your text, the images, and the particular framework. However, in a blog you can write just a few lines, or you can write several paragraphs depending on the length and the chosen topic. I like the flexibility of blogging and I plan to do more of it in the future. Blogging enables you to add things like pictures or video, kind of on the fly. If you're reporting somewhere, and you happen to quickly want to post, it enables you to do it in a really easy way.

With respect to spending time online, for journalists, obviously the Internet has radically changed the nature of how we do our jobs. The bulk of what we are doing is gathering information, and doing that with a resource like the Internet is often a thousand times more efficient than trying to do that with old-fashioned books.

When it comes to blogs and the PR pitch, I would suggest the PR person develop a dialogue outside the context of a journalist's blog. I think the blog is really the medium for the journalists to communicate with readers, rather than to field PR pitches. I would say that a better way of communicating would be to e-mail separately and then reference a blog post, if it's relevant.

Q: Have you seen any interesting pitches using social media that have come across your desk?

A: The video product pitch I mentioned earlier, I found interesting. In this one case, it happened to be particularly useful as it successfully demonstrated how the product would work in real life and showed creatively what the product could do, and why it would be useful. I find that many pitches offer a piece of information; for instance, this is a new product we have, this is a new service that's coming out, and here's how we're launching our campaign. What they often leave out is the significance of why the product is important, why a reader should care, and what benefits it has for consumers.

However, most of the pitches I get now are by e-mail. I'd say the most effective ones are very brief and lay out three things. The first is that the information is very clear, simple, and straightforward. The second most important factor is to identify why the product or service is significant now, or what's happening now that's different. Last, it's important to spell out why the new product/service is relevant to *TIME* magazine's audiences.

I get a lot of pitches about local events that might be of great interest to a small number of people in a particular area, but might not be appropriate to the national audience of *TIME*. It's particularly helpful when the PR person has thought about what *TIME* is, what we've done in the past, and why our readers would be particularly interested in the subject. Those three things are really helpful in PR pitches, in any format, but particularly by e-mail.

Q: How do you feel about the use and value of the social media release?

A: I see the social media release as a second step. I think the first step is to receive the 'what and the why' e-mail. What is the service, why is it relevant, what's the context, what's the benefit, why would I be interested, and how is it relevant to what I've done or what I might be working on at the time? If there's a huge amount of information and videos, audio files, and pictures, which appear to be cumbersome, then what this whole thing is about is not clear to me. I'm not going to want to take the time to dig into all the information provided.

On the other hand, if a journalist is interested in a subject and they've already expressed an initial interest or curiosity about that subject, or a journalist makes it clear that it's relevant to something they're working on, then, yes, I think it could be a useful set of resources. But I haven't really come into contact with that as of yet.

Q: How do you feel the advancement of technology has changed the relationship between the PR person and the journalist? Do you think technology has made it weaker or stronger?

A: It certainly made it easier for PR people to get in touch with journalists and to get more of their pitches read even though journalists get an overwhelming amount of e-mail every day. Journalists tend to read the pitches because they want to make sure they are not missing anything important. I think technology has made it easier for PR people to get their information in front of journalists.

On the other hand, it has also made it increasingly difficult to capture the attention of a journalist, as I mentioned before, who is overwhelmed with information and e-mail. It's even more important for PR people to learn the art of being concise, and that's something that I find is lacking most often. I get a huge number of news releases or PR people contacting me in writing. They send numerous paragraphs of information, which most of the time isn't really necessary. E-mail might have made it easier for people to be in touch, but it's definitely harder to maintain the attention.

I think the e-mail subject line is worth addressing. The subject line is a very important way to capture someone's attention and is also a quick way to lose their attention too, if it's clearly not relevant, or if it hasn't been targeted to the person appropriately. If the subject line doesn't grab my attention, why would I bother reading the e-mail?

Just one other tip while we're on the point about e-mail and technology. I often get e-mails with huge attachments and all kinds of extraneous materials. Unfortunately, some media outlets are still using systems that are unable to digest all the attachments and additional information that PR people send. I would say that, unless PR people are absolutely certain that the journalists on the receiving end can digest whatever attachment they're sending, they should just keep it plain and simple. If it's a jpeg, then most e-mail software will identify it as a jpeg. That's not so much a problem, but sometimes if it's a high-resolution image, unsolicited, that will clog the system. Today, there's less of a problem worrying about viruses, and more of a problem with the size of the files.

Q: Is there any advice you'd like to offer PR professionals as they continue to use new media to build relationships?

A: One tip I would offer the PR pro is to have a simple way for a journalist to contact you, whenever it's convenient for them. One method I've experimented with, and I would recommend, is a service Grand Central. Grand Central basically gives you a universal contact number. It enables people who have seven different phone numbers, three different e-mails, and two different fax numbers to be contacted through one telephone number. For a journalist, having many numbers for a single PR person gets unmanageable. A universal number automatically forwards to whatever number you happened to be at so that you avoid the problem of missed connections. For journalists, time is particularly precious; I'm sure for PR people as well. Right now the Grand Central services are free, so it's a good tool to try to keep everyone connected when time is of the essence.

Another tip: It's easy for a PR person to find out what someone has written about, his/her interests, and background information. This intelligence should be used to tailor a pitch appropriately and to show that you have some understanding of what is of interest to that person based on what they've done in the past. Even if it just means spending a couple minutes acquainting yourself with a person's body of work, it's probably a good idea to take advantage of that. It lets people know that you've taken the time to see what they do.

The cost benefit equation comes into play. It might not be worth it every time you send a pitch, to spend hours at the library finding someone's articles. But, with the Internet, if you can do it in a minute or two, which you can often do, it might be worthwhile. However, there is a line not to cross as it's important to reference only strictly professional information that you find. I've had occasions where someone will find something out or look for something that might not be relevant to the professional context of the communication. I would say it's probably better to stick to finding out what the person has written about rather than where they spend their summer vacations. We all know that information is out there about us. In the same way that you wouldn't mention personal matters in a professional meeting, it's inappropriate online to do the same.

This is actually one of the dangers of social networks online like Facebook and MySpace, which can be useful for finding information or networking. But, this is a place where the lines between professional and personal can be blurred. I know a PR person who recently posted a button that said they support a particular politician in an election. For some people that's fine and they are comfortable with including this type of information in a personal profile. Mixing political and personal life with professional life is a personal choice.

However, it's worth thinking about how that might impact your professional communications with people if that doesn't suit them, or if it's in conflict with them in some way. It's tricky because people have online identities in the social networks they use in their off hours. They are communicating with their friends and there's nothing wrong with that necessarily, but if they're using that social networking for professional purposes the lines can become blurred.

PR 2.0 Means Great PR

If you are *not* providing the media with the knowledge and expertise to help them reach their deadlines, there isn't a social media application available that will help you to get their attention. You should use social media tools to reach the influencers once you've proven that you understand what it is they are trying to accomplish and what their audiences want from them. Then, these new media interactions will enhance their stories or your brand in their eyes. It always has to make sense and, above all, it must be a useful interaction. Your journalists require great PR. Nothing has changed; this goes back to the early days of Edward Bernays.

Back in 2000, I interviewed Frazier Seitel. Seitel is a well-known PR counselor and the man who practically wrote the book on PR, the author of *The Practice of Public Relations*. He said that we were returning to the Golden Age of PR. According to Seitel, PR professionals can be much more focused on strategy because the Internet enables them to be less of the "paper pushers" and more of the strategic thinkers who counsel C-level executives. And, now we have enthusiasm and excitement about PR 2.0. There is a reason to be excited because just like other eras in PR,

2.0 is meant to get PR people practicing great PR. It's always been about great PR (and always will be). You need to keep the following in mind:

- Journalists, regardless of a level of technological acceptance or a desire to engage in social media, still expect and require a few very important characteristics, including your ability to deliver excellent information that's timely, credible, and accurate.

- Some journalists would forego the fancy social media interactions just to obtain the best, most relevant information and a deeper level of understanding from their trusted PR sources.

- Your use of social media tools with the media should also be used to augment their ability to obtain the information that's critical to their deadlines.

- Today's savvy PR 2.0 professional knows the type of communication to use in a media outreach program. It is truly the individual preference of the recipient.

- Communications professionals should not allow themselves to get lost in the "looseness" of the Internet. Good communication skills shouldn't stop in 2.0.

- When it comes to social media, journalists want to remain impartial and don't necessarily want to connect with PR people in what could be perceived in a social way.

- Social networking has dangers; it can be useful for finding information or for networking with contacts. However, this is a place where the lines between professional and personal can be blurred.

- Blogs are a really good medium for journalists to communicate with readers, or to research topics rather than to field PR pitches.

- The social media release might be used as a second step in the case of journalists wanting to receive the 'what and the why' e-mail as a first step.

Chapter 14

A PR 2.0 Plan

The PR 2.0 plan should bring the "Public" back into public relations. Your plan needs to get information directly to your customers so that you can help them make meaningful decisions and hopefully influence their behavior to begin using or maintain the usage of your product/service. When constructing your PR plan, or strategizing for your campaign, you need to proceed with a fine balance; that of traditional PR strategy and that of your new social media approach. You've already heard the perspectives of some of your influencers, the media such as Jeremy Caplan at *TIME* Magazine and Jeffrey Chu at *Fast Company*, who don't rely on social media from PR people, or the brands they represent, when researching or writing a story. Remember that you have the online consumer and professional audiences who want to receive, organize, and share your content in the many communities they belong.

The Best PR 2.0 Planning Approach

What's the best approach to a successful PR 2.0 plan? For now, keep traditional PR strategy in the back of your mind and open your frame of reference as to what is the right amount of social media to make your stakeholders feel content satisfied. The companies in this chapter all understand that proper PR 2.0 strategy and planning includes using social media applications that are

- An innovative means to drive business

- An effective way to communicate to employees, customers, prospects, other stakeholders with less expensive techniques

- An opportunity to increase the reach of your brand's messages

- An interactive forum to position your company and its executive team as thought leaders or your brand as a thought leadership company

- A chance to communicate with audiences in ways that were never possible in the past

- A means to hear firsthand customer comments, concerns, and insight into what influences their thinking and decision-making

Creative PR 2.0 Planning and Strategy

Today's companies are using PR 2.0 and social media to enhance communications to capture the attention of many different groups. They understand that social media sites (for example, MySpace and Facebook) and social networking are no longer for younger audiences. People of all ages and all professions are reading blogs, joining online communities, tagging articles, listening to podcasts, enjoying their RSS feeds, and have profiles on social networking sites such as Facebook and LinkedIn. What's the best way to get started?

Adverb Media

I spoke with Scott Delea, President of Adverb Media, and was so impressed when he told me one of his PR 2.0 strategies. Adverb Media was a sponsor of the ad:tech conference in New York City in November 2007. Delea moderated a panel session at the conference called "Thriving in the New Digital Marketing Ecosystem," which had leading marketers in attendance with the latest thinking on how they can best leverage the Internet to stay ahead of the competition. The panel tackled this topic by hearing the perspectives of Glen Whiting, Executive Director of DigitalGrit, a leading digital agency; Gordon Henry, CMO at Yellow Book USA; Safa Raschtchy, Former Managing Director, Internet Media and Marketing, Piper Jaffray and Company; and Jodi Kahn, President, Digital Business, Reader's Digest Association, Inc. The session answered several interesting questions on the minds' of executives: How is the

Internet changing the way a company communicates with its customers? What is an example of an innovative way you have seen a company engaging with prospects using Web 2.0? What role does consumer generated content and social networks play in effectively communicating or serving customers?

Certainly all these topics take more than a simple hour's worth of discussion.

Delea wanted to provide more than "the panel discussions, which are show up and throw up." In this type of forum, panelists present their PowerPoint slides and call it a day. The conversation shouldn't begin and end with the one-hour presentation. Delea thought it would be much more powerful and relevant if they leveraged Web 2.0 technologies to facilitate a dialogue before the event. His idea was to devote more time and create early interest in the topics by setting up a networking group on Facebook and by announcing the event on the social networking site prior to the panel session. "Interested parties would get to know the panel members, be able to view bios and ask questions they want answered even prior to the actual event," Delea explained. After the conclusion of the event, Delea wanted the discussion about Facebook to continue so that more interested parties become engaged in the marketing conversation. What a great idea! It costs next to nothing (with the exception of the time it takes for executives to participate). We also discussed how video-taping the ad:tech panel session could lead to video clips posted on Facebook. These clips could be shared by the group and provide firsthand insight from the experts on the topics.

Adverb Media is the parent company to a family of companies— Temel, DigitalGrit, and RelevantNoise—which are entrenched in new media and digital marketing solutions. As many organizations are contemplating to blog or not to blog, DigitalGrit's blog dates back to November 2004. It was developed as a part of the company's early PR 2.0 strategy. Now, DigitalGrit has employees on Twitter (www.twitter.com), the micro blog that gives play-by-play, up-to-the-minute actions of the person who is "Twittering." DigitalGrit also communicates to its audiences through RSS feeds, podcasts, and on-demand Webinars. When it comes to PR 2.0 and social media, Adverb Media and its family of companies is a group of companies to watch.

TOMY International

The use of the Internet as a means of creating strong product "buzz" and building awareness for products and services continues at a rapid pace as more marketers look to leverage active online communities to differentiate products and services. In today's world, many marketers will use online campaigns in advance of product launches and retail availability as a means of stimulating buzz and creating a demand for products or services as they become available.

One such example is an international campaign being coordinated by a leading U.S. public relations firm, Southard Communications, in partnership with its European partner Threepipe Communications on behalf of TOMY International,[1] a leading marketer of toys and games.

Overview

Eternity II is a geometric puzzle solved by placing its 256 square pieces into a 16" × 16" grid. The pieces are bordered by colored patterns, each of which must be correctly aligned with its neighboring side to correctly fit into place. Unlike most puzzles, which only have one correct way of completing the final solution, there are thousands of ways Eternity II can be solved to win the $2 million prize.

Eternity II was developed by the original inventor of Eternity I, the well-known British publisher and former policy advisor to Margaret Thatcher and Lord Christopher Monckton. Eternity I was launched in Europe in 1999 and sold more than 500,000 puzzles worldwide becoming the fastest-selling puzzle ever. A Cambridge student successfully solved the puzzle in 18 months and was awarded the UK £1 million prize.

Contestants submit their possible solutions to the puzzle by registered mail. All submissions are time-stamped and sealed inside a safe until the first scrutiny date of December 31, 2008. If no correct solutions are opened, submissions for the following year would be kept until December 31, 2009, and lastly 2010. The first correct solution will win the prize of US $2 million.

For the first time, the puzzle has been made available to American consumers, distributed by TOMY USA. For this launch, the company is not engaging in any traditional print or outdoor advertising to support the product launch. Instead, TOMY is relying on the $2 million prize and viral, word-of-mouth promotion to duplicate the frenzied success it once had in Europe.

Opportunities

Some of the advantages of Eternity II lie in the marketability of the product and its incredible and unprecedented prize offering of $2 million. Never before has a game or puzzle been introduced in the U.S. with such a life-changing prize prospect. Consumer excitement around the game can be more easily aroused and sustained because of this very unique offering.

Another benefit of Eternity II is the wide appeal to a broad demographic of consumers who enjoy low-intensity puzzles or games. Grandparents to college students, PhDs, blue-collar workers, and teenagers find the game appealing. Mainstream empty nester puzzle players will be motivated by the prize fund. Students 20–30 years old have time to play but no money. Mathematicians and other intellectuals will be stirred by the challenge of finding the solution. Eternity II's simplicity of play also makes it more attractive because the incredible prize is perceived as being a bit more attainable.

Because Eternity II is being rolled out internationally, the creators behind the puzzle did well to create a compelling and dynamic Web site to serve as the online headquarters for Eternity II. EternityII.com features an interactive demonstration of the puzzle and visually appealing graphics. There, enthusiasts can learn about the story behind the Eternity II and news updates. A real-time ticker is featured that counts down until the first solution scrutiny date of December 31, 2008, continually provoking players to return to the puzzle and keep trying for their own chance to win.

Finally, only 5,000 Eternity II puzzles have initially been made available in the U.S., exclusively at Toys "R" Us retail stores and ToysRUs.com during the product's launch period. This restricted availability of the puzzle, in turn, will help instigate a higher demand among consumers.

Challenges

Marketers of Eternity II are also faced with a number of challenges to achieving successful sales of the product in the U.S. Generally, American consumers are a more skeptical group and to achieve buy-in, TOMY will have to overcome the perceptions of an impossible prize, a puzzle that might be too difficult to finish, and a general distrust of a company claiming to offer $2 million for playing a game. The retail price for Eternity II is another obstacle. The game retails for $49.99, which is a price point much higher than American consumers are used to paying for a board game or jigsaw puzzle.

The Campaign

Recognizing the advantages and disadvantages of Eternity II in relation to the U.S. market, Southard Communications in partnership with Threepipe UK have implemented an online, social networking and viral marketing campaign that capitalizes on the opportunities presented by the puzzle while conquering the challenges to achieving a successful sell-in stateside.

Videos of the official unveiling of the puzzle at a toy industry conference and the worldwide launch were posted to YouTube.com and tagged with various keywords for engine searches. The videos, which feature the branded game and exciting footage of a Mr. Universe contender destroying the laptop that held the solution to the puzzle, have received more than 15,000 viewers and have been e-mailed between friends and colleagues a countless number of times.

The marketing team identified influential blogs that focus on puzzle gaming and started chatting to them about Eternity months before the game was launched. Teaser messages discussing the coming of a new puzzle with an unbelievable $2 million prize were posted, which inspired an ongoing online dialogue that has resulted in placement on about 5,000 blogs to date.

A Facebook site was developed early on with new content and news drip-fed to build excitement. Links to the EternityII.com Web site were offered in advance of its official launch and videos were posted. An online demo of the puzzle was created and e-mailed to thousands of people and

international media, which linked back to the interactive Web site http://
us.eternityii.com/. The game demo and countdown to the first scrutiny
date was included with the easy ability to forward the game demo to
friends.

Active discussion exists today about Eternity II on online groups and
chat rooms, including Yahoo!. The Yahoo! group has almost 1,500 members. Chatter about Eternity II was monitored as much as possible, and
responses are crafted by marketing team members when and where they
can. The viral campaign has also included targeting a great deal of online
sites to help with natural search-through engines and also to drive people
to the online retailers. The online campaign has spawned software programs created by computer whizzes to help solve the puzzle. One example
is a man from New Zealand who created a program and a Web site
(www.eternity2.net) about Eternity II. In addition, International media
covered the story extensively.

Finally, an online campaign targeting the Toys "R" Us customer database included a direct HTML e-mail with the game demo included and a
"buy it now promotion" to encourage traffic to the stores and
ToysRUs.com. The game was made available for presale on ToysRUs.com
and sold 1,000 units before the product was officially launched.

Quality Technology Services

Quality Technology Services (QualityTech) currently positions itself as
a full service technology infrastructure company providing Managed
Services, Data Center Services, and Professional Services to business in the
United States (www.qualitytech.com). The company, which is less than
two years old, has built its business quickly through a series of acquisitions, including edeltacom and Globix, as well as securing several data
center facilities across the country to increase its national footprint.

However, with every acquisition, and with continued company
growth, QualityTech faces communication challenges. QualityTech must
take the strengths from each acquired company, as well as the roots of a
strong "Quality" brand, and meld them into one concise and cohesive
message to the market; to convey its state-of-the-art services and facilities,

and to present a strong, intelligent, and credible organization that pro-vides *World Class People, Processes and Facilities* to the businesses it serves.

The main objectives of QualityTech's PR 2.0 thought leadership com-munications plan are to introduce a young, intelligent, world-class com-pany to the market; to increase editorial coverage (and third-party endorsements) through trade journals, vertical media, and business publi-cations; to engage in direct dialogue with customers and prospects to pro-vide them with targeted information that presents QualityTech as a thought leadership company; and to convert sales leads into customers.

To achieve the company's 2.0 objectives, QualityTech's PR strategies consist of the following programs:

Media Relations. The media relations program includes several tried and true PR outreach strategies, including news release development and distribution to trade, business, newspapers, online and syndicated media, editorial calendar review and angle development (to pitch different edi-tors on targeted stories), and a meet-the-media program at the grand opening for one of QualityTech's datacenter facilities. To accommodate those media influencers who are engaged in social media, both the tradi-tional and the social media news release template will be available on QualityTech's Web site. Social media releases will have bulleted informa-tion with approved quotes from executives but will also provide video, RSS, social book marking, hyperlinks to other sources, and audio down-loads to help the media and general audiences to quickly and easily gather and organize information.

Online Media Kit Development. QualityTech will set up an interac-tive newsroom that enables visitors to access video news style interviews with the company's executives, as well as testimonials from customers who are willing to discuss how QualityTech helped to solve their hosting chal-lenges. The media kit will also include a full interactive slideshow or video of QualityTech data centers and information for download on its national facilities. Media kits will contain executive information (bio and photos). All executive and sales team members will have links to social networking profiles, including LinkedIn and Facebook. Members of the QualityTech sales team will also have bios that are linked to their forums and groups where they actively discuss hosting and managed services topics.

Blogging. A blog on the QualityTech Web site is an ideal way to engage customers and current prospects in dialogue to learn more about their concerns and business issues they face everyday with respect to outsourcing their hosting and managed service. Because marketing is one big conversation on the Internet, social media enables QualityTech to start a dialogue with prospects and/or clients on its own Web site. Blogging alone enables QualityTech to engage their customers and prospects in a discussion, and be privy to conversations between their customers. Blogging is a low-cost form of research for QualityTech—it's the greatest focus panel they could ever implement for only a fraction of the cost. By developing a blog, QualityTech will select interesting topics for discussion, including what keeps executive up at night. The company can key into the many issues that concern customers who are looking for a colocation, hosting, or a managed services company. These topics might include security, privacy, power, cooling, green datacenters, and so on.

Video Series. QualityTech's Web site was developed to display video and flash presentations in the large, open graphical area on the home page. It's important for customers, prospects, the media, and other influential audiences to see and learn first-hand about the company's state-of-the-art facilities and meet the intelligent team behind the QualityTech brand. Video can be shared and passed along to interested parties. Incorporating video into the framework of the Web site is a first phase step. A more advanced video platform would be an area of the QualityTech Web site called QualityTech Forum[2], a place where all audiences would access an online repository of searchable multimedia, including detailed information on colocation, hosting, and managed services.

Podcasting. Podcasting enables QualityTech to capture the attention of those audiences who prefer to spend a minimal amount of time on their Web site and would rather download information to a handheld device to "listen on the run." A podcast series could provide highlights from speaking engagements, company meetings, or interviews on compelling topics such as the green movement in hosting, the future of hosted services, maximizing customer relationships with managed services, and so on. Podcasts can also be clips from any industry presentations from QualityTech's speaking engagement program. For QualityTech, podcasting is an effective way beyond blogging that provides an inauthentic company voice. As a social media tool, it enables the company to reach a highly mobile audience—customers and prospects who seek valuable content for listening on their own terms and at the time most convenient to them.

RSS Technology. RSS technology will be an easy means for QualityTech's online audiences to access news, updates, and valuable industry information. QualityTech will offer three feeds from its newsroom, company blog, and from the QualityTech Forum. These feeds are a great way to let audiences know that new information is available. A feed also enables customers, prospects, employees, analysts, media, and other influential parties to share the information with other audiences (through "e-mail a friend"). The RSS technology feeds are, of course, optional to users. Users will have to opt into the RSS feed to participate in the program. RSS feeds provide targeted communication to those interested parties, and will keep QualityTech's brand and expertise top of mind.

PR 2.0 Monitoring. Monitoring is one of the most important parts of the QualityTech plan, especially because there are so many concerns regarding PR 2.0 and the loss of control of communication. If a company is going to send out its messages to audiences, it needs to monitor and assess the level of positive and negative communication, as news is disseminated. With so many sophisticated monitoring services from Cision and Delahaye to PR Newswire's eWatch and MarketWire, QualityTech will be able to freely discuss topics on its blog and in news releases, and feel comfortable when audiences share the content. QualityTech will be able to listen closely to what's being said. Listening is the only way to take the proper actions. Positive information is confirmation that the PR 2.0 plan is a success and can be placed back into the company's research and service development cycle. Any negative talk on the Internet will be monitored for a period of time and then positive messaging will be developed to combat any harmful chatter.

The PR 2.0 portion of QualityTech's plan makes sense. Its audience, comprised of CIO, CTO, and technologically savvy professionals, is online and comfortable with Web 2.0 and for the most part, familiar with social media applications. Enabling audiences to organize and share information will ultimately result in more conversations with prospects and customers, greater visibility as information is shared, and credibility as an industry leader, with knowledgeable resources provided through social media applications. The end result—qualified leads turn into customers. QualityTech is on the right track. It might take a year or so to get their PR 2.0 plan completely launched and fully functional, but they are no different from a number of companies that are just getting their feet wet with social media and PR 2.0.

ASCO Power Technologies

ASCO Power Technologies (www.ascopower.com), a division of Emerson Electric, is a company best known for keeping the power "on." As a world leader in Automatic Transfer Switches and Power Systems, ASCO protects data and information and safeguards critical installations whether it's that of a healthcare facility or a financial institution.[3]

The company recently began the development of ASCO Power University[4], a completely new concept and area of its Web site. From a marketing perspective, the underlying motivation was to establish ASCO as a thought and innovation leader within their industry. To do this, the University is built with two main objectives. The first objective is to use the site as an educational portal for all external audiences, and the second objective is to educate ASCO Power Technologies' engineers (internally). Phase I of the initiative launched in early 2008.

ASCO Power University, through its use of social media applications, is a PR 2.0 communications concept. Users are able to search, organize, and share content. The site provides informational presentations from basic power to advanced power systems through Web streaming—video-on-demand (VOD) and RSS technology. This online repository of materials provides visitors not only a wealth of information but also the ability to view materials and then take a quiz to test their knowledge on the subject matter. Then, RSS feeds let engineers know when specific information of interest is available for their review. ASCO intends to focus on the external launch of this site for audiences including the media. The company wants to reach out to journalists to invite them to take advantage of the rich content on the site for research and story-building purposes.

According to Brian Phelan, Director of Marketing Services at ASCO Power Technologies, this type of social media application was long overdue. Phelan discussed his thoughts about ASCO's use of social media and how it would change the nature of their organizations' communications moving forward.

Q: Is ASCO Power University your company's first foray into social media?

A: No. We were the first company in our industry to develop multimedia interactive marketing tools to describe applications for our products, as well as educate engineers on our product features. In fact, in 2000, we won the prestigious Axiem award for "Absolute eXcellence in Electronic Media."

However, with respect to Web-based initiatives, yes. Unfortunately, we haven't put much energy and resources into our Web efforts to date. However, we've been encouraged in recent months by a steady increase in traffic to our site, Web sponsorship opportunities that are presenting themselves, and a stronger push by companies within our industry to take a more aggressive Web-based marketing strategy. Interestingly, for an industry that literally provides the resources to power the Web, as a whole we've lagged far behind the curve in terms of how best to utilize it. With ASCO Power University, we're helping to propel forward not only our own company, but also the entire industry.

Q: How do you think ASCO audiences will benefit from ASCO Power University?

A: We're not planning on ASCO Power University being an advertising vehicle. Although future segments might include "how to" topics for effective usage of ASCO products, the early content releases will be based on topics that engineers would be concerned with and could learn from. Many engineering universities simply have not offered courses in the basic fundamentals of power that build the foundation of our industry. At the same time, there are established engineers who have been in the industry for years, but haven't had the time or resources to keep up with the rapid changes that are part of electrical engineering.

We're building ASCO Power University to fill these gaps. Through an ongoing series of 30-minute content modules ranging across a variety of topics, we're going to be the premier learning center outside an accredited university where both new and established engineers can gather the information they need quickly and easily.

Q: What are the most useful tools for engineers or other groups on the site?

A: We'll be developing each instructional module with a mixture of video, Flash animation, and PowerPoint to maintain a high level of instructional and entertainment value. Ease of navigation and interactivity will also be inherent in all modules. Each learning module will be followed up by a quiz so that engineers can check their knowledge on a given topic, and feel confident that they have completed the learning module with a reasonable understanding of the material.

In addition, users will have access to information as to which quizzes they've taken and how well they did, plus the users are able to see which modules they have only partially seen so that they can revisit them at a later time. The convenience factor and self-testing capabilities will prove to be a tremendous benefit to our audience.

In the future, we might use this tool to begin a certification course with credits. This will take the entire University effort to a new level, helping to boost engineers' credentials and promote career advancement, while firmly establishing ASCO as a knowledge-based resource.

Q: Was there any resistance from upper management with respect to this initiative or any other social media efforts?

A: No. On the contrary, we have always maintained a cutting edge mentality in developing marketing initiatives for our industry. In fact, we received the Emerson Technology Award for our cutting edge marketing initiatives.

Q: Would you ever consider expanding ASCO Power University to include a blogging tool for ASCO to communicate directly with its audiences?

A: We are already considering this and plan to include blogging technology in future updates to the University. We've already discussed the possibility of having our call center in Manilla be responsible for moderating and controlling blog usage. Initially, our biggest concern regarding blogging was the fear that people posting comments would give wrong information on a topic. Worse yet was the danger of a competitor leaving negative comments about ASCO. However, once we gained a greater understanding of how blogs work, and realized that we can police and filter the comments before they get posted, we saw a clearer vision of the great benefits a blog would provide.

Q: Discuss your vision for ASCO Power University as an external educational portal.

A: We anticipate that ASCO Power University will be focal point for seasoned engineers as well as recent graduates to gather information that will help them achieve greater understanding of important topics within the electrical power industry. By making content easy to find, enjoyable to review, and valuable in terms of its content, we expect that users will utilize the site and ongoing educational resources, while at the same time establishing in their minds that ASCO is a leader in its industry.

Moving Forward with Your PR 2.0 Planning

If you're looking to put the "public" back in public relations, venturing into direct-to-consumer communication through social media applications will not only jumpstart your communications, but also increase the reach of your marketing conversation. Some of your audiences will always rely on you for traditional communication, but for those audiences that are active online and want their information delivered in a 2.0 fashion, you need to focus on the following:

- Your campaign requires a fine balance between traditional PR and social media tactics to reach your audiences.

- People of all ages and all professions are reading blogs, joining online communities, tagging articles, listening to podcasts, enjoying their RSS feeds, and have set up profiles on social networking sites.

- Social media enables online consumers to gather, organize, and share information to make informed decisions and purchases.

- PR 2.0 and the use of social media applications provide an effective way to communicate to employees, customers, prospects, the media, analysts, bloggers, and other stakeholders with less expensive techniques.

- PR 2.0 enables you to hear firsthand customer comments, concerns, and insight into what influences their thinking and decision-making.

- Social media sites and social networking enable you to keep the marketing conversation going with the opportunity to increase the reach of your brand's messages.

- Brands adopt PR 2.0 and social media strategies at all different rates. As some companies are just beginning their foray into social media, other organizations are employing strategies that enable audiences to share content which leads to increased marketing/PR buzz.

Endnotes

1. The TOMY International case study was provided by Southard Communications, New York, New York, October 2007.

2. QualityTech Forum is a concept developed by PFS Marketwyse.

3. ASCO Power Technologies Web site Homepage is at www.ascopower.com.

4. PFS Marketwyse created ASCO University's software shell.

The Future of 2.0

Chapter **15**

The Path to Great PR

Does anyone really know the future? I've heard some interesting predictions, but like all predications, I take them with a grain of salt. Some communications professionals are forecasting the onset of PR 3.0. How could there be talk of PR 3.0? I don't remember successfully accomplishing a fraction of what there is to accomplish in PR 2.0. Ask yourself, have you perfected your PR 2.0 strategy for your brands? In this fast-paced Web world, occasionally you need to slow down, take a deep breath, and put everything into perspective. It's really important to review everything you know about PR 2.0 from the research and monitoring to new social templates and social networking. Then, you'll be able to figure out the best way to apply all your knowledge and experiences to create powerful Web/PR communications.

Your Path to Great Communication

At this point, most likely you've realized it's not just the Web 2.0 technological platform or a cool multimedia application that "makes" the communication. No, it's so much more. The technology will always enhance the communication; however, it doesn't matter if it's 2.0, 3.0, or someday 5.0. Regardless of the platform, it will always be your job to make sure that your public relations and marketing communication are done for the right reasons, at the right time to reach your stakeholders with information, in a manner that gets their attention. You need to interact with them where they thrive the most—in their communities—and always remember that marketing is one big online conversation.

PR 2.0 is not just about good communication; it's about finding the path to the conversations. Traveling this path will enable you to directly reach and communicate with the people who will influence decisions and ultimately help carry the brand forward, which ultimately leads peer-to-peer + influencer driven customer loyalty. I had a discussion with Brian

Solis[1], founder of FutureWorks in San Francisco, and also someone whose work I respect in PR 2.0. Solis is one of the "Founding Fathers" of the PR 2.0 movement. He is a firm believer that PR 2.0 leads to not only great PR, but also a new era of outbound customer service.

You've Come a Long Way

Solis was thinking about PR 2.0 back in the 1990s when many of us were only just experimenting with brand communication online. Reflecting on the past, he feels that although PR 2.0 has been around for years, it's only just popularized now. He pointed out that in the late 1990s, there were a series of Web sites that started to take off as "next-generation bulletin board services and user groups that appealed to the early market majority population." These included Yahoo! Groups, Copy Serv, AOL, and all the places dedicated to people with a particular and similar interest.

Solis' first experience with PR 2.0 was when he really started to get involved in reaching people who were considering jumping into digital photography. "Digital photography at the time was all so new and met with notable resistance from those who didn't believe film would be anything less than the mainstream. But, digital photography wasn't just about pros or early adopters. It had mass appeal and it was going to affect families who wanted to take pictures of their kids playing soccer or photos of family outings, picnics, or daytrips to the beach," he said. Solis became interested in social media, although at the time it wasn't called social media; instead it was referred to as new media and represented new opportunities to reach people. It was then that he realized he could actually go into a Web community and start fostering conversations with people, not as a marketer, but as a fellow photography enthusiast. He was able to get their feedback, hear their input, and also at the same time become a part of that community—an evangelist to help them understand the world in general digital photography. "I was just calling this whole thing PR 2.0; to document how the Web was changing the game for PR and opening the doors for knowledgeable communications folks to reach people directly. We participated in a way that helped them make decisions, based on the experience that we had as peers, not even as marketers at the time," explained Solis.

For Solis, PR 2.0 really is about doing two things. "First, it was a call from people to 'stop the bullshit' and it was also an opportunity for those who didn't buy into this process of PR, to find a new channel to connect with people and get back to basics, which was all about cultivating relationships." PR has and always will be about relationships—whether practiced well or not. At the same time, Solis feels that while PR is supposed to be about Public Relations, it was the advent of Social Media that really changed everything at the mass level. Solis experimented early on with multimedia, CDs, enthusiast sites (now known as blogs), streaming video, and then Web conferences. He invited users to come in and have conversations about products and chat with them over the Web. He knew it was a fantastic opportunity to meet groups of customers, as well as traditional media.

Even though this has been in practice for about ten years, one of the biggest challenges is getting brands to embrace PR 2.0 and social media. Although Solis feels that he fights a battle everyday with some of his clients with respect to implementing PR 2.0 strategies, he knows they will soon realize that "New PR" really helps companies connect with people through their channels of influence and conversation. "It's no longer about messages or audiences, it's about discovering the people that matter, where they go for information, and why what you represent matters to them specifically. But it's not just PR's responsibility to engage. It's a critical requirement for all corporate marketing up to the executive level, to participate," he said.

"I've been having the same conversations for ten years, and I still come back to an identical argument. For example, blogging is an important aspect of social media and it is important for a company, whether they are B2B or B2C to blog. I'm still having tireless conversations where I am blue in the face trying to explain the benefits."

I can relate to Solis' frustrations. An entry from my blog at www.deirdrebreakenridge.com reads:

It's Time to Get Started

What I found to be the most interesting about discussing Web 2.0 and social media with technology companies is that I expected more businesses to be incorporating social media into their communications programs. As I listened closely to the comments from many of the audience members (throughout the two-day Tier1 Research Hosting Summit), I heard many executives ask questions including: How do I engage in a dialogue with a prospect? How do I develop a relationship? What keeps my clients up at night? What are the most important characteristics potential customers look for in a hosting or managed services company?

It amazed me to hear all these questions. They had the answer at their fingertips. *Marketing is Conversation.*[2] Social media allows you to start a dialogue with prospects and/or clients right on your own Web site. Blogging alone enables you to engage your customers and prospects in a dialogue, and be privy to their conversations with your other customers. Blogging is also your cheapest form of a research—it's the greatest focus panel you could ever implement for only a fraction of the cost. By developing a blog, you can select interesting topics for discussion including what keeps executives up at night, and you can key into the many issues that concern customers who are looking for a colocation, hosting, or managed services company. These topics might include security, privacy, power, cooling, green datacenters, and so on.

When I look at the technology sector and the companies that provide hosting and managed services, I immediately think that these companies should automatically be ahead of the curve with respect to Web 2.0. In terms of the platform, they definitely are. However, when it comes to communication and PR 2.0, they realize that they need to provide the right information to their customers to help them make important decisions, yet they're behind the curve in terms of the communications strategies.

Now, I'm sure there are many tech firms that are blogging, social networking, and podcasting. I guess they just weren't attending this conference. My reaction to the tech companies not using social media: get onboard and start getting up to speed. If companies like Cisco, BMC, and Sun Microsystems can blog without red tape and restrictions from their communications departments, then similar or smaller organizations have no excuses. It's time to get started!

Solis admitted that many companies still don't see the value of blogs. "They think blogs are just rants and diaries of what people do on a day-to-day basis. They completely underestimate the fact that a blog can become a destination, an aggregate of knowledge and expertise that helps customers make decisions while also building relationships with them. It just blows me away." Solis explained that there's also a misunderstanding of how to use blogs. "Some executives will say 'let's do it' and then have their PR people ghost write blogs for them, as if they were computer articles. Or, they use a blog as a marketing channel and start pumping news releases into their posts. But to me, the best thing a company can do is to get in that conversation and let people within that organization represent the brand. Technically everyone within an organization should be responsible for public relations, whereas media or analyst relations are specific responsibilities of communications professionals. Those conversations are going to happen out there with or without them, and if companies aren't on the radar screen, then they're missing opportunities," he commented.

Solis stressed the importance of how PR professionals need to embrace social media—including podcasts, blogs, lifestreaming, livecasts, social networking, social bookmarking, and many other social tools to join the conversation—not as marketers, but as people. It all starts with listening and reading. You need to hear what's going on out there before you can participate. Every community has its own culture, so you can't simply expect to come in and start spamming it with PR. It all starts with becoming an expert. There's no reason why PR shouldn't truly understand what they represent, why it's important and different, and how it helps people.

At any time a conversation can pop up about your company or a competitor, or its technology, or your product or service. Whatever it is, those conversations happen all the time and it's fairly easy for you to find those conversations to join. "Every time you place a noncommercial piece of information with valuable insight or expertise or simply answer someone's questions and help them out, those types of interactions bring people back to your site and introduce them to something they might not have known before," Solis said.

PR 2.0 Hot Topics

Because PR 2.0 is a different approach to public relations, it has caused confusion and excitement at the same time. This different approach also spawned some very hot topics in the communications industry. For Solis, the hottest topic is this whole social media movement, which includes blogging, blogger relations, Social Tools, community relations, the social media news release, and social media newsroom. Solis says he's in a different camp when it comes to the social media release. For him it's just a platform to present information and spark conversations, with or without journalists and bloggers. Many are under the impression that the social media release is the driving force behind PR 2.0, yet it is only one of the many tools that help conversations and relationships flourish.

At the same time, of course, the SMR opens up the possibility to enable people to embrace it in conversation. However, most don't realize that the social media release with pictures and links and all these things have been done for years by PR newswire under the MultiVu brand. Solis reminded me, "It's a multimedia news release. The point where I got passionate about the social media release just like social media in general, is the ability to engage with people directly, which by default forces PR people to stop acting like traditional PR people. News releases are notorious for being lumped in with BS hype and 'spin.' Social media is an opportunity to break the stereotype, to become experts, and create conversations directly and indirectly. This is our chance to evolve public relations into a more valuable branch of marketing, making everyone smarter and hopefully more passionate in the process." Solis proves a point. Now, with social media, everyone is basically socially empowered to do something with the information they create or discover. In the case of the Social Media Release, it's a social tool, which can be great for journalists to gather information and also ideal for customers to gather, organize, and share content.

According to Solis, "Stripping the garbage out of the release and sticking with the important facts and benefits" makes a good news release regardless of format. You're able to produce a credible, newsworthy resource that's unique and helpful. With the social media news release, the corporate legal speak is removed and the essence of the release is the information that helps journalists to build better stories. Releases are to the point and also offer information for the citizen journalists. Solis believes that maybe there isn't just one type of release for everybody. He references *The Long Tail* by Chris Anderson and says, "If *The Long Tail* has taught us anything, it's that there are many segments to markets and perhaps the same is true of today's business of information." Solis admits that the PR industry, like most age-old professions, has difficulty with change. "The most important thing is that once you start to experiment with New PR and Social Tools, it has less to do with replacing a news release and more to do with a concept that enables professionals to reach people and bring them into the conversation. It starts to become more about sociology than the technology forcing change."

Solis' favorite topic in our discussion was the future of PR 2.0 and what it means to professionals today. As a matter of fact, when *PR Week* came out and said the PR profession is entering into the "Age of PR 3.0," Solis stopped what he was doing at the time and as he puts it "just ripped the idea apart." For Solis, he hopes that PR 3.0 never sees the light of day again, and he'll keep fighting his fight. A big misperception is that PR 2.0 is a result of Web 2 0 and suddenly everything is 2.0. Solis wrote an article about this very topic. The article explains that PR 2.0 is more of a call for change than creating a new iteration for PR sociology. "This is about the renaissance of public relations and the ideas behind PR 2.0 will simply fold into 'PR' once the industry embraces the changes." Solis also stressed, "In the new game of PR, messages are dead, pitches are dead, and people no longer comprise one audience. There is no market for messages or pitches, only how something benefits those who you're trying to reach through the culture of the communities in which they participate."

I agree with Solis that PR 2.0 brings a new breed of public relations professionals. Now the real test is how professionals embrace the renaissance and the sociology of the communities out there. Through PR 2.0, brands are going to know how to talk to people; whether it's a journalist they need to reach or whether it's a customer or even a partner. Solis builds a strong case and it's true. As you practice PR, you're going to understand where to go and how to bring the information to people in the way they want to hear it. That's the mission of PR 2.0—it's to build relationships with reporters, bloggers, and customers. At the end of the day, it's all about people, although some are confusing the tools with the concept. Social media tools or applications (blogging, podcasting, RSS, social networking, and the like) are the tools that help better your job performance.

According to Solis, there's a problem and we need to admit it and do something about it. PR has become very bureaucratic and practically hands off. The larger the company, the harder it is to get the communication approved—so how timely does that enable you to be? PR 2.0 is about making PR better. Once you recognize there are things that need to be fixed, you can evaluate your approach. Although social media seems like advanced technology, it's actually in theory a back-to-basics approach as it enables you to go out and listen and in turn, participate. You know there are important conversations taking place. For those brands that think those conversations are unimportant or simply ignore them, think again. According to Solis, "Why give up opportunities to connect with customers and instead allow your competition to win their attention? Social media isn't a spectator sport." Solis' final words on PR 2.0: "For me, the inspiration behind all this is to someday walk into a room and be introduced as more than just some PR guy—to be proud of the PR profession and get a proper introduction. 'This is **THE** PR guy, the one you need to meet!'"

More Expert 2.0 Advice

I called on Brian Cross, who is the Director of Fleishman-Hillard's Digital Group in Saint Louis, and serves as one of the Global Practice Group Leaders. He has more than 12 years of experience in innovative, online customer-centric solutions, with expertise ranging from online marketing and outreach, search strategies, technology consulting, and Web 2.0/social media campaigns.

Before Cross answered my question about the future of PR 2.0, he wanted to discuss the confusion over the definition of the concept. If you look at the social media club (www.socialmediaclub.com), you will see there is still a big debate as to exactly what the definition of social media is and therefore, what the roots of PR 2.0 are. "But, if you boiled down social media, I look at it as collaborative communication. If you think about it, you've been collaborative all your life. How much different is writing a rough draft of your paper in grade school and sending it off to your teacher for comments? This is a similar concept to the wiki or a blog. You're sending out information for feedback. Social media can be a large focus group of sorts. Look at the group paper—isn't that a wiki?" Cross asked.

The conversation is what makes PR 2.0. For Cross, it's not about targeting your audience. He gave an example of advertising—advertisers want to target their audience, launch their campaign, and barrage the consumer. "Instead of targeting your audience, you're targeting yourself. PR 2.0 teaches you that you don't target audiences—you draw an irresistible bull's-eye on yourself, on your brand. Today's online audiences will target your brand. If you think about it, that's why the online search is so big. Audiences are changing. PR pros are used to targeting journalists to reach their audiences. Now you can go directly to the public, or better yet, they can come to you. You just have to make yourself as attractive as possible so that they find you." I asked Cross what's the best way to be found and he said to simply identify the right Web communities and have the members of the community agree to have a relationship with you.

Your Brand and PR 2.0

Cross makes a strong point about who controls the brand. Is it the executives who plan the marketing and advertising program? No, it's today's consumer who controls the brand. Because the Web is a conglomeration of what everybody else is saying about your brand, it's your consumer who dictates your brand's every move. That's why companies are engaging their consumers in their marketing. For example, during the Super Bowl, Frito Lay had ads created by their consumers. "Office Max allowed a consumer to upload his or her face and to become a dancing elf and then send it out to their friends. M&Ms allows you to make your own M&M candies. You can even make an M&M look like you," recalled Cross. These are all opportunities for the consumer to be closer to the brand, to be intimately involved, and to control what they want to see from their brands.

Cross believes, "One of the hottest PR 2.0 topics is trying to legitimize social media. There's an entire industry trying to figure out what the hell is going on. It's not like they know it so well that they are having a major debate about any one particular thing. There's a fundamental change in the way media is defined and delivered." Cross remembers a speech given by his CEO at Fleishman-Hillard. His CEO read a quote to the audience from a publisher of a New York newspaper. The publisher being quoted was complaining about a disruptive new technology and its impact on his newspaper. The publisher goes on to say that newspapers might as well accept their fate. They're going out of existence. He continued to say that there's been a lot of talk of layoffs at the newspaper. After hearing the quote from the newspaper publisher, most of the audience thought that the publisher of this New York newspaper was complaining about the introduction of the Web. The CEO then lets his audience know that the quote was from 1852, and to everyone's surprise, the new technology was the telegraph—same problems, different century.

According to Cross, the Internet poses the same problem, as did the telegraph in 1852. However, social media and the ability to share information is a great asset to society. Cross gave an example of the military dictators of Myanmar. Nothing can stop the world from witnessing oppression—not even by cutting off television transmission. Citizens used cell phones on the Web to beam out images of bloody Buddhist monks as soldiers were beating protestors. Certainly not a fun topic to point out but an excellent example of how a military dictatorship shut off TV; however, also an example of how they could not shut off the flow of information being shared by countries. People flipped on their cell phones and captured the atrocities and sent the images around to the world. As another example, Londoners were panicked by the terrorist subway bombings of 2005, and there was no way for traditional media to cover the story. People who'd been in the subways started beaming text messages and video clips to their families and friends, the BBC found out, and set up a cell phone news channel. Soon the whole country knew what was happening, and panic was replaced by information.

PR Has Changed for the Better

Today, with this ability to gather, share, and organize content, you no longer have the same traditional PR process. PR people used to write news releases and then send them to the newspaper. However, citizen journalists are now sounding off on their blogs and sending content to Twitter. As much as PR people are the middlemen, it appears that with PR 2.0 and social media, there's less of a role as middleman. Embracing this type of change when you've been performing in a role for so long is difficult. According to Cross, there are three trends feeding into this transitional role: exhibitionism, an erosion in formality and civility when communicating, and voyeurism. Cross suggests looking at other methods and other channels to understand the changes we're experiencing.

One of biggest trends you see in television is reality programming. "There is this increasing trend for informality. There are a lot of people who don't want the formality. We're an extremely informal society right now," Cross said. There is also the desire to lay it all on the line. Online consumers want their 15 minutes of fame, but with an audience of only 15 people and giving full details on the Internet, in their blogs, and in social networks. "It's crazy. I mean you can talk about anything on a personal blog. The rules have changed even when it comes to job interviews. Laws exist that say you can't ask about the candidate's age, religion, and the like; however, a prospective employer can log on to Facebook or other social networking sites and find extremely personal information about a job candidate and more," he said. The third trend is voyeurism—not the kind of voyeurism that makes people snicker, but the fascination with watching the lives of others. People love looking at other people. Cross believes that these three trends feed into the desire to move toward more social media online. "The truth of it is that we've gone beyond just liking social media. In fact, it's been given to us, we've seen it, we've consumed it, and now we definitely expect it."

Cross gives a good example of basic building blocks with three distinct layers. He describes the top layer as "your assets." So, for example, consumer generated media is your asset, whether it's a post, a blog, or a photo you uploaded or a video or link to a document. He refers to anything that you take and share with people, what you put out there, as an object. As for the next layer, the middle layer, Cross describes it as the area where people can vote, comment, subscribe, share rate, and collaborate. The bottom layer is for the tools, whether that's Wizard, wiki, blog, tag, IM, a poll, and so on. The third layer is the one that is always going to change. This is representative of the future. There will always be new tools. Even though the tools will continually change, PR professionals will always start the conversation, facilitate that conversation and then, of course, monitor the conversation. It's that feedback or marketing conversation that's meant to go back into the brand development life cycle.

Cross said, "I think that there's going to be a whole lot more direct conversations with the consumer and I think the consumer is going to gain more and more control, but not control in a bad way—control in a way that they're going to ask for exactly what they want." This will definitely help the brand. That doesn't mean that PR and advertising are going to go away because suddenly companies can bypass the communications professionals and just go direct to the consumer. He believes that when companies decide to go direct-to-consumer, they often have trouble figuring out which niches are right for them. The many different Web communities today make it more difficult. That's where PR is crucial. PR is going to basically come in and say, "These are the right target audiences for you in these communities, and we're going to now show you how to walk into that community and make yourself attractive enough that they are going to want to strike up a conversation with you." PR 2.0 and social media tools enable you to do this and do this successfully.

Don't Just Go with It—Go for It!

As a result of PR 2.0, the changes are immense, somewhat overwhelming, but definitely exciting for communications professionals. PR 2.0 and social media applications are here to stay. The PR profession is still evolving with the many new social media tools available and the means to engage more people in conversations. If people in their Web communities are craving information a certain way, it's not for professionals to ignore or deny these requests. Remember the target is the brand and brands need to be found. There's a big bull's-eye on your brand, and your customers have plenty to say and share with you. So, as a communications professional you need to inform your brands that it's time to evolve, be flexible, and deliver information in a way that can be gathered, organized, and shared in Web communities.

PR 2.0 is not a fad and as it continues to develop, so will the brands that adhere to these new rules of communication. You need to look at PR 2.0 with a fresh set of eyes. You'll never abandon what you've learned as a communications professional, but you will need to apply the rules of 2.0 to every part of the communication process. That means looking at research and monitoring with PR 2.0 techniques and selecting partners who have the technology that enables you to have better visibility in the blogosphere. You also need to reevaluate your PR templates. Perhaps use a blended approach and have the traditional pyramid style news release along with a PR 2.0 social media template in your interactive newsroom. You will also be reconsidering how you approach blogs and social networking. These social media applications will take on a whole new meaning for your brand. And, there are tools like RSS that provide you with the reach and targeting that communications professionals only dreamed about years ago. Video and podcasts will soon become a part of your brand's strategy and planning. Video tells an incredibly compelling and visual story, and podcasts relay information for audiences on the go. Today's consumers are looking for quick and easy ways to obtain information on the run. Of course, all these new PR 2.0 approaches will be strategic and used to accomplish your objectives, not just because they are cool multimedia applications.

Last, but most importantly, you will reexamine your role as a professional. For those of you just starting out or for the many who have watched the industry evolve, you have found your path to the greatest communication in the 21st Century. Blazing this path is PR 2.0 and all the incredible social media resources that go along with it. By nature, you might feel apprehensive about releasing communication in a different fashion. But if you've listened and absorbed the messages in this book, then you will walk away with a newfound strength. You will realize that with the risk of PR 2.0 and not as much control over communication is the tremendous opportunity to interact and build relationships with journalists, bloggers, and customers. Your brand will engage in dialogue that has never been experienced before.

PR 2.0 is an approach that translates into excellent communication. But, a word to the wise: Don't get hung up on the number sequence. In ten years, the rest of the world might be calling it PR 5.0; who knows. It's definitely not about a number. It's about the best communication you and your brands can achieve. Technology will enable the tools to continually change to better suit the online consumer's preferences. You'll find better conversations in communities that at one time never would have invited you to enter, to listen, and to engage in intimate communication. PR 2.0 is today and it's the future.

Endnotes

1. For more information on Brian Solis, go to www.briansolis.com.

2. Ynema Mangum stated that "Marketing is conversation" in her blog excerpt presented in Chapter 12, "The Pro's Use of PR 2.0."

Index

W

X

Y

Z